A Feast of
FISH

A Feast of FISH

IAN McANDREW

Photography by MARTIN BRIGDALE

A Little, Brown Book

Little, Brown and Company
Boston · New York · London

DEDICATION

*Peter and Shaun, this book is for you, thank
you both for your faith. Shaun, thank you for
your help with the research and the recipes, but
most of all thank you both for your friendship.*

A Little, Brown Book

First published in 1999
by Little, Brown and Company (UK)

Text copyright © Ian McAndrew 1999
Photographs © Martin Brigdale 1999

The moral right of the author has been asserted.

A CIP catalogue record for this book is available
from the British Library

ISBN 0 316 84773 9

Designed by Janet James

Little, Brown and Company (UK)
Brettenham House
Lancaster Place
London WC2E 7EN

Printed and bound in Italy

contents

The recipe collection

Foreword

When I first arrived in this country, over twenty years ago, Ian was one of the first chefs I had the pleasure to work with. Indeed he had himself just returned from working abroad and what first struck me about him was the enthusiasm and energy with which he seemed to approach life, in particular cooking, and above all eating. He simply loved it, and these were very exciting times at the end of the seventies and beginning of the eighties.

Cooking was undergoing a fundamental change and everything was becoming possible. There was a move away from the rigidity and classical values which had been upheld during the past decades. This change was led by chefs, not by hoteliers or restaurateurs.

Ian was at the forefront of this change – a young English chef opening a restaurant in Canterbury and achieving national acclaim and with it a Michelin star.

It was then that he wrote the first of many cookery books and they all have one thing in common: they are all very user-friendly.

Originating from the North East of England, Ian has always resolutely followed his own uncomplicated, direct and enthusiastic approach to cooking. And to nobody's surprise this is once more reinforced in this, his latest book. It has a wonderfully wide range of recipes covering all varieties of fish from around the British Isles and beyond.

The dishes are well thought out, the emphasis being on depth of flavour and freshness with an often surprising combination of ingredients making the recipes truly exciting and mouth-watering. Some are old-time favourites and others are contemporary but all are simple to prepare. The ingredients are easily obtainable and their preparation is carefully explained, making the recipes a pleasure to follow. Above all, with this book Ian has given a new meaning to Rudyard Kipling's 'Teach us delight in simple things'.

Anton Edelmann
Maître Chef des Cuisines
The Savoy Hotel, London

Introduction

It is some twelve years since the first edition of *A Feast of Fish* was published, way back in the mid eighties. Fish, having been through a bit of a decline in popularity, was just starting to become fashionable again. Now, at the beginning of the new millennium, it is probably more popular than ever. These days almost every supermarket has a fish counter and fish shops are starting to reappear in our high streets, making it so much easier to find good quality fish. And there's a far wider choice than ever before!

In my first edition I found myself concentrating on what we chefs call prime fish. These are the fish that always fetch a high price and are highly sought after, such as turbot, John Dory, sole and sea bass. This time, although I still include these fish (I could hardly leave them out!) I have considerably widened my horizons.

Food has changed at an incredible rate in Britain over the last decade and as a nation we have become much more adventurous with our food. The new wave of TV programmes bears witness to this. They have produced a renewed interest in food and how it is prepared, which has to be a good thing. It is very much because of this interest that we have a better and wider range of products available to us. To the professional chef, fish such as mackerel, cod, haddock and skate would at one time, and not too long ago at that, have been too lowly to include in any *real* menu. These days you are more likely to see the humble cod on a restaurant menu than a turbot. Now used by the great and the good everywhere, fish such as cod would not have been touched by any self-respecting chef, not even with someone else's barge pole! Yes, I was one of that breed – I would happily eat it myself away from work but I wouldn't even consider putting it on the menu.

Cost is of course a great contributor to the rise of what we once considered to be inferior fish. Quality prime fish now fetch such a premium that many restaurants cannot afford to buy them, forcing the cook to turn to cheaper alternatives. Cheaper they may be, but that doesn't mean they are not as good. How I wish I had had the courage to use fish such as mackerel on my menus fifteen years ago! Courage sounds a strong word to use, but believe me, in the late seventies and almost throughout the eighties, it would have needed immense bravery. I doubt that the man from Michelin would have considered many of the fish I use in this book as suitable for a one star restaurant back then. Let us all be thankful that times have changed – I can now own up to the fact that cod is one of my favourite fish!

In the past I also concentrated on dishes that in many ways mirrored the food I was serving in my restaurant. Basically, I was writing a book for my peers, a book that featured dishes that were more suited to professional chefs with one or two easier ones interspersed to try to appeal to a wider audience.

Here too I have changed my approach and this time I have tried to make my dishes much more accessible. That is not to say I wouldn't have included them in a restaurant menu – far from it. Many of these recipes have appeared on my menus over the last few years. They are tried and tested and have stood the test of time and demanding customers. But they do show how food has changed; almost everyone's approach to food and the whole eating experience has altered considerably.

Over the years my recipes have also become more straightforward, more varied, lighter, and easier to prepare. Presentation is not as ostentatious although, to be fair, my food has never been as complicated as some I could mention. I have always preferred to err on the side of simplicity and I think this book bears that philosophy out.

My beliefs are straightforward: use good, honest ingredients, cook things simply, do not over-garnish or over-sauce your food, and let the ingredients speak for themselves. One of my favourite dishes in this book is also one of the easiest to make (and, incidentally, one of Martin Brigdale's favourite photographs) – Curried Turbot. The turbot is lightly dusted with curry powder, pan fried and served on buttered cabbage – no fuss, just excellent food!

Never forget, if you are in a hurry and don't really have time to cook, try using fish, nature's original convenience food. It cooks in minutes, often only seconds – quicker than soft boiling an egg, for heaven's sake! These days there is absolutely no need to worry about skinning or filleting or any of those tedious jobs, as most, if not all, retailers will do the preparation for you. In fact, if they don't then change shop! The only time you may need to do the filleting is if you caught the fish yourself, and if that's the case then you probably don't mind anyway!

In the introduction to the first edition of *A Feast of Fish* I said 'By all means follow the recipes in this book – that, after all, is what it's for – but also improvise. If there is an ingredient in a recipe you cannot get hold of, don't just give up – substitute it. Good food and good cooks are created and creative not made from books. I hope you will use my book as a guideline and as a source of inspiration – not a bible.' This holds as true today as it did then; all too often recipes are followed to the letter. I want this book to inspire you to experiment and be creative. So what if your first attempt doesn't work? Who cares, try again, they are not all going to be disastrous. Cooking should be fun, so enjoy!

Acknowledgements

My thanks have to go to certain people without whom this book would probably never have appeared. There was a time when I swore that I would never write another book. So if a couple of friends had not, over the intervening years, nagged at me to start tapping away at the typewriter again, this book would never have appeared. Although Shaun and Peter have never met each other, I have both of you to thank for having faith in me and for browbeating me into submission – I am glad I listened to you both (eventually). Shaun deserves a special thank you as he has been a tremendous help with the research, accompanied me at ungodly hours on trips to Lowestoft market and even occasionally bought breakfast!

Thank you also to Gordon Hall, proprietor of Hall Batson Wines in Norwich for his wine notes and suggestions. Wine and food pairing is something we both believe in, and too often it is an aspect of dining that is taken for granted, with chance playing a huge part in whether or not the wine complements the meal. Good luck in changing attitudes, Gordon!

Norwich has played a sizeable part in the writing of this book, mainly because I moved to Norfolk shortly after starting work on it. Being new to an area can be traumatic but the people of Norfolk have been both friendly and helpful. Gary Howard of Howard's Fishmongers in Norwich was one of these. Gary, you have been a tremendous help in supplying fish for the recipe-tasting and for the photographs, as well as giving me an insight into the problems a high street fishmonger faces. I also managed to glean a lot of information by visiting Lowestoft fish market, so thanks to all those who unwittingly helped there.

For years now I have used the same fishmonger in a number of different places and over time he has become a friend. Richard Organ of Simson's Fisheries of Coulsdon supplied me with fish while I was in Canterbury and continued to do so when I moved to London as well as numerous other places along the way. It was natural that I should turn to him when looking for supplies for the photography and, as I knew would be the case, Richard came up trumps for me. Truly some of the best fish I have ever seen, thanks mate!

I must also thank Martin Brigdale. This is the second book I have worked with him on and what photos! The man is a genius behind the lens and his taste in wine is pretty good too! Superb Martin, let's do it again!

Thank you also to Clare and Julia at Little, Brown for their faith in the book and patience with me. And last but by no means least, thanks to my wife, Jane, for being my guinea pig and eating fish night after night after night. All the recipes in this book have been cooked by me at home so I know they work!

Buying and Preparing Fish

Choosing Your Fish: Freshness and Quality

Choosing your fish is probably the most important and crucial part of your intended dish: without good quality fresh fish, your dish will be ruined before you start.

My first rule is: do not use anything frozen. However, before I go any further, I must admit that this is as much a personal preference as it is for any other reason. Let me clarify my reasoning before the frozen food industry accuses me of overreacting.

Firstly, I have a policy (and always have had) of not using anything frozen, tinned, bottled or preserved in any way unless I have either done it myself or it is absolutely necessary. Secondly, there are a lot of dishes where frozen fish is definitely unsuitable. Mousselines are a prime example of this. The freezing of fish seems to break down the gluten content of the meat and therefore a good binding of egg white and cream cannot be achieved.

Thirdly, have you ever noticed how much ice you get with frozen fish (or glaze as the manufacturers call it!)? Prawns and scallops are both heavily-glazed items; when defrosted, see how much smaller, limp and tired-looking they are compared to those lovely, plump, shiny examples of their species sold fresh.

Now I come to the last, most controversial and yet most important reason why fresh fish is preferable to frozen. We all know that the majority of fish caught is frozen at sea when it is at its best. However, it is equally true that a lot of fish landed fresh today finds itself unsold in a few days' time – then what? In my experience, it finds its way into a freezer and then, of course, it is sold as frozen. How old was it before it was frozen? In fact, it may even have been frozen once already, thawed, then refrozen to extend its shelf-life. That glaze on it, is it natural sea slime? Or is it slime from decomposition? I know this is a little hard-hitting and certainly the exception rather than the rule, but I make no apologies. After all, it is definitely harder to tell how fresh a fish is when it's frozen!

Now that I have, I hope, persuaded you not to buy frozen fish, how can you tell whether the fresh fish you are looking at is really fresh? Well, most of it is common sense. A fresh fish looks fresh (obvious, isn't it?), bright and shiny; an old fish looks dull and lifeless. The first sign is the skin. It should look shiny, have a slight natural slime, and the scales should look bright and fresh. The eyes should be nicely rounded and once

again have a good shine. The gills should be bright red. As the fish ages, the gills go very grey and dirty-looking. Another way to test for freshness is to press the fish quite firmly with your forefinger. If it springs back and leaves no mark, you have a good fish. If it leaves a mark that will not go away, then the fish is old. There is, of course, another way to test for freshness. I once read in a book on fish that you should bend down so that your nose is about 5cm/2 inches away from the fish, then inhale deeply. Believe me, if that poor fish is bad you will know about it long before you get that close!

Choosing Shellfish

Choosing shellfish is easy – if it's alive, then it's fresh. However, shellfish can also be bought cooked. Once again, as with frozen fish, I would strongly advise against buying cooked shellfish. I have heard of cases where they have not been completely cooked; not only that, but whoever cooked it probably didn't take as much care over the court bouillon as you would, assuming, of course, that a court bouillon was used at all, which is very doubtful. More than likely, the shellfish were only cooked in plain boiling water and, therefore, their flavour must be affected.

Crabs and lobsters should be alive and feel heavy in relation to their size. A lobster or crab with only one or even no claws is classed as a cripple and is more often than not cheaper. Decide what you want it for and it may be better to use a cripple. Oysters, clams, scallops and mussels should always be tightly shut or, if not, should snap shut as soon as they are disturbed.

Choosing and recognizing good quality fish is the easy part! The hard part is finding a good supply. Basically, find a good fishmonger and let them know you will not accept second best. It may take time, but if they care about what they sell, your efforts will pay dividends in the long run.

Preparing Fish

Probably what puts most people off fish is having to prepare it. Yes, it can be a smelly and messy business, but at least in doing it yourself you will know how fresh the fish really is. The alternative is either to buy fish pre-prepared or ask your fishmonger to prepare it the way you need.

Here I have described the basic methods of preparation. The most important tool in fish preparation is the knife. Without a sharp knife the job becomes a chore. It should have a blade of at least 15cm/6 inches and be slightly flexible; in other words, a filleting knife. The fish cook's filleting knife is as indispensable as a boning knife is to a butcher. It

SCALING FISH

1 Holding the fish by its tail, scrape away from you with a knife towards the head

2 Place the fish under running water to wash off the scales.

must, however, be kept sharp at all times. A blunt knife will not cut but tear and slip; more pressure is then needed in using it, and this can result in more cut fingers than when using a sharp knife.

Scaling

There are three basic preparations for fish: scaling and filleting, then, depending on the recipe, skinning. Scaling should always be your first step; it is an important part and one that people often try to get out of doing, but believe me it must be done – why spoil a beautiful dish just because you cannot be bothered to do the job correctly? If the fish is not scaled before filleting, then the knife, no matter how sharp it is, will not cut through the scales, which are always very tough. This is not, however, the only reason for scaling; as well as being inedible, scales are also quite loose and some will come off during cooking and removing them from the meat or sauce before serving will be impossible. To scale, hold that fish by the tail using a cloth to keep a grip, then, using the back of a knife, scrape the skin with the knife from tail to head. This is best done over a sink full of water or under running water as the scales do have a tendency to fly off in all sorts of directions. Once scaled, the fish should be rinsed to remove any remaining loose scales.

Filleting

Depending on the recipe, the fish may require filleting. Although most fish can be bought ready filleted, it is just as well to know what to do. As fish come in two basic shapes, round and flat, there are also two ways of filleting. Flat fish are probably the easiest to cope with as they have a flat bone that is easy to negotiate, and there is also a line, the lateral line, down the fish from head to tail, which acts as a cutting guide. This line runs from the centre of the tail up the middle of the fish towards the head; just before the head, it curves off to one side around the pectoral fin and finishes behind the gills. Round fish have a curved rib cage, which makes them more difficult to negotiate, and a line of small bones that have to be freed from the backbone.

For flat fish, first cut round the side of the head, then down the centre of the fish following the line once it straightens out. Slide the knife under each fillet, angling it towards the bone as you go. For round fish, lay the fish on its side and make a cut just behind the gills at an angle towards the head, then cut along the back just above the dorsal fin from head to tail. Using the point of the knife, carefully cut the fish away from the bone, turn the fish over and repeat on the other side.

FILLETING FLAT FISH

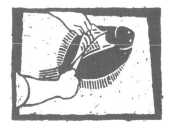

1 Lay the fish on the work surface with its head away from you. Make an incision along the dark line through to the bone from head to tail.

2 Slide the knife under each fillet, angling it towards the bone as you cut.

3 Continue cutting until free.

4 Remove the other fillet, turn the fish over and repeat.

FILLETING MONKFISH

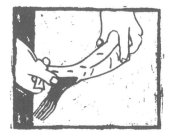

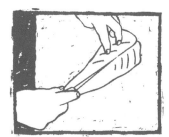

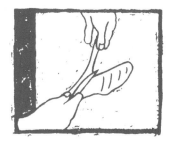

1 Holding the fish firmly, pull away the skin.

2 Put the fish flat on its back and cut the fillet away from the bone.

3 Repeat with the second fillet.

PREPARING FLAT FISH

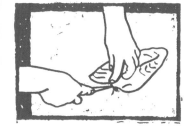

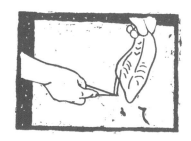

1 Using a heavy knife, cut off the head at an angle.

2 Trim off the fins and tail with a pair of kitchen scissors.

3 With the point of a knife, scrape away the blood clot from just behind the head.

4 Pull out any roe. Wash the fish well, especially the cavity, and pat dry.

FILLETING COOKED SOLE

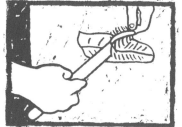

1 Lay the cooked fish on a flat surface and, using a palette knife, scrape away the skirt on both side.

2 With the head of the fish towards you, run the knife down the centre line of the fish. Slide the knife under the fillets and lift off.

3 Slip the knife under the bone and carefully lift it out. Replace the top two fillets on the bottom two.

Once filleted, always wash the fish and pat dry. There is a line of small bones that runs down the centre of each fillet on a round fish, and these should always be removed before cooking. Depending upon the fish, these bones may only run for about an inch or they may run for two-thirds of the fillet. Bass, mullet, haddock and cod have only a few bones, four or five, whereas salmon and trout have a line of over 20 bones in each fillet. If you do not know where they are – and they are hard to see – run your finger down the length of the fillet from head to tail and they will be easily found. I find it best to remove these with a small pair of pliers.

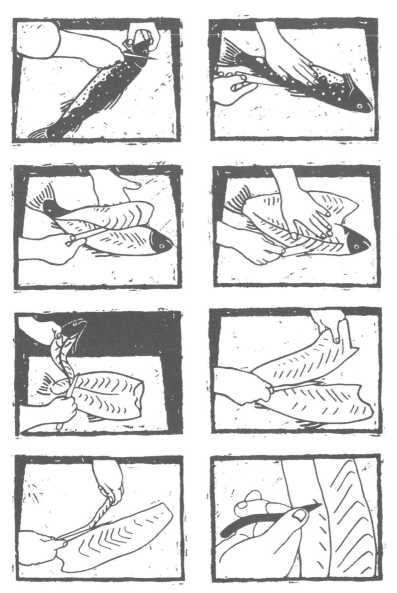

FILLETING ROUNDFISH

1 Lay the fish on its side and make a cut through to the bone at an angle just behind the gills. Turn the fish over and repeat.

2 Starting just above the dorsal fin, cut in one movement towards the tail, finishing just above the tail fin. Finish by cutting from the dorsal fin to the cut behind the gills.

3 Using the point of a sharp knife, carefully cut along the bone towards the backbone, moving from head to tail, until the top fillet is free but still attached to the bottom fillet.

4 Insert the knife under the bone at the tail end and slide it towards the head.

5 Free the bottom fillet by gently lifting away the bone.

6 Cut the fish down the middle into two fillets.

7 Trim the edges of the fillets.

8 Using a pair of pliers, remove the line of small bones that runs two-thirds of the length of the fillet. To make the bones easier to find, run your fingers or the back of a knife down the fillet.

SKINNING FILLETS

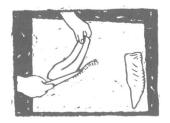

1 Lay skin-side down and cut through the flesh at the tail end. Grip the skin and work towards the head with the knife.

2 Trim off the skirt.

SKINNING DOVER SOLE

1 Make an incision through the skin on the tail and scrape away enough skin to hold onto.

2 Hold the tail with a cloth and pull the skin towards the head.

Skinning

Again, depending on the recipe, the fillets may need skinning. Lay each fillet on the board, head end away and skin side down, then make an incision at the tail end through the flesh but not the skin. Work the blade from side to side between the flesh and the skin, pushing with the knife and at the same time pulling the skin with the other hand. Once filleted, the skirt that runs around the edge of all flat fish should be removed.

Once scaled, filleted and skinned, the fish is then ready for cooking. All that needs to be done now is to portion it if it is too large. When cutting a fillet into two or more pieces, I always cut across the fillet holding the knife at a slight angle; this tend to give it a more attractive shape. Sometimes I also cut at an angle diagonally across the fillet; this is normally when the fillet is narrow and a longer strip is required.

Preparing Shellfish

The preparation of shellfish is a little more varied than that of other fish because there are so many types and so many ways of using them.

Lobsters, when bought alive, must first be killed before using. Depending on the recipes, there are a number of ways of carrying this out, some of which are definitely not for the squeamish. If cooking the lobster whole, it should first be killed by plunging a trussing needle deep into its head between the eyes; this method is supposed to be quick and humane, although I am a little dubious as to whether it is or not. Crabs are treated in the same way, because if a live crab is plunged straight into a boiling liquid it has a tendency to shed its claws. When roasting or grilling a lobster or removing its meat for a mousseline, cut through the head with one swift movement using the point of a heavy, sharp knife. Whichever way you prepare the lobster, once killed it will not just lie still. Nervous reaction will make the fish jump and move about, sometimes quite considerably, so it is best to be mentally prepared for this happening.

Many people are understandably a little frightened of handling a live lobster or crab, and live crayfish are particularly active. As long as you remember to hold the fish behind the claws, there is no cause for alarm, as it will not be able to reach your hand. Both crabs and lobster, if bought really fresh, can normally be kept alive for a couple of days by wrapping them in wet newspaper and keeping them in the refrigerator. Crayfish will also keep for several days; put them in a covered container and store in the refrigerator.

FOLDING FILLETS OF SOLE

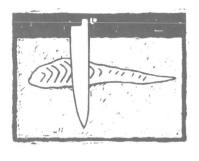

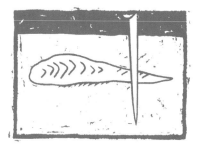

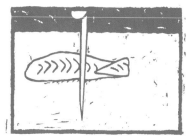

1 Lay the fillet skinned side up and lightly flatten with the side of a heavy knife.

2 Using the blade of the knife, tap the fillet across its width about 2.5 cm (1 inch) from the tail end.

3 Fold the tail over.

4 Tap the fillet again with the blade of the knife but this time across the middle.

5 Fold the head over towards the tail.

6 The folded fillet is now ready for use.

REMOVING THE INTESTINAL TRACT FROM CRAYFISH

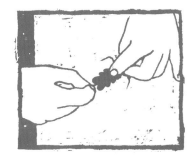

1 Hold the crayfish firmly behind the head and claws.

2 Grip the middle of the tail with your thumb and forefinger.

3 Twist and pull.

SHELLING DUBLIN BAY PRAWNS OR LOBSTERS

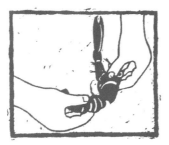

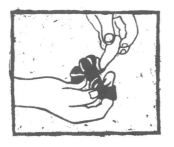

1 Pull away the head.

2 Crack the shell with the palm of your hand.

3 Carefully pull away the shell.

When preparing mussels, scallops and clams, it is as well to remember that they are always full of sand and therefore cannot be washed too often. With both mussels and clams, allow them to sit in clean water for about 15 minutes, having first checked that they are alive, then change the water, allow them to sit for another 15 minutes, and repeat the process once more. Mussels should always be scraped to remove any barnacles and the beards pulled away. If a mussel feels too heavy for its size, then it is probably full of mud and should be discarded. Mussels and clams can also be kept for a couple of days before cleaning and cooking; simply cover them with wet newspaper, place a heavy weight on top, and store them in the refrigerator. A few will die, but the majority will be alive and perfectly good.

Scallops are quite difficult to clean, so it is probably best to buy them ready cleaned, although even then they will still need a good wash. It is important to remember that although all fish, especially shellfish, must be washed, they should not be left standing in water for too long as this will impair their flavour.

Oysters, although molluscs, do not need the same careful cleaning as, for example, mussels. The shells should be scrubbed, especially if they are to be eaten raw straight from the shell, but soaking is not necessary. When using them for cooking, always save their juice; strain it though muslin and add it to the sauce. Oysters can be stored for a few days in exactly the same way as mussels, but always check that they are still alive before using.

KILLING LOBSTER

1 Using a heavy-bladed knife, place the point just behind the head.

2 With one swift movement, push the knife through the head.

3 Alternatively, plunge a trussing needle between the eyes.

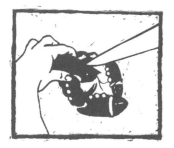

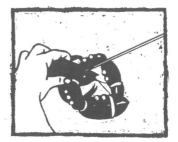

PREPARING CRAB

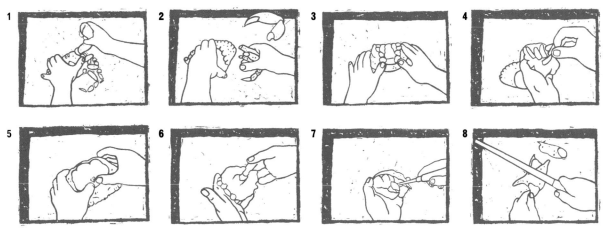

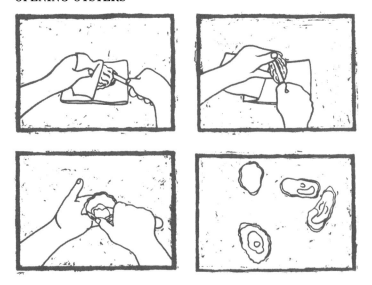

1 Turn the crab onto its back and break off the claws.

2 Pull off all the legs.

3 With the crab still on its back and with the eyes away from you, push the body up and away with your thumbs to separate it from the carapace.

4 The gills, or dead man's fingers, can now be pulled away from the body and discarded.

5 The only inedible part of the crab is its stomach. To remove this, press down on the mouth part of the crab until it cracks off. It can now be pulled out and

discarded. All the remaining meat can be removed and eaten.

6 Any brown meat in the centre of the body can be eaten.

7 Using a thin-bladed knife or oyster knife, pick the white meat out of the body where the legs have been pulled away.

8 Using the back of a heavy-bladed knife or mallet, carefully crack the claws and legs to remove the meat.

OPENING OYSTERS

1 Hold the oyster in a cloth so that the flat side is uppermost. Using an oyster knife, push into the hinge and twist.

2 Slightly prise the shells apart down the inside of the flat shell.

3 Remove the oyster from the concave shell by freeing it with the knife.

4 The oyster is now ready for use. If liked, keep the shells for decoration.

Cooking Fish

The actual cooking of the fish is probably the most difficult and crucial part of any of the recipes. Fish is so easy to overcook and so difficult to get just right – it is almost done, just needs a few seconds more and it will be ready, when the telephone rings or the door bell goes, you answer it and, too late, you are having dry, tasteless fish again!

Fish is cooked at a much lower internal temperature than other meats and therefore it cooks quicker – when it reaches about 63°C/145°F, it is ready; once over that temperature, the water in the structure of the fish runs out, the meat very quickly becomes dry and, since the flavour is contained in the water, very tasteless.

There are many ways in which fish can be cooked, but one way that should be avoided is boiling unless you are cooking shellfish or making soup, and even then they should only simmer. You will see in the recipes that my preferred ways of cooking are poaching and steaming, although I also use grilling, baking and frying. The cooking times mentioned in the recipes work for me, although there are a few variables that must be taken into consideration. The efficiency of your oven or grill will be a major factor in determining the cooking time; if the thermostat in your oven is not working properly, then the cooking time may vary slightly. The thickness of the fish will also play its part in upsetting your timing. Where I have called for a 150g/5 oz fillet of turbot, for example, it could be 1cm/$\frac{1}{2}$ inch thick and 12.5 cm /5 inches long or, if the fish it came from is larger, it may be 2cm/$\frac{3}{4}$ inch thick by 10 cm/4 inches, and this extra depth will mean that it must be cooked a little longer. Use the cooking times supplied as a guide, but do not take them as being absolutely correct in every case. They do, however, emphasise how little time fish needs to cook, and even if the fish is not cooked after the specified time, it will probably only take a matter of seconds more, rather than minutes, to finish the process. Once the fish has been cooked, it must be served as soon as possible. Remember that while it is being kept warm, the fish will continue to cook and that if it is kept too warm for too long, it will overcook and become dry and flavourless. At all times be aware, and take care not to overcook!

Finally, you can tell whether the fish is cooked or not in a number of ways: its colour will change and become opaque and even; it should just give to the touch; or, if on the bone, the meat should just pull away, not fall off easily.

Poaching

To poach means to cover or partially cover the fish in liquid, such as stock
or court bouillon, which is then gently heated until the liquid just starts to
tremble. The liquid should then be held at this point until the fish is
cooked. I find it best to transfer the pan to the oven to complete the
cooking process; this will prevent the liquid from boiling, which must be
prevented if the fish is to poach correctly and retain its flavour and
moisture. If the poaching stock is allowed to boil, the fish will toughen and
shrink considerably. It is important when poaching that the pan or tray
used is large enough to take the fish without them touching or overlapping.
If you do not have a pan large enough, use two pans rather than using the
same one twice. If the fish is to be served cold once poached, it is best to
allow the fish to cool in its stock until ready for serving; this will greatly
improve its flavour and is particularly good for shellfish. When cooking
shellfish, they should always be plunged into boiling liquid and then the
heat turned down and the liquid allowed to just simmer, not boil.

Steaming

Fish is steamed by placing it in a tightly fitting perforated container over
a pan containing boiling water or stock so that the steam produced by the
boiling liquid envelopes the food. It is a quick and clean method of
cooking that was, until recently, much maligned in the West as being fit
only for invalids, but it is a method that is extensively used by the
Chinese. Its main advantage over other methods is that it retains more of
the natural flavour, moisture and nutrients of the food, needs nothing
added to facilitate cooking, and is, therefore, better suited to those on
calorie-conscious diets. Another advantage is that more than one food can
be cooked in the container at the same time without any loss of individual
flavours. It is important when steaming not to allow the boiling liquid to
touch either the fish or the steaming basket, and to keep the liquid boiling
continuously and not to allow the pan to boil dry.

Grilling

Grilling is suitable for both small, whole fish, such as mullet, or for fillets
of fish, and even for some shellfish such as prawns or lobsters. It also
takes two forms: over heat on a charcoal grill or barbecue; or under a grill
giving top heat only. If the fish is thin or only a fillet, the flesh or cut side
should be done first to seal in its juices; alternatively, a tray can be used
instead of a rack, in which case the fish will not need turning. Always
preheat the grill to its highest setting so that the fish seals quickly,
trapping its juices; if it is a large piece, then turn the heat down a little so

that the fish cooks gently and without burning. When grilling a whole fish, it is best to score the flesh a few times so that the heat can penetrate more effectively, and remember that it will need basting occasionally. If it is not scored, the outside of the fish will dry and burn before the inside is cooked.

Shallow-frying or sautéeing

This method is often called pan-frying and differs from deep-frying in that only a small amount of fat is needed; in fact, since the arrival of the non-stick pan, food can be sautéed dry, which is a lot more acceptable to the health-conscious. When using fat to fry in, a combination of oil and butter is best; butter for the flavour it gives, and oil to prevent the butter from burning. If you wish to use only butter, then it must be clarified first; clarified butter will not burn, whereas unclarified will. The food should always be started in a very hot pan to seal in its juices, then the heat reduced to allow it to finish cooking gently. It is a very quick way of cooking and is more suited to thinner cuts than to whole fish.

Baking

Baking is cooking in an oven with butter or oil and with a little liquid, although the addition of fat or liquid is not strictly necessary. It is normally reserved for whole fish or thicker cuts of fish, and also includes cooking fish in pastry or foil, such as en papillote.

Braising

Braising is another a method of cooking in an oven; the fish is normally braised on a bed of vegetables with the addition of stock and wine. Braising is a slower method of cooking, and it is always carried out in a covered pan in a moderate oven (160-180°C/325-350°F/Gas Mark 3-4). The fish must be basted occasionally with the cooking liquor and it is normally served in its own liquor or with a sauce made from it. As with baking, this method is more suited to whole fish or cuts of firm fish such as turbot and brill.

Roasting

This is probably a method that not many people would associate with the cooking of fish. It is, however, very good for cooking whole fish and cuts of firm fish. It is also an excellent way of cooking lobster, and a few recipes for roasting lobster are included in this book. Roast lobster has a far different flavour to that of poached, one that, to my mind, is superior. To roast, a fairly hot to hot oven is needed (200-230°C/400-450°F/Gas Mark 6-8). If the oven is not hot enough and the roasting pan not heated up first, the juices from the fish will escape and it will boil rather than roast.

Basics

Carrot Essence

This recipe has many uses so I have included it in this section; not only can it be used in the recipes in this book but it is also good with other fish as well as rabbit or chicken.

METHOD Peel the carrots and roughly chop them up along with the leek, celery and onion. Heat the oil in a pan and add all the vegetables, then cover and sweat them without colouring for about 10 minutes. Add the water and the sugar and season with a little salt. Bring to the boil and very gently simmer for 1 hour. Liquidise and strain. Pass the liquor through muslin and return to the pan and reduce till only 1 pint remains.

Makes 600ml/1pt

15ml/½fl oz olive oil

2k/4½lb carrots

115g/4oz leek

2 celery stalks

1 peeled onion

3pts water

2tbsp sugar

salt

Celeriac Purée

METHOD Cut the celeriac into small rough dice. Place them in a saucepan along with the other ingredients and seasoning. Cover with a tight-fitting lid or tin foil, bring to the boil and then simmer for 20 minutes until the celeriac is soft. Purée in a food processor until smooth.

Serves 4-5

350g/¾lb celeriac, peeled

¼ lemon, juice of

25g/1oz unsalted butter

60ml/2fl oz cream

30ml/1fl oz fish stock

salt and freshly ground white pepper

Court Bouillon

Makes 4¹/₂ litres/8pts

1 large onion

4 stalks celery

1 leek

3 stalks lemon grass

3 cloves garlic

300ml/¹/₂pt white wine vinegar

4¹/₂ litres/8pts water

55g/2oz sea salt

1 bay leaf

¹/₂oz coriander seeds

3 star anise

25g/1oz black peppercorns

METHOD Peel the onion and roughly chop. Roughly chop the rest of the vegetables and the lemon grass. Peel and chop the garlic. Combine these together with the vinegar, water and the remaining ingredients. Bring to the boil and simmer for 10 minutes. Remove from the heat, allow to cool and strain. Store in the refrigerator until needed.

Cous cous

Serves 5-10

280g/10oz cous cous

salt and freshly ground white pepper

425ml/³/₄pt fish stock

75ml/2¹/₂fl oz olive oil

METHOD Put the cous cous in a bowl and season it well. Bring the fish stock to the boil and pour over the cous cous. Allow to soak in and go cold. Once cold, stir in the olive oil.

Curry oil

1 onion

3 stalks celery

1 leek

4 cloves garlic

1 apple

2 tomatoes

25g/1oz ginger

2 stalks lemon grass

zest ¹/₂ lemon

55g/2oz raisins

3 star anise

15g/¹/₂oz coriander

4tbsp curry powder

1tsp Thai red curry paste

2tbsp tomato purée

600ml/20fl oz olive oil

1.2lt/2pts vegetable oil

salt

Flavoured oils have long been a favourite of mine, and this one is no exception. Once bottled it will keep almost indefinitely.

METHOD Roughly chop the onion, celery, leek, garlic, apple, tomato, ginger, lemon grass and lemon zest.

Heat a little of the olive oil in a saucepan and add the vegetables; sweat them in the oil with the pan covered until they are soft. Add the raisins, star anise and the coriander, cover and continue sweating for a few more minutes. Stir in the curry powder and paste along with the tomato purée. Cook this for a couple of minutes stirring occasionally. Stir in the oils, season with the salt and allow to simmer very gently on a very low heat for a couple of hours. Strain and bottle, then use as required.

Fish Stock

About 1 litre/1¾pts

Fish stock is essential if you are going to do anything other than just grill your fish. Although the stock can be made from any fish bones the best ones to use are those of flat fish, monkfish and possibly whiting. Once made it will keep in a refrigerator for up to 7 days but can always be frozen. Freeze it in usable quantities and defrost it as needed.

450g/1lb fish bones

900g/2lb white vegetables (white of leek, celery, onion, fennel)

45ml/1½fl oz olive oil

85g/3oz mushrooms

150ml/5fl oz dry white wine

½ lemon

bouquet garni of parsley, or parsley stalks, thyme and bay leaf

1 tbsp white peppercorns

METHOD Remove any blood from the bones and, if using the heads, remove the gills. Wash the bones really well in a few changes of cold water. Peel and wash the vegetables and roughly chop them. Heat the oil in a saucepan, add the vegetables and mushrooms and sweat for a few minutes until the vegetables start to soften, with the pan covered. Add the white wine and reduce slightly. Cut the lemon into two and add to the pan with sufficient water to just cover the bones. Bring to the boil and skim frequently. Once it reaches the boil reduce it to a simmer. When no more scum comes to the surface, after about 5 minutes, then add the bouquet garni and the peppercorns and simmer for 20 minutes. After 20 minutes strain the stock through muslin or fine cloth and allow to cool.

There is no point in cooking the stock for more than 20 minutes, as no more flavour will be extracted from the bones after this time. If the stock is not very strong then reduce it to the desired level after straining.

Garlic Confit

METHOD Peel the garlic cloves and place these in a saucepan with the peeled onion cut into three pieces. Add the remainder of the ingredients. Cover tightly and bring to the boil.

Transfer the mixture to an oven pre-heated to 180°C/350°F/Gas 4 for 20 minutes.

20 cloves garlic

½ small onion

½tsp black peppercorns

½tsp coriander seeds

1 bay leaf

½ star anise

small sprig rosemary

30ml/1fl oz dry white wine

30ml/1 fl oz chicken stock

60ml/2 fl oz olive oil

salt and a pinch of sugar

Gazpacho

1 medium red pepper

1 medium yellow pepper

225g/8oz cucumber

115g/4oz shallots

3-4 small red chillies

15ml/1tsp Worcester sauce

1 clove garlic, crushed

600ml/1pt tomato juice

salt and freshly ground white pepper

This sauce is great to use with any cold fish dish, from smoked salmon to crab. Once made it will keep for up to three days in the refrigerator. It is best made at least 1 hour before needed to allow the ingredients time to infuse with the tomato juice.

METHOD Quarter and de-seed the peppers, and cut them into very fine dice. Cut the cucumber into fine dice, discarding the central core of seeds. Peel and finely chop the shallots. Split the chillies in half length-ways, scrape out the seeds and discard, and then finely chop them. Combine all the ingredients together with the tomato juice and season to taste.

Lobster Sauce

To make about 1.2 litres/2pts

675g/1½lb lobster shells

85ml/3fl oz brandy

25ml/1fl oz oil

225g/8oz mirepoix (leek, celery, carrot, onion, fennel)

½ stick lemon grass roughly chopped

1 clove crushed garlic

1½tbsp tomato purée

1.7lt/3pts fish stock

1 bay leaf

1 star anise

1 sprig fresh rosemary

10g/¼oz fresh tarragon

pinch saffron

It will sound a little strange to most people and it may just be me but I think the best part of buying a lobster is the by-products one is able to get from it. Lobster sauce, soup, oil and coral are all possible by-products, with their own uses. Whatever you do, never buy a lobster, eat the meat and discard the shell – you would be better off discarding the meat and using only the shell!

METHOD Preheat the oven to 180°C/350°F/Gas 4.

Chop the lobster shells up quite small, place them in a roasting tin and sprinkle them with the brandy. Place in the oven and roast for 20 minutes.

Heat the oil in a large ovenproof saucepan and add the vegetable mirepoix, the lemon grass and the garlic, cover with a lid and sweat over a medium heat stirring occasionally, until the vegetables start to soften. Add the lobster shells and continue to sweat for another 5 minutes. Stir in the tomato purée, swill the roasting tin out with some of the fish stock then add this and the rest of the stock to the shells. Add the herbs and saffron and bring to the boil. Transfer to the oven and continue to cook for 1½-2 hours (the liquid should just simmer). Once cooked, strain through muslin or a very fine strainer.

Once made this sauce has many uses for recipes such as the one on page 154, as the base of a consommé or reduced with cream to make a richer sauce (great with poultry).

Lemon Vinaigrette

This very simple to make vinaigrette has such a clean taste that it will go with any manner of dishes. Perfect for a light dressing for mixed leaf or green salads, fish or even chicken dishes.

METHOD Zest both of the lemons. Pick the dill leaves and roughly chop, saving the stalks. Cut the zest of one of the lemons into a fine short julienne, place it in a saucepan of cold water, bring to the boil, drain and refresh. Squeeze the lemons and put the juice into a saucepan with the remaining zest, the dill stalks, sugar, peppercorns, star anise, water and olive oil. Add the salt and gently warm through to infuse, for about 15 minutes; do not allow to get too hot. Strain onto the lemon zest and allow to cool.

2 large lemons

15g/½oz fresh dill

1tbsp sugar

1tsp black peppercorns

½ star anise

75ml/2½fl oz water

150ml/5fl oz olive oil

pinch salt

Mash

'Mash to die for' is the way my mash has been known by many of my customers over the years, and who am I to argue? Although I tend to use reds such as Desirée I do also use other varieties depending upon their quality at the time of making. Some people use only oil. Others only use cream and others still, only butter; some prefer other combinations. Hang the expense, I use all three! No matter what potatoes you use or the amount of cholesterol you add you really need a mouli to make good mash. If you do not possess one then I recommend you go buy one.

METHOD Peel the potatoes and boil in salted water. Once cooked, drain well, return to the pan and heat for a minute to dry them out properly. Pass though the mouli. Stir in well 45ml/1½fl oz of the oil. If you cool the mash it can be stored in the refrigerator like this for 24 hours and reheated as needed.

To reheat the mash place the remaining oil, the butter and the cream in a pan and bring to the boil; add the mash and seasoning and reheat, working in the oils until they have been absorbed and it is really smooth and silky.

The amount of oil, butter and cream you add will depend very much on the type of potato used. If your potato comes out lumpy after storage in the refrigerator it means you did not add sufficient oil to the mix initially.

Serves 6

1.25k/2lb 12oz red potatoes

100ml/3½fl oz olive oil

salt and freshly ground white pepper

150ml/5fl oz whipping cream

55g/2oz unsalted butter

Pasta

600g/1¼lb plain flour

6 egg yolks

7 eggs

30ml/2tbsp olive oil

salt

METHOD Place the flour in a food processor and switch on. Slowly add the eggs and yolks using pulse setting. Add the olive oil and salt, mix briefly. Knead for a few minutes and rest for at least one hour.

Serves 6

350g/12oz yellow peppers

550g/1lb 4oz red peppers

175g/6oz onion

1-2 cloves garlic

45ml/1½fl oz olive oil

2oz tomato purée

salt and freshly ground white pepper

Pepperonata

This is a great accompaniment to any grilled fish and can be served either hot or cold. Try serving it on a crostini as a snack or a nibble before dinner.

METHOD Blanch, skin and deseed the peppers, and cut them into strips. Halve the onion, remove the root and slice as thinly as possible. Peel, halve and finely slice the garlic.

In a saucepan heat the oil, add the onions and garlic, cover and sweat over a medium heat for about 3-4 minutes stirring occasionally until the onions are soft but not browned. Add the peppers and seasoning, cook over a medium heat for about 5 minutes then stir in the tomato purée. Continue cooking slowly for a further 15 minutes, stirring occasionally so as not to brown or dry out.

Once made, the pepperonata will keep for up to three days in the refrigerator.

Pesto

2 large bunches of basil

140g/5oz grated Parmesan

100g/3½oz pine kernels

2 large cloves of garlic

300ml/½pt olive oil

salt and pepper

METHOD Place all of the ingredients in a food processor and blend to the desired consistency.

The pine kernels can be toasted if you wish.

Polenta

METHOD Season the water and bring it to the boil. Whisk in the polenta and continue to whisk until it starts to thicken. Whisk in the butter and parmesan until melted. Pour the mixture onto a greased tray and allow to set. Cut out as needed.

1.7 litres/3pts salted water

225g/8oz polenta flour

115g/4oz unsalted butter

115g/4oz grated **Parmesan**

Puff Pastry

The amount of water needed to make a paste will depend on the quality of flour used. Do not add all of the water at once; save a little and add a few more drops if it seems too dry.

1.25kg/2lb 12oz

450g/1lb plain flour

2tsp salt

225ml/8fl oz cold water

450g/1lb cold unsalted butter

METHOD Sieve the flour and form into a mound on the work surface. Make a well in the centre. Dissolve the salt in the water and pour into the centre of the well. Gradually mix together using your fingers. When the ingredients are thoroughly mixed, work the dough with the palms of your hands until completely smooth. Wrap the dough in a cloth or greaseproof paper and leave to rest in the refrigerator for at least two hours.

Dust the work surface with flour and roll out the dough to form four flaps of about 10cm/4in wide, each at right angles to one another, and leaving a piece of dough in the middle. Knead the butter to form one supple slab and place in the centre of the dough. Fold over each of the four flaps to enclose the butter. Return to the refrigerator, covered, for a further 30 minutes.

Again, lightly flour the work surface and gently roll the dough into a rectangle about 60cm/24 inches long and 40cm/16 inches wide. Always roll the pastry away from yourself. Mark the rectangle into three equal sections. First fold one end section over the middle section and then fold the final section over the other. This is called a 'turn'. Now turn the dough through 90 degrees and roll it into a rectangle as before, flouring the work surface as you go. Once again mark out three equal sections and fold. The pastry has now had two 'turns'. Cover and leave the pastry to rest and firm up again in the refrigerator for at least 30 minutes.

Give the pastry another two 'turns', cover and refrigerate for a further 30 minutes. Give the pastry two final 'turns' so that it has now had six 'turns' in total. After resting for 30 minutes the pastry will be ready to use. It will last up to four days in the refrigerator or for weeks in a freezer.

Red Tomato Chutney

1.3kg/3lb ripe tomatoes
225g/8oz onions
15g/½oz salt
1tsp paprika
pinch cayenne pepper
150ml/5fl oz malt vinegar
175g/6oz brown sugar

Try making this tomato chutney to serve with your grilled or deep fried fish, or use it instead of tomato ketchup next time you bring home the fish & chips. Great to make when you have a glut of tomatoes or at the height of the season when they are cheap. If potted and sealed properly this chutney will keep a long time, but it does need to mature for about four weeks before using so try not to be too impatient.

METHOD Blanch the tomatoes then roughly chop them either with or without the seeds, whatever your preference. Peel and finely chop the onions. Place the onions and the tomatoes in a saucepan, bring them to the boil and simmer for 20 minutes. Add the salt, the spices and half of the vinegar, then cook gently for about 40 minutes or until quite thick. Add the sugar and the remaining vinegar, stir until the sugar has dissolved; simmer for a further 10 minutes stirring occasionally. Pot and seal.

Risotto Base

3 finely chopped shallots
100ml/3½fl oz olive oil
350g/12oz arborio rice
200ml/7fl oz dry white wine
600ml/1pt stock

METHOD Sweat the shallots for a couple of minutes in the oil. Add the rice and sweat for a further two minutes. Add the white wine and reduce by half. Add the stock and simmer until just cooked and almost all of the liquid has been absorbed.

Remove from the pan onto a tray to cool.

This risotto base can be made up to 24 hours in advance.

Yoghurt Dressing

65ml/2½fl oz natural live yoghurt
65ml/2½fl oz whipping cream
juice of ½ lemon
pinch of caster sugar
freshly ground white pepper

This dressing is great for all sorts of uses: as a light, fresh-tasting dressing that livens up green salads and as an accompaniment to terrines, mousses and the like. Try it with the addition of a few mixed herbs or chopped chives.

METHOD Mix together the yoghurt and the cream, and add the lemon juice to taste. Season with a pinch of sugar and freshly ground pepper.

Salsa Verde

METHOD Blend all of the ingredients together and season.

2 cloves of garlic

1 large bunch flat leaf parsley

1 bunch basil

6 leaves mint

25g/2tbsp capers

55g/2oz **Dijon** mustard

15ml/1tbsp white wine vinegar

150ml/¼pt olive oil

Sauce Jacqueline

Serves 4-6

I have included this recipe in the book because I think it is one of the sexiest sauces you will ever eat. It is loosely based around Louis Outhier's Sauce Jacqueline and I have therefore kept the name as a tribute. Outhier's Jacqueline is based on carrots and a lot more butter than I use here and itself is truly magnificent. It is a wonderful sauce for most poached fish and deserves to be here if only for that reason. It is also the basis for Fricassee of Scallops in Pimento Butter (see page 182).

METHOD Remove the stalk from the peppers, peel the carrot, the onion and the garlic, and wash the celery and the fennel. Chop all of these very small in a food processor.

Melt 25g/1oz of the butter in a saucepan and add the vegetables, cover and sweat for 5 minutes without colouring, stir in the paprika and the sugar then add the wine, the stock and the remaining butter. Bring this to the boil and simmer until reduced by two thirds.

Strain through a very fine strainer or muslin and allow it to go cold. Once cold the butter will have separated from the stock and set on top. Scrape it off.

When ready to use, return the stock to the boil and reduce by about half then gradually add the butter, whisking continuously until it is all melted. Do not return the sauce to the heat once the butter has been added.

400g/14oz red pepper

115g/4oz carrot

1 small onion

1 clove garlic

55g/2oz celery

55g/2oz bulb fennel

115g/4oz unsalted butter

½tsp paprika

1tsp sugar

300ml/white wine

600ml/1pt fish stock

Sauce Vierge

100ml/3½fl oz olive oil

30ml/1fl oz lemon juice

1tsp crushed coriander seeds

8 shredded basil leaves

9 tomatoes, blanched seeded and diced

METHOD Combine all ingredients together and season.

Scallop Sauce

Makes 900ml/1½pts

1½kg/3½lb scallop roes, skirts and trimmings

½ fennel

1 leek (white only)

2 medium onions

4 sticks celery

3oz mushrooms

2 cloves garlic

3 plum tomatoes

4dsp olive oil

2 bay leaves

2 star anise

10g/¼oz black peppercorns

200ml/7fl oz dry vermouth

50ml/1½fl oz brandy

1.7 litres/3pts fish stock

pinch saffron

This sauce is a great way of using the trimmings from the scallops. So often these are wasted but the flavour they contain is very intense.

METHOD Wash the scallop trimmings really well. Cut the fennel, leek, onion, celery and mushrooms up small. Crush the garlic and slice the tomatoes.

In a heavy saucepan heat the oil, and when hot add the fennel, leek, onion, celery and mushrooms, cover with a lid and sweat them down for about 10 minutes stirring occasionally.

Add the garlic, tomato, bay leaves, star anise and peppercorns, and continue sweating them for a further 5 minutes. Add the scallop trimmings and sweat for a further 10 minutes.

Pour in the vermouth, the brandy and the fish stock. Bring this to the boil and skim well. Add the saffron and simmer for 20 minutes.

Strain through a fine strainer and reduce by half.

Shortcrust Pastry

Makes about 350g/12oz

225g/8oz plain flour

1tsp salt

150g/5oz butter

1 egg

25-50ml/1-2fl oz cold milk

This light crumbly pastry is mainly used for flans and tartlets and will keep well in the refrigerator for four or five days. The amount of milk depends on the quality of the flour; the better the flour the more liquid.

METHOD Sieve together the flour and the salt, then rub the butter and the flour together with your fingertips. Add the eggs and the milk and mix together. When they are mixed in, knead the pastry into a smooth dough, but do not overwork; the finished dough should be quite firm.

Wrap in greaseproof paper or in a polythene bag and store in the refrigerator. Allow to rest for at least 1 hour before using.

Sweet Red Pepper Fondue

This sauce makes a really good accompaniment to grilled fish. Try mixing a little of the base into mayonnaise to serve with prawns, crabs or grilled lobster.

METHOD Remove the seeds and stalk from the peppers and cut the flesh up small. Peel the onion and finely chop it. Heat the oil in a saucepan and add the peppers, onion and garlic, season with the salt and pepper and cover the pan. Gently sweat this off without colouring for 10 minutes. Add the stock or water, bring to the boil then reduce to a simmer for 2 hours. Process in a blender until smooth and pass through a sieve.
Once made this will keep in the refrigerator for 4 days.

450g/1lb sweet red peppers

115g/4oz onion

45ml/1½fl oz olive oil

2 cloves crushed garlic

salt and freshly ground white pepper

15ml/½fl oz stock or water

Tapenade

METHOD Blend all of the ingredients together except the oil, until really smooth.
  Gradually add the oil.

250g/9oz pitted black olives

55g/2oz anchovies

25g/1oz capers

1½ cloves garlic

30ml/2tbsp olive oil

Thai Spice Mix

This recipe can be used in all sorts of different ways: in a risotto as on page 54, as a marinade for hot smoked prawns on page 159 or cooked in a sauce to accompany most fish or even chicken.

METHOD De-seed the peppers, peel the garlic and the ginger. Roughly chop the peppers, garlic, ginger, chillies and lemon grass then place in a food processor with the other ingredients and blend together. It will never be totally smooth due to the nature of the ingredients but this will not affect the final flavour.

2 red peppers

2 green peppers

6 cloves garlic

55g/2oz fresh ginger

2 bird's-eye chillies

1 stalk of lemon grass

1 teaspoon ground turmeric

2 green cardamom pods

¾tsp cayenne pepper

½tsp ground cumin

½tsp ground cinnamon

4-6 portions

5 medium plum tomatoes

60ml/2fl oz olive oil

25g/1oz chopped shallots

1 clove of garlic crushed

15g/½oz tomato purée

60ml/2fl oz dry white wine

125ml/4fl oz white wine vinegar

1 bay leaf

salt and freshly ground white pepper

possibly a little sugar

Tomato Vinaigrette

Use this either hot or cold with any grilled or roast fish; with the addition of some fresh basil it is great with poached salmon.

METHOD Blanch, skin and deseed the tomatoes then cut them into dice of about 1cm/½in. Heat the oil in a saucepan, add the shallots and garlic and gently fry without colouring for about 1 minute. Add the tomatoes, tomato purée, wine, vinegar and bay leaf. Season and add sugar to taste, then simmer over a low heat for 20 minutes. Remove from the heat and allow to go cold. Re-heat as necessary or use cold.

Makes 850ml/1½pts

½ head fennel

1 stick celery

1 medium onion

4 cloves garlic

½ leek

½ medium red pepper

10g/¼oz ginger

1.1kg/2½lb plum tomatoes

55g/2oz sun dried tomatoes

50ml/1½fl oz olive oil

1dsp black peppercorns

½ star anise

1dsp crushed coriander seeds

2 bay leaves

1dsp tomato purée

50ml/1½fl oz red wine vinegar

1.7 litres/3pts water

25g/1oz sugar

55g/2oz fresh basil

Tomato Essence

METHOD Roughly cut the fennel, celery, onion, garlic, leek and red pepper fairly small, wash and allow to drain. Slice the ginger.

Cut up the tomatoes into small pieces along with the sun dried tomatoes.

Heat the oil in a saucepan, and when hot add the vegetables along with the peppercorns, star anise, coriander seeds, bay leaves and ginger. Cover with a lid and sweat these down over a medium heat for about 5 minutes, stirring occasionally to prevent browning.

Add the tomatoes and sun-dried tomatoes, re-cover and continue to cook for a further 5 minutes.

Stir in the tomato purée and cook for another two minutes. Add the vinegar, the water and the sugar. Roughly cut up the basil and add to the pan. Bring this to the boil and simmer gently for one hour.

Strain through muslin and reduce by half.

Tomato Sauce

This easy to make tomato sauce can be used in lots of different ways, not only for fish but also for chicken, vegetables, lamb, anything!

METHOD Roughly cut up the cherry tomatoes and the sun dried tomatoes. Peel and slice the shallots and crush the garlic. Heat the oil in a saucepan then gently soften the shallots and the garlic in this without colouring. Add the tomatoes and the tomato purée and stir it through. Add the vinegar, sugar and seasoning then the water. Bring to the boil and simmer for 1 hour. After 50 minutes add the basil.

Gently rub the sauce through a sieve. Once made the sauce will keep for about three days in the refrigerator.

Makes 425ml/³/₄pt

450g/1lb cherry tomatoes

15g/½oz sun dried tomato

115g/4oz shallots

2 cloves garlic

15ml/1½fl oz olive oil

1½tbsp tomato purée

30ml/1fl oz white wine vinegar

1tsp sugar

salt and freshly ground white pepper

600ml/1pt water

stalk of fresh basil

Veal Stock

Veal stock needs to cook for a minimum of 8 hours as it takes at least 6 hours for the bones to give up their natural jelly and even longer to extract all the flavour. You could use beef bones as an alternative, or chicken bones with slightly more pig's trotters to help create the jelly a good stock needs. This stock can be used as a base sauce for all meat dishes as well as fish. It will freeze very well and will keep in the refrigerator for at least a week.

METHOD Pre-heat the oven to 230°C/450°F/Gas 8. Brown the bones in a roasting tray in the oven, turning from time to time. When lightly browned dot the tomato purée over them and continue browning for a further 10 minutes. Drain the bones of any fat and transfer them to a large saucepan, then add the water and bring to the boil. Once the stock comes to the boil, lower the heat and skim; a lot of fat and scum will have risen to the surface and this all needs to be removed. Allow to simmer, skimming as is necessary for about 5 hours or so then add the vegetables, mushrooms, tomatoes and garlic, simmer for a further hour then add the herbs. Continue to simmer up to a total of 8 hours. After this time, strain off the stock through a muslin or fine strainer. Reduce it down till only about 1.2 litres/2pts remains.

To make about 1.2lt/2pts

2.5kg/5½lb chopped veal marrowbones

1 pig's trotter split lengthways

25g/1oz tomato purée

app. 4.5 litres/8pts water

2 medium carrots, chopped

2 onions, chopped

2 small leeks, chopped

4 sticks celery, chopped

55g/2oz mushrooms, chopped

3 medium tomatoes, chopped

1 head garlic, chopped

1 sprig fresh thyme

1 sprig fresh rosemary

1 bay leaf

1 tbsp black peppercorns

Recipes

Bass

French: *Bar, Loup de Mer* • Italian: *Branzino, Spigola* • German: *Seebarsch*
Spanish: *Lubina*

Strangely the sea bass has always been much prized by anglers, yet only in more recent times has it been favoured by gourmets. Soft fleshed and delicately flavoured, it is one of my favourites and I like to eat it grilled and strewn with fresh dill. The Chinese and Japanese have always admired this fish and it appears on the menu in Chinese restaurants the world over. Popularity inevitably means that the price rises and the sea bass is no exception to this rule.

When swimming, sea bass appear remarkably silver (they are sometimes known as salmon bass because of their colouring) but once caught they seem to be more blue/black across the back, silver on the flanks and white on the under belly. A shoaling fish, they tend to be caught in huge numbers, especially during the summer months when they are often found gorging on smaller fish such as sardines and herring.

Farming sea bass has been very successful and the price of a farmed bass tends to be much more affordable than that of a wild one. The flavour of a farmed fish is not in the same league as its wild cousin though, and although good, I much prefer the real thing. Wild bass are increasingly line-caught these days and are also better for being caught this way – look out for them! As a guide, if you see lots of bass in a shop together, all the same size, then they will undoubtedly be farmed and not wild.

Bass is a remarkably good and versatile fish that can be used in so many ways – raw as the Japanese like it, baked, poached, steamed, grilled or fried. I always leave the skin on as it is thin enough to eat and since the flesh is very soft it helps to hold the fish together.

Sea Bass with Braised Fennel and Cucumber

Serves 4

1 x 1.3-1.6kg/3-3½lb sea bass

a little oil to grease
a grilling tray

55g/2oz unsalted butter,
melted

To braise the fennel:

1 bulb of fennel weighing
about 175g/6oz

55g/2oz unsalted butter

juice of ¼ lemon

100ml/3½fl oz fish stock
(see page 23)

4-6 cardamom pods

pinch of sugar

salt and freshly ground
white pepper

15ml/1tbsp Pernod

Sauce:

60ml/2fl oz dark soy sauce

300ml/10fl oz fish stock

175ml/6fl oz veal stock
(see page 33)

30ml/1fl oz sesame oil

For the cucumber garnish:

40g/1½oz unsalted butter

1 cucumber

a good pinch of sugar

salt and freshly ground
white pepper

I have never been a great admirer of cucumber but it works quite well with fish a lot of the time. I prefer my sea bass grilled, but this dish will work just as well with the fish poached.

METHOD Begin by scaling and filleting the sea bass, then removing the line of pin bones. Cut each fillet into two portions, as even as possible.

Trim the fennel of any discoloured or dry areas; cut the bulb in half and then chop each half into wedges. You will need at least 4 wedges per portion. Place these in a saucepan along with the butter, lemon juice, fish stock, cardamom pods, sugar, seasoning and Pernod. Tightly seal the pan either with a well-fitting lid or with foil, as you do not want any of the liquid to evaporate. Bring to the boil and cook rapidly for 10 minutes. Keep warm.

In a saucepan bring to the boil the soy sauce and the fish stock. Reduce this down over a high heat until only about one tablespoon remains. Add the veal stock, return to the boil then keep warm.

Lightly oil a grilling tray. Lay the bass on it meat-side up. Brush the fish with the melted butter and season. Place the fish under a pre-heated grill for about 4 minutes or until it is just cooked. Sea bass is a very soft fish and will cook very quickly. While the fish is cooking, heat the butter for the cucumber in a saucepan, and just as it starts to sizzle (it is important not to get the butter too hot as the cucumber should almost be poached in the butter not fried) add the cucumber, the sugar and seasoning. Stir this over the heat until it just becomes limp.

Arrange four wedges of fennel in the middle of each plate. Lay a fillet of fish on top of this. Spoon the sauce around and divide the cucumber onto the top of the fish in neat piles. Pour the sauce with a little of the sesame oil on each plate.

> **Wine Note** • Montagny, Louis Latour *(Burgundy)* • Fennel is always happier with white wine, and the delicate yet aromatic flavours here suggest a fragrant, French Chardonnay such as this excellent example which is both herbaceous and slightly nutty.

Grilled Sea Bass with Capers

Quite often with fish the simple approach is the best, especially when using a fish as good as sea bass. It has such a wonderful flavour and texture that it is almost a sin to put anything with it.

METHOD Lightly oil a grilling tray with some of the olive oil; season the fish on the meat side then lay the fillets on the tray skin side up. Brush the fish with the melted butter.

Place the fish under a pre-heated grill for about 4 minutes until just done, depending upon how thick the fish is.

Place all of the remaining ingredients together in a small saucepan and gently warm through; the idea is not to heat or cook the ingredients but rather to apply a little heat to help the flavours infuse throughout the oil. Check the seasoning and serve spooned over the fish.

Serves 4

150ml/5fl oz olive oil

4 fillets of sea bass each weighing about 175g/6oz

salt and freshly ground white pepper

25g/1oz melted butter

15g/½oz chopped parsley and dill

55g/2oz tiny capers

1 shallot finely chopped

1 clove garlic, finely sliced

2tsp grain mustard

juice of ¼ lemon

Wine Note • Concha y Toro, Sauvignon Blanc *(Chile)* • A delightfully simple dish that simply needs a refreshing glass of thirst-quenching dry white, which is exactly what this good value Sauvignon represents. From the central valley of Chile, the wine is fresh, herbaceous and perfectly balanced with just the right level of acidity to look after the 'tang' of the capers and mustard.

Sea Bass with Girolles

Serves 4

4 x 140-175g/5-6oz fillets of
sea bass

45ml/1½fl oz olive oil

25g/1oz melted butter

salt and freshly ground
white pepper

550g/1lb 4oz girolles

115g/4oz streaky bacon

2 shallots, finely chopped

1 crushed clove of garlic

100ml/3½fl oz Madeira

1tbsp chopped mixed herbs
(dill, tarragon, parsley and
chervil)

225ml/8fl oz veal stock
(see page 33)

Girolles are a fantastic mushroom but of course quite expensive. If you are lucky enough to live somewhere like the New Forest or Speyside, for instance, then you will be able to pick your own – that is if you know where to go. Normal button mushrooms could be used instead or a combination of mixed wild mushrooms or wild and cultivated; either way the dish will still work, although it does work best with girolles.

METHOD Make sure the sea bass is properly scaled and that the pin bones are removed. Using about 15ml/½fl oz of the oil grease a grilling tray. Lay the bass on it skin side down and brush with the melted butter then season the fish with the salt and pepper.

Scrape the girolles of any dirt and grit and cut off the roots; only wash them if they are too dirty to use, and then squeeze them dry and lay them on kitchen towel to dry thoroughly. Blanch the bacon in boiling salted water for a few seconds, drain and cut it into lardons. Fry the lardons in a little of the oil until they just start to crispen.

Cook the bass under a pre-heated grill for about 3 minutes until it is just cooked then keep warm.

Heat the remaining oil and the fat from the bacon in a frying pan; when hot add the girolles, the shallots and the garlic, season well and toss over a high heat for about two minutes; half way through add the lardons. Add the Madeira and allow to cook for a further minute. At the last second add the herbs. Drain the mushrooms and keep them warm. Set the mushroom juices in a saucepan over a high heat and reduce until almost gone. Add the veal stock and reduce until it just starts to thicken.

Arrange a pile of the mushrooms and bacon in the centre of each plate with a fillet of the fish on top then pour the sauce around.

Wine Note • Fleurie, Les Garants, Thomas la Chevaliere *(Beaujolais)* • Something fruity and not too heavy is the order of the day with this dish, which seems light in style yet has some underlying strong flavours. The girolles add a certain earthiness, which this well-balanced Fleurie will complement well since it has plenty of fruit and a good long finish.

Bream

French: *Dorade or Daurade* • Italian: *Pagro or Pagello*
German: *Nordischer Meerbrassen* • Spanish: *Besugo*

There are many different fish that can be categorised as sea bream. The names I have given above are those commonly used for Red Sea bream; the other main types are black bream, gilt head sea bream, Ray's bream and in the USA they are known as porgy or scup. The recipes that follow all use Red Sea bream, as this is the one I prefer, although the gilt head bream is generally regarded to be better.

Red bream is easy to recognise as it has very noticeable large round eyes. It also has a dark mark just behind the gills (similar to the 'thumb print' on a dory or haddock). The body of the fish is a grey colour with a pinky-red tinge. It can be found along the south and southwest coasts of the British Isles and it occasionally ventures further north if the weather is warm enough.

Most sea bream are on the small side – only about 30cm/12in long on average – and grow to a maximum of 50cm/20in, so a normal fish should be sufficient to serve two.

Red Bream with a Citrus Dressing

Serves 4

Once again this dish is suitable with many other fish: try it with salmon, halibut or John Dory. There are a lot of people who do not like fruit with either fish or meat, but if you are one of these please do not write this off; try it first, you may be surprised. We all know lemon works with fish, and so does a dressing like this.

METHOD Ensure that all of the scales and bones are removed from the bream then cut 6 or 8 slashes in the skin. Grease a grilling tray with the olive oil, season the meat side of the fillets and place them meat-side down on the tray. Brush the skin side with 40g/1½oz of melted butter and season the skin too.

Zest one orange and one lemon; cut the zest into a fine julienne. Place the zest in a saucepan, cover with water, bring to the boil, strain and refresh. Segment both the lemon and the orange. Juice the remaining oranges and the lemon.

In a saucepan combine together the juice, the fish stock and the white wine. Bring this to the boil and reduce until only about a third remains.

Put 55g/2oz of the butter into a pan along with the spinach, season and set over a high heat to cook the spinach very quickly, stirring occasionally. Once cooked, squeeze out the excess water and keep warm.

Place the fish under a very hot pre-heated grill for about 3 minutes until cooked.

Return the sauce to the boil and add the shallots, then gradually add the remaining butter, whisking the sauce until the butter has melted. Add the tomato dice and the spring onions and allow to warm through. At the last minute add the marjoram leaves.

Divide the spinach into the centre of the plates and place a fillet of the fish on top. Spoon the sauce over and around the fish.

Ingredients

4 x 175g/6oz fillets of red bream

30ml/1fl oz olive oil

Salt and freshly ground white pepper

40g/1½oz melted unsalted butter

3 oranges

2 lemons

250ml/9fl oz fish stock (see page 23)

100ml/3½fl oz dry white wine

115g/4oz unsalted butter

450g/1lb picked and washed spinach

2 shallots finely chopped

2 plum tomatoes, blanched, seeded and cut into small dice

2 spring onions sliced

16-20 leaves fresh marjoram

Wine Note • Château La Gordonne, Rosé, *(Côtes de Provence)* • Citrus fruits in any dish need to be balanced by a wine of equal acidity such as this deliciously fragrant wine that is very clean and refreshing. The colour will also complement the appearance of the fish.

Bream with Spinach and Saffron Potatoes

Serves 4

15ml/½fl oz olive oil

4 x 175g/6oz fillets of red bream

salt and freshly ground white pepper

25g/1oz melted butter

20 small new potatoes

600ml/1pt fish stock (see page 23)

good pinch saffron

125ml/4fl oz whipping cream

125ml/4fl oz red wine

150ml/5fl oz veal stock (see page 33)

25g/1oz unsalted butter

450g/1lb spinach, picked, well washed and drained

The colours of this dish are just so wonderful. Turbot, brill, sea bass, halibut, snapper or cod would work just as well as bream.

METHOD Grease a grilling tray with the olive oil. Make a few slashes in the skin of the bream to prevent curling and to speed cooking. Season the fish on the meat side and lay the fillets on the tray. Brush the skin sides of the fish with the melted butter and lightly season the skin.

Turn the potatoes into small barrel shapes and combine them together with 350ml/12fl oz of the fish stock, the saffron and a pinch of salt in a saucepan and cook them. When the potatoes are cooked remove them from the pan and cover. Reduce the stock by three quarters. Once reduced, add the cream and return to the boil, reduce until it just starts to thicken then remove from the heat.

Place the fish under a very hot grill for 3-4 minutes depending upon how thick the pieces are. Once cooked, remove and keep the fish warm.

Combine the red wine and the remaining fish stock and reduce until almost all gone; add the veal stock and reduce slightly more. Keep the sauce warm.

Heat the remaining butter in a saucepan and add the spinach and season. Cook this over a high heat until just limp; squeeze the spinach of all excess liquid. Place a pile of spinach in the middle of each plate. Return the potatoes to the boil. Place five potatoes on each plate in a circle around the spinach, then dribble a little of the saffron sauce over each one. Lay a fillet of bream on the spinach and spoon the red wine sauce around the saffron sauce.

> **Wine Note** • Heggies, Viognier Australia • Why not try a different grape variety here. Viognier is more usually seen from the Rhone Valley and this Aussie version has a lovely full, fruity style with flavours of peach and apricot that will accompany the aromatic saffron influence very well.

Red Bream with Stewed Onions and Black Turtle Beans

Serves 4

This particular recipe is suitable for so many different fish it was difficult deciding which one to choose. Try it with snapper, red fish, monkfish, even cod; it will work just as well with them all.

METHOD Soak the beans in cold water 24 hours before needed, remembering that they will swell to three times their size.

Drain and wash the beans. Place them in a saucepan along with the onion, bacon, carrot, leek and garlic. Cover well with water and bring to the boil. Allow to simmer until cooked. Once cooked allow to cool in the liquid, drain and discard the vegetables and bacon, then lightly rinse the beans in fresh water and drain well.

Peel and finely slice the onions. Place these in a saucepan along with the rest of the ingredients listed under Stewed Onions and season. There should be just enough liquid in the pan to cover the onions; if not then add more stock. Bring this to the boil and allow to simmer, stirring occasionally and making sure the onion is in the liquid all the time, until all the liquid has gone but the onions are still very moist. This will take up to 2 hours depending upon how fast you allow the pan to boil – the slower the better.

Reduce the red wine and fish stock in a saucepan over a high heat until almost gone then add the veal stock; reduce slightly to thicken.

Grease a grilling tray with the olive oil. Make a few slashes in the skin of the bream to prevent curling and speed cooking. Season the fish on the meat side and lay the fillets on the tray. Brush the skin sides of the fish with the melted butter and lightly season the skin. Place the fish under a very hot grill for 3-4 minutes depending how thick the pieces are.

Add the black beans to the sauce and warm through. Spoon the stewed onions into the centre of the plates and place a fillet of fish on this skin side up. Spoon the sauce around and drizzle with the pesto.

Ingredients

115g/4oz black turtle beans

½ medium onion, peeled

25g/1oz streaky bacon or a bacon bone

½ carrot, peeled

½ leek, white part only

1 peeled clove garlic

175ml/6fl oz red wine

350ml/12fl oz fish stock (see page 23)

225ml/8fl oz veal stock (see page 33)

30ml/1fl oz olive oil

4 x 175g/6oz fillets of red bream

Salt and freshly ground white pepper

40g/1½oz melted unsalted butter

60ml/4tbsp pesto (see page 26)

Stewed Onions:

900g/2lb onions

225ml/8fl oz dry white wine

600ml/1pt fish stock

20g/¾oz sugar

Wine Note • Sutter Home, Zinfandel *(California)* • A seriously robust and wintry dish with a degree of sweetness coming from the onions. There is only one grape variety to put with a dish that is rich or spicy yet slightly sweet. This Zinfandel has sufficient body, having been aged in oak for 12 months, together with aromas of raspberries and black pepper that are reflected on the palate.

Brill

French: *Barbue* • Italian: *Rombo liscio* • German: *Glattbutt* • Spanish: *Remol*

Although brill is related to turbot the two fish are only superficially similar. Brill has a much more elongated body than its rather round cousin and has small scales and no 'stones'. It's best described as a smaller, slightly inferior, shallow-water version of the turbot. The skin colour of both fish changes according to where it lives and how much light it gets, so a fish that has been living on a very sandy seabed in shallow water will be quite pale, whereas a darker, almost black skin indicates that it has been living in a muddier environment. Like the turbot, the brill is confined to the European side of the Atlantic and although it is not found in American waters it is fast becoming more popular in restaurants over there.

Brill never grows as big as turbot – a large fish normally weighs no more than 2.7kg/6lb and will be approximately 60cm/24in in length (although I have occasionally bought bigger). For this reason it will never be very meaty and you should always check the underside of the fish for bruising as any blood in the meat will render it unusable.

A good brill is a fine fish and it can be substituted for turbot (or any other flat fish for that matter) in most of my recipes. It has wonderfully tasty, firm, white flesh and for this reason it can actually command as much money as turbot these days.

Grilled Fillet of Brill with a Tomato, Courgette and Chickpea Broth

Serves 4

METHOD Cut the courgettes into dice about 1cm/½in square discarding the core. Blanch and skin the tomatoes, cut them into quarters and remove the seeds, cut the quarters into dice similar in size to that of the courgettes. Cut the onion into similar-sized dice.

Grease a grilling tray using the oil, season the fillets of fish, lay them on the tray and brush with the melted butter. Place under a pre-heated grill to cook for about 3-4 minutes depending upon how thick the fish is. Remove once cooked and keep warm.

Heat the butter in a saucepan till sizzling, add the onion and gently cook until translucent. Add the courgette and the garlic at this point and continue to fry gently for about 15 seconds, then add the chickpeas and the tomato sauce. Bring to the boil, add the cream and simmer for about 2 minutes until the courgette is cooked. Meanwhile reheat the mash as described on page 25.

Place a spoonful of mash in the centre of each plate; at the last minute add the chopped tarragon to the sauce, spoon the sauce around the mash and place a fillet of brill on top of the potato.

175g/6oz courgette

3 plum tomatoes

¼ medium onion

4 x 175g/6oz fillets of brill cut from a thick fish

15ml/½fl oz olive oil

salt and freshly ground white pepper

25g/1oz melted butter

40g/1½oz unsalted butter

1 crushed clove garlic

175g/6oz cooked chickpeas

225ml/8fl oz tomato sauce (see page 33)

45ml/1½fl oz whipping cream

½ recipe for mash (see page 25)

2tsp chopped tarragon

Wine Note • Viognier, Pere Anselme *(Rhone Valley)* • A wine from Languedoc Rousillon will marry very well with this dish that feels part French, part Spanish. The flavours are rich yet rustic.

Brill with a Wild Mushroom Consommé

Serves 4

Consommé:

800g/1lb 12oz flat mushrooms

½ leek

4 sticks celery

1 onion

2 cloves of garlic

1 tomato

30ml/1fl oz oil

4fl oz dry white wine

1.2lt/2pts water

1tbsp coriander seeds

1tsp black peppercorns

½tsp fennel seeds

1 bay leaf

salt

Clarification:

200g/7oz mushrooms plus wild mushroom trimmings

½ stick celery

½ small onion

¼ leek

1 tomato

1 clove garlic

1tbsp tomato purée

few sprigs parsley

few tarragon stalks

1 egg white

60ml/2fl oz Madeira

salt and freshly ground white pepper

This recipe will work with turbot and halibut just as well as it will with brill. This is a dish for the early autumn when the mushrooms are available in abundance and there is still fresh tarragon in the garden. It is not one of the quickest dishes to produce as the consommé needs to be made first. Try not to make the consommé today then use it tomorrow, as I think it is better all completed on the same day.

METHOD To make the consommé, chop the flat mushrooms up finely. Wash the vegetables and roughly cut them up, including the garlic and the tomato. Heat the oil in a saucepan and add the vegetables; sweat them with the pan covered for about 8 minutes until they go quite soft. Add the flat mushrooms and continue sweating until they have come down by half. Add the wine, the water and the herbs with a little salt. Bring to the boil and simmer for 1 hour. Drain through a fine strainer squeezing the mushrooms as dry as possible to extract the maximum amount of flavour. Allow to cool.

Trim the wild mushrooms saving any trimmings for the clarification. Wash and roughly chop the vegetables for the clarification, place these along with the mushrooms in a food processor and chop them quite fine. Tip into a saucepan and mix in the rest of the ingredients. Stir in the cold mushroom stock. Set the pan over a medium heat and bring it to the boil. As it heats stir occasionally, making sure it is not sticking. Just before it comes to the boil stop stirring it, as to stir now will cause the consommé to cloud. Turn the heat down as it comes up to the boil, so it is barely simmering. Allow to simmer very gently for about 45 minutes then carefully strain it through a muslin.

To finish the dish, season the fillets of brill. Place these along with 175ml/6fl oz of the consommé in a shallow pan large enough to hold the fish without overlapping. Bring to the boil, cover just as the liquid starts to tremble, and place in an oven pre-heated to 220°C/425°F/Gas 7 for 6-8 minutes until the fish is almost cooked. Remove and keep warm.

Make sure the mushrooms are really clean then reheat the remaining consommé with the mushrooms. Once hot, add the tarragon leaves, season, and divide the consommé, tarragon and mushrooms across the serving dishes, arrange the garnish around the edge and place a fillet of brill in the centre.

> **Wine Note** • Burglayer Schlosskapelle (blue bottle) *(Germany)* • A light fruity wine would nicely complement the earthiness of the wild mushrooms here without detracting from the delicate nature of the dish.

To serve:

4 x 175g/6oz of brill fully trimmed

600ml/1pt consommé (the above recipe makes about 600ml)

150g/5¼oz mixed wild mushrooms, e.g. mousserons, girolles, oyster, chanterelle, morels

20 leaves tarragon

salt and freshly ground white pepper

Fillet of Brill Poached in Red Wine with Shallots

Serves 4

METHOD Butter an ovenproof pan large enough to take the fillets of brill without overlapping. Cover the base with the sliced shallots, season the fillets of brill on the undersides and place them on top of the shallots. Add the red wine and the fish stock, cover with buttered paper or foil and bring up to almost boiling. Transfer to an oven pre-heated to 200°C/400°F/Gas 6 and cook for about 4-6 minutes depending upon how thick the fish is. Once cooked remove the fish and the shallots, cover and keep them warm.

Return the stock to the heat and reduce by three quarters. Add the veal stock and return to the boil; reduce until it just starts to thicken. Divide the shallots between the plates, place a fillet of fish on top and pour the sauce around. Garnish the plates with sprigs of fresh chervil.

4 x 150-175g/5-6oz fillets of brill

10g/¼oz unsalted butter

175g/6oz shallots, finely sliced

salt and freshly ground white pepper

175ml/6fl oz red wine

300ml/10fl oz fish stock (see page 23)

225ml/8fl oz veal stock (see page 33)

sprigs of fresh chervil

> **Wine Note** • Rockford, Dry Country Grenache *(S. Australia)* • Clearly the red wine sauce requires a red wine to accompany it, but it needs to be of good quality to equal the power of the reduced sauce. Grenache is *the* grape variety of the moment and this example from one of the most respected winemakers in the Barossa Valley is made from 40-60 year old vines and packed with spicy, ripe fruit.

Poached Brill with Potato, Celery, Bacon and Marjoram

Serves 2

175g/6oz new potatoes

85g/3oz streaky bacon

15ml/½fl oz olive oil

2 stalks of celery

2 x 140g/5oz fillets of brill

salt and freshly ground
white pepper

225ml/8fl oz fish stock
(see page 23)

100ml/3½fl oz dry white wine

175ml/6fl oz whipping cream

app. 30 leaves marjoram

A bit of a treat this one, best saved for when you are out to impress someone, or for that romantic dinner for two. The sauce is quite rich, as is evident from the amount of cream, but it is sheer elegance. If marjoram is unavailable then oregano, which is almost identical, will do. If neither is available then thyme is a good substitute, but as with all herbs only use it when fresh.

METHOD Boil the potatoes in salted water still in their skins until almost, but not quite cooked, refresh and peel. Cut them into 1cm/½in dice.

Cut the bacon into lardons and blanch for a second in boiling water; fry these in the oil until nicely browned. Peel the celery of its strings and cut into 5cm/2in batons.

Lightly season the undersides of the fillets of brill. Combine the fish stock and the white wine in a pan large enough to hold both fillets of brill flat and without overlapping each other. Lay the fish in the stock, cover and gently bring to the boil; just as it starts to simmer transfer the pan to an oven pre-heated to 200°C/400°F/Gas 6 for about 3-4 minutes, depending upon the thickness of the fish. When the fish is just slightly undercooked, remove from the stock and keep warm. Set the stock over a high heat and reduce by two thirds; as it reduces add the celery. Once reduced far enough add the cream, the potatoes and the bacon, return to the boil and reduce again until it just starts to thicken. By now the celery should be cooked but still slightly crisp and the potatoes will have finished cooking. Return the fish to the oven for a minute to reheat.

At the last second add the marjoram to the sauce then spoon the sauce onto the plates arranging the garnish in a circle towards the edge of the plate. Place a fillet of fish in the centre so the garnish surrounds it.

Wine Note • Pinot Blanc, Domaine Runner *(Alsace)* • If not Chardonnay, then pinot blanc is a good companion for any cream-based sauce and this full-bodied, fruity wine also has sufficient intensity to stand up to the bacon and celery. The domaine is family run by three generations that take great pride in their vineyards, which total just 11.5 hectares.

Clams

French: *Palourde, Clovisse* • Italian: *Vongola*
German: *Sanddklaffmuschel/Venusmuscheln* • Spanish: *Almeja/Clame*

Clams are well known, highly-regarded and loved in America yet they have never really found great favour this side of the Atlantic, with the French, Spanish and Portuguese probably the biggest users in Europe. There are many types to choose from, but in my opinion the cockle is far superior to the clam and if you can get them fresh (a task that is almost impossible in Britain), they can be used instead of clams in all of the following recipes. Just like oysters clams can be eaten raw, although you will experience a slightly unpleasant abrasiveness caused by sand if you eat them this way.

Clams are among the easiest of shellfish to produce on a commercial basis, and although they take four years to grow (almost as long as an oyster), they apparently are less of a risk. There have been attempts to grow them in British waters over the years, some successful, but the majority are grown in the waters around France.

When buying clams the same rules apply as when buying oysters or mussels. Make sure they are tightly shut and alive and that their shells are not cracked or broken. Thorough washing before cooking is absolutely essential, even more so than mussels, as they always carry more sand. I like to sit them in at least three changes of clean fresh cold water for about 15 minutes each time, but even then they will still be gritty.

Carrot Mousse with a Sauce of Clams

Serves 4

This will be the third book this recipe has now appeared in – that is three that I recall, it may be more! It was originally in the first edition of **A Feast of Fish** *and now it is in this edition; between times it also appeared as one of my dishes in Kit Chapman's book,* **Great British Chefs.** *I liked it first time around and still think it worthy of inclusion.*

METHOD Preheat the oven to 200°C/400°F/Gas 6. Clean the clams thoroughly. Heat the oil in a saucepan, then add the mirepoix of vegetables and sweat until soft. Add the fish stock, white wine and parsley stalk and bring to the boil. Once boiling, add the clams, cover and cook over a high heat until they open: this will take 4-5 minutes. Tip the clams into a colander, allow to drain until cold, then remove the meat from the shells. Strain the liquor through a very fine strainer or muslin and reserve.

Cook the carrots in the orange juice with the zest and a little water and seasoning. Drain and place in a food processor or blender until a smooth purée. If the resulting purée is a little wet then dry it out by placing it in a saucepan over a low heat, stirring occasionally, until some of the moisture has evaporated. Allow to go cold. Beat the eggs and, when the carrot purée is cold, mix in the eggs together with 60ml/2fl oz of the cream. Season to taste. Butter four 85ml/3fl oz round or oval moulds and fill each one with the carrot mixture. Top each mould with buttered foil and poach in a bain-marie in the oven for 20 minutes.

While the mousses are cooking, bring the clam liquor to the boil and reduce until almost gone. Add the remaining cream, return to the boil and reduce again until it just starts to thicken.

Once the carrot mousses are cooked, tip them out of their moulds, placing one in the centre of each plate. Add the clams to the sauce and allow to soak for 1 minute over a very low heat. At the last minute, add the chopped parsley to the sauce, and then pour it over the mousses.

225g/8oz clams

a little oil

85g/3oz mirepoix (celery, leek and onion)

150ml/5fl oz fish stock (see page 23)

150ml/5fl oz dry white wine

1 stalk of parsley

450g/1lb carrots, roughly chopped

½ orange, juice and zest

salt and freshly ground white pepper

2 eggs

225ml/8fl oz whipping cream

a little butter

1tsp chopped parsley

Wine Note • Le Clos Chardonnay, Clos du Val *(California)* • Unequivocally Chardonnay is required here. The sweetness of the carrots together with the rich clam sauce and that tricky customer, the egg, all cry out for a rich, buttery, fruity wine which, of course, means New World Chardonnay. This example from the Napa Valley is simply bursting with ripe 'melony' fruit and plenty of sunshine, with a pleasing crisp finish to keep the palate clean.

Thai Spiced Clam Risotto

Serves 2

1kg/2lb 4oz clams

300ml/½pt fish stock

1 clove crushed garlic

2 finely chopped shallots

40ml/1½fl oz olive oil

1tbsp Thai spice mix
(see page 31)

175g/6oz arborio rice

100ml/3½fl oz dry white wine

55g/2oz unsalted butter

40g/1½oz freshly grated
Parmesan

2tbsp mixed chopped herbs
(chervil, dill, parsley,
tarragon, basil, and chives)

This recipe is a bit of a mix of cultures but it does work. Both the clams and the risotto base can be made up to 24 hours in advance then brought together as and when needed.

METHOD Clean the clams thoroughly. Heat the fish stock along with the garlic and half of the shallots and bring to the boil. Once boiling, add the clams, cover and cook over a high heat until they open; this will take 4-5 minutes. When cooked tip the clams out into a colander and allow to drain until cold, then remove the meat from the shells. Strain the liquor through a very fine strainer or muslin.

Sweat the rest of the shallots for a couple of minutes in the oil. Add the Thai spices and stir in, then add the rice and sweat for a further two minutes. Add the white wine and reduce by half. Add the stock reserved from cooking the clams and simmer until the rice is just cooked and almost all of the liquid has been absorbed.

Add the clams to the rice; allow these to heat through. Add the butter, which should be cold and cut into small pieces, and the Parmesan. Gently stir the risotto until it has all melted. At the last minute add the herbs.

Wine Note • Chardonnay, Grand Ardèche, Louis Latour *(Ardèche)* • This fairly exotic risotto needs a wine of considerable character to cope with the spicy flavours. Many experts have been fooled by this fabulous wine from the Ardèche, so rich and complex it thinks it's a top quality Burgundy.

Spaghetti with Clams

Gone are the days when you could only buy one type of pasta and one quality: there are so many now! Only buy the best as cheap pasta is not very good and can be difficult to cook. Spaghetti served with clams and tomatoes (alle vongole) is one of Italy's best known fish pasta dishes. Here I have included red peppers and a little chilli to give it more life.

METHOD Clean the clams well, discarding any that are damaged or open. Rinse in a few changes of clean water. In a large saucepan bring to the boil the white wine and the fish stock; once boiling add the clams and cover with a tight-fitting lid. Continue boiling until all the clams have opened; this will take 4-5 minutes. When cooked, tip the clams out into a colander, allow to drain until cold, then remove the meat from the shells. Strain the liquor through a very fine strainer or muslin. Over a high heat reduce the clam liquor until only 60ml/2fl oz remains.

Heat 60ml/2fl oz of the oil in a saucepan, add the onion and garlic and sauté lightly without colouring until soft. Add the chopped peppers and chilli along with the reduced clam liquor and continue cooking gently for about 10 minutes, still without colouring. Add the tomatoes and the tomato purée, stir in well and continue cooking for about another 10 minutes until the sauce has started to dry out a little. Transfer the sauce to a food processor and purée lightly; it shouldn't be too smooth, but thick and not too dry. Add the clams to the sauce and gently reheat while the spaghetti is cooking.

Cook the spaghetti in lots of boiling salted water with the remaining oil until al dente, tender but still with a firm bite, which would normally take 8-10 minutes. Drain in a colander and return to the pan. Pour the sauce over the spaghetti and toss through. Serve immediately.

2kg/4½lb venus or palourdes clams

125ml/4fl oz dry white wine

125ml/4fl oz fish stock (see page 23)

75ml/2½fl oz olive oil

2 medium onions

2 cloves garlic

2 skinned and seeded red peppers, roughly chopped

1 small red chilli, seeded and chopped

450g/1lb plum tomatoes, skinned, seeded and roughly chopped

1tbsp tomato purée

350g/12oz best quality spaghetti

Wine Note • Chianti Classico, Il Ghirlandaio *(Italy)* • Italian of course and red or white goes well with pasta, the choice depending on the sauce. Here we could go either way although the chilli and peppers really need something red with plenty of fruit and perhaps a hint of spice, which suggests one of the Italian classics – Chianti. Full-bodied, rich and ripe, this one has a warm, lingering finish and, combined with the spaghetti, will transport you straight to Tuscany.

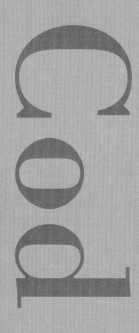

Cod

French: *Cabillaud, Morue* • Italian: *Merluzzo* • German: *Kabeljau*
Spanish: *Bacalao* • U.S.A.: *Atlantic Cod*

The ubiquitous fish and chip shop started in the mid 1800s, probably in London, when Jewish merchants sold fried fish, although a long time before anyone thought of including chips with it. Fish and chips then went on to become part of the British staple diet. Although spurned by the restaurant trade for many years for being too cheap and common, the cod is now making a strong comeback and rightly so. It is probably my favourite fish, because of its versatility and those enormous succulent and meaty flakes.

The cod has been revered for centuries. It has had wars fought over it, diets of whole countries built around it and livelihoods based upon it. Cod is a truly remarkable fish, so much so that it was, in 1998, the subject of an in-depth book simply entitled *COD* by Mark Kurlansky. This book traced its importance across four continents, from the Vikings who pursued the fish across the Atlantic right through to Clarence Birdseye who founded a whole industry on frozen cod in the 1930s.

There is no waste on a cod. Some think that the head is more flavoursome than the body, the tongue and cheeks are used, the swim bladder is used in clarifying agents and in some glues and the roe is eaten both fresh and smoked. The milt, stomach, tripe and liver are all eaten in one part of the world or another. Even the skin is either eaten or cured as leather, and anything left gets used to make fertiliser. Icelanders soften the bones in milk and eat them too! The liver has long been used for oil because of the vitamins it contains.

Thankfully, cod reaches maturity quite rapidly, although this seems to be a recent phenomenon. A female about 100cm long can produce three million eggs in one spawning, and a larger fish can produce some nine million. All species that spawn so prolifically do so because very few eggs manage to survive to maturity. If each female was to produce two mature adults then the population would be stable.

During the Second World War there was little deep sea fishing. This meant that stocks of ground fish such as cod recovered, but sadly these fish are now at an all-time low and it is hard to see just how this decline is to be halted.

Fillet of Cod with a Herb and Parmesan Crust and Parsnip Mash

Serves 4

METHOD Wash the herbs. Squeeze off the excess water and chop them fine. They should still be damp. Combine the herbs with the Parmesan and the breadcrumbs. Season with salt and pepper and mix in the melted butter. Roll this mixture out between two sheets of cling film to about 4cm thick. Place in the freezer until firm. Cut into pieces the same size as the cod portions.

Boil the potatoes in lightly salted water. Roughly cut up the parsnips. Place these in a saucepan along with 40g/1½oz of the butter, sugar, a little salt, pepper and half of the fish stock. Put this on to boil with the pan covered. Simmer until cooked, stirring occasionally. Most of the liquid should have been absorbed but tip off any excess. Combine the potatoes and the parsnips and mash well.

Heat 1dsp of the oil in a frying pan until smoking. Season the meat side of the cod portions, add a knob of the butter to the pan and place the cod in meat-side down and sear until golden brown. Turn them over and cook for about ½ minute on the skin side. Transfer them to an oven tray; place a sheet of the breadcrumb mix on top of each piece of cod, having first removed the cling film. Place in a hot oven and bake until cooked. This will take about 6-10 minutes, depending on the thickness of the fish. Once cooked, remove from the oven and keep warm.

Bring the remaining fish stock to the boil with the white wine and reduce by three quarters

In a saucepan, heat 85ml/3fl oz of the cream and the remaining olive oil. Once boiling, add the potato and parsnip mix. Stir in well and heat through. Check the seasoning.

Add the remaining cream to the reduced stock, return to the boil and gradually add the remaining butter which should be cut into small cubes and well chilled, whisking continuously until melted. Place a spoon of the parsnip mash in the centre of each plate. Place a fillet of cod onto the mash and pour the sauce around.

25g/1oz chopped mixed herbs (chervil, dill, parsley, chives, and tarragon)

40g/1½oz freshly grated Parmesan

140g/5oz fresh white breadcrumbs

salt and freshly ground white pepper

55g/2oz unsalted butter, melted

175g/6oz peeled potatoes

350g/12oz parsnips

155g/5½oz unsalted butter

1½tsp sugar

350ml/12fl oz fish stock (see page 23)

30ml/1fl oz olive oil

4 x 175g/6oz of cod

60ml/2fl oz dry white wine

150ml/5fl oz whipping cream

Wine Note • Dr. 'L' Riesling *(Germany)* • On the whole herbs are happiest with white wines and the parsnip mash here gives a degree of sweetness which leads us very directly to this fresh, fruity, floral wine from the famous Doctor – very good medicine!

Brandade of Salt Cod with a Saffron, Black Olive and Tomato Dressing

Serves 6

350g/12oz cod fillet, skin and bone removed

4tsp sea salt

200g/7oz potatoes

60ml/2fl oz olive oil

1½ cloves crushed garlic

freshly ground white pepper

125ml/4fl oz whipping cream

½ head curly endive

a little olive oil and salt and pepper for dressing the curly endive

Dressing:

200ml/7fl oz fish stock (see page 23)

100ml/3½fl oz dry white wine

good pinch saffron

1 finely chopped shallot

3 plum tomatoes

40g/1½oz pitted black olives

1tbsp chopped chives

100ml/3½fl oz olive oil

To serve:

4 sprigs of fresh chervil

*This recipe does not use proper salt cod or **Bacalhau** as it is known in Portugal. Instead I use fresh cod, which I salt for a couple of days; this leaves the finished product very white and not as salty as it would otherwise be. Brandade can be served cold as an interesting and colourful first course.*

METHOD Sprinkle the cod on both sides with the salt and leave to stand in the refrigerator for 48 hours. When ready to use first soak the cod for at least two hours in cold water then wash it well in a few changes of water to remove the salt, and then dry the fish.

Peel the potatoes and boil; once cooked purée them.

Heat the oil in a large pan; once hot, but not so hot that it is smoking, add the garlic and gently cook without colouring for a few seconds then add the cod and season with the pepper. Cook, almost poaching the cod, in the oil and garlic turning it often in the fat until it starts to flake. It is important that the cod does not fry in the fat and that it is only just cooked. Add the potatoes to the cod working with a spatula to a coarse paste. Allow it to go cold. You could purée it all in a food processor but I prefer mine with the coarse finish working it by hand gives.

Half whip the cream and fold into the cod once cold. Allow it to set in the refrigerator.

To make the dressing, bring the stock and the wine to the boil, reduce by two thirds and add the saffron and the chopped shallot. Keep the stock warm for 3-4 minutes while the saffron infuses then allow to go cold. Blanch, peel and deseed the tomatoes, cut the flesh into 1cm/½in dice. Cut the olives into similar-sized dice and combine all of the ingredients, including the chives and oil, together.

Break up and wash the endive, toss in a little olive oil and seasoning. Form a nest of this in the middle of each plate. Using a large spoon scoop a quenelle of the brandade and place on the salad. Spoon the dressing around. Top each quenelle with a sprig of chervil.

Wine Note • Château de Bord, Blanc *(Rhône Valley)* • Reds are best avoided with a salty dish such as this since the salt will simply enhance the effect of the tannin and create a clash. Soft reds, low in tannin would be acceptable but best of all is a dry, herbaceous and fairly intense wine like this white Rhône or a white Rioja.

Paprika Seared Fillet of Cod with a Warm Potato Salad

Serves 4

METHOD Wash and scrub the new potatoes well. Put these on to boil until cooked, then refresh in cold water until cold. Peel the potatoes and cut them into a dice about 2cm/³⁄₄inch square.

Blanch, skin and deseed the tomatoes and cut them into fingers.

Remove the outer leaves from the spring onions and discard. Cut the onions into pieces at a slight angle. Mix these with the potato along with the tomato fingers, mustard, chives, fish stock and half the olive oil. Season with salt and pepper to taste.

In a frying pan heat the remaining oil. Season the cod portions on the meat side then dip them on the meat side only in the paprika to coat them. Shake off the excess.

Once the oil is smoking add the butter. Place the fish paprika-side down in the hot fat until they are golden brown. Turn them over onto the skin side and transfer them to a very hot grill to finish cooking, for about 4 minutes depending upon the thickness of the fish. Once cooked remove from the pan and allow to rest in a warm place.

Gently heat the potato salad through over a low heat until warm. Place a spoon of this in the middle of each plate. Place a portion of cod on top then spoon the pesto around.

450g/1lb new potatoes

2 plum tomatoes

4 spring onions

15g/½oz whole grain mustard

10g/¼oz chopped chives

60ml/2fl oz fish stock
(see page 23)

100ml/3½fl oz olive oil

salt and freshly ground
white pepper

4 x 175g/6oz of cod fillet

10-15g/¼-½oz paprika

55g/2oz unsalted butter

60ml/4tbsp pesto
(see page 26)

Wine Note • Bon Vallon, Chardonnay "sur lie", de Wetshof *(South Africa)* •
The hint of paprika here, reminiscent of Hungary maybe, might lead us to an Eastern European grape variety but the safest bet is undoubtedly a good, New World Chardonnay. Danie de Wet specialises in Chardonnay and this unwooded version is a perfect match for a dish which, although lightly spicy, is not so powerful as to demand lashings of oak.

Fillet of Cod with Roasted Courgettes, Spinach and Curry Oil

Serves 4

225g/8oz courgettes

30ml/1fl oz olive oil

4 x 175g/6oz cod fillets

55g/2oz unsalted butter

salt and freshly ground
white pepper

225g/8oz picked and
washed spinach

125ml/4fl oz curry oil
(see page 22)

2tsp chopped coriander
leaves

METHOD Cut the courgettes in half lengthways, then cut them into slices slightly on the angle. In a frying pan heat half of the olive oil. Season the cod fillets, add half of the butter to the pan and place the cod in meat-side down. Brown over a very high heat until golden. Once well browned, turn the cod over and place under a very hot grill or in a very hot oven for 3-4 minutes. Remove once cooked, and keep warm.

In a frying pan or wok heat the remaining oil; when smoking add the butter and the courgettes, season lightly and brown them well. Once browned add the spinach and toss through the courgettes until limp. Gently warm the curry oil through. Return the cod to the oven or grill to re-heat. Place a pile of the courgette and spinach mixture in the centre of the plates, with a fillet of cod on top. Once the curry oil has warmed through add the chopped coriander to it and spoon over and around the fish.

Wine Note • Bin 555, Shiraz *(Australia)* • A robust wine for a robust dish. Curry flavours work best with Alsatian wines or powerful, fruity New World reds. The substantial 'weight' of this dish undoubtedly suggests a powerful Shiraz and Bin 555 really packs a punch!

Smoked Cod, Leek and Black Pepper Fish Cake with a Tomato Chilli Sauce

6 fish cakes

350g/12oz potatoes

115g/4oz leek

30ml/1fl oz olive oil

½ clove garlic crushed

350g/12oz smoked cod skinned and all bones removed

salt and freshly ground black pepper

10g/¼oz chopped parsley

15g/½oz unsalted butter

a little flour for dusting and rolling the fish cakes in

Tomato Sauce:

4 plum tomatoes

45ml/1½fl oz olive oil

½ small onion, finely chopped

1 clove of crushed garlic

½ oz sun dried tomato, finely chopped

2-3 small red chillies

30ml/1fl oz dry white wine

1tsp tomato purée

salt and freshly ground white pepper

There are many ways to make a fish cake and several different kinds of fish can be used - salmon, crab, smoked fish, roes, or just plain fresh fish. Most are made with mash but I prefer more texture and therefore like my potatoes simply crushed.

METHOD To make the sauce, blanch, skin and seed the plum tomatoes. Cut the flesh into a rough dice. Heat the oil in a saucepan, add the onion and the garlic and cook this out for a minute without colouring. Add the remaining ingredients and stir in well and season. Gently cook for about 20 minutes then leave to cool. The sauce can be served hot or cold.

Peel and boil the potatoes in salted water till cooked and drain well.

Cut the leek into dice and wash well then drain. Heat just under half of the oil in a small saucepan; when hot add the leek and garlic and season lightly. Carefully cook the leek without colouring until it is just done. Remove from the pan, drain and cool. Using a little of the remaining oil grease a grilling tray. Lay the fish on this, season heavily with coarsely ground black pepper but not with salt as the smoked fish will be salty enough. Lightly oil the fish and grill under a very hot grill until just cooked. Put the cooked potato, the leek and the cod and parsley into a bowl and mix together well, adjust the seasoning as necessary.

Divide the fish into 6 equal amounts, each about 85g/3oz. Form these, using the flour so they do not stick, into cakes about 7.5cm/3in by 1cm/½in.

Heat the remaining oil in a frying pan; when hot add the butter and gently fry the cakes in this for about 1½ minutes per side until golden brown. Serve with the tomato sauce either hot or cold. Try them on a bed of French beans tossed in butter or on a bed of frizzy salad tossed in a little olive oil.

Wine Note • Valle de Vistalba, Chardonnay • Lots of fruit and flavour as well as tremendous value for money, this South American Chardonnay will cope well with the smoky nature of the dish. Alternatively, if you prefer red, try the Cabernet Sauvignon from the same stable.

Roast Fillet of Cod with Pepperonata, Topped with Garlic Mayonnaise

Serves 6

Raw crushed garlic can be used, but I much prefer the flavour once cooked, as it is so much softer and smoother and will not stay on the breath for so long. If using raw garlic then 2-3 cloves would be sufficient for this amount of eggs.

METHOD Peel the cloves of garlic and place in a saucepan along with the star anise, the bay leaf, peppercorns, white wine and sea salt. Add 30ml/1fl oz of the olive oil. Cover with a tight-fitting lid or foil, bring to the boil and simmer gently for about 15 minutes until the garlic is really soft. Allow to cool. When cold, remove the star anise, the peppercorns and the bay leaf. Purée the garlic along with the mustard. Add the egg yolks then gradually add the oils, whisking continuously. As the mixture thickens use the lemon juice to thin it out. Continue adding the oils until gone. Season with salt and pepper as required. Add more lemon juice if needed. If the mayonnaise becomes too thick and all of the lemon juice has been used you can always add a little warm water dribbled in to thin it down. The finished mayonnaise wants to be quite thick, as it will be spooned on top of the fish as a quenelle.

In a frying pan heat the oil; season the fish. When the oil is smoking add the butter. Place the fish in the pan meat-side down and brown it really well. Once well browned turn the fish onto its skin side and place either under a very hot grill or in an oven pre-heated to 230°C/450°F/ Gas 8 for about 4-6 minutes. This cooking time will vary depending upon the thickness of the fish used. Once cooked the fish will feel firm and have a very slight give to it. Leave to rest in a warm place.

In a saucepan gently warm the pepperonata through. Place a spoonful of this in the middle of each plate, spoon a little of the pesto around and arrange a piece of cod on top. Finish the dish with a spoonful of the mayonnaise on top of the fish.

6 x 175g/6oz of cod

30ml/1fl oz olive oil

25g/1oz unsalted butter

salt and freshly ground white pepper

pepperonata (see page 26)

4tbsp pesto (see page 26)

Garlic mayonnaise:

55g/2oz cloves of garlic

½ star anise

1 bay leaf

½tsp black peppercorns

30ml/1fl oz dry white wine

pinch sea salt

330ml/11fl oz olive oil

3 egg yolks

300ml/10fl oz salad oil

25g/1oz English mustard

juice of ½ lemon

salt and freshly ground white pepper

Roast Fillet of Cod with Wilted Rocket, New Potatoes and Chorizo with a Balsamic Jus

Serves 2

This has to be one of my favourite dishes; it's always been popular with the customers too. The spicy sausage blends very well with the peppery rocket and the new potatoes add a little earthiness. Using balsamic vinegar is very trendy but it also gives an extra richness. The truffle oil to finish is pure opulence but worth it. It may seem like I use a lot of potato in this recipe but if you turn them as I suggest you will need this amount. If you do not want to turn them then halve the quantity and chop each potato in half.

METHOD Turn the new potatoes into small pointed barrel shapes then cook them in boiling salted water; refresh in cold water and drain. Slice the chorizo and cut into fingers. Combine the vinegar, fish stock and wine in a saucepan; bring to the boil and reduce until only about 2tbsp remain. Add the veal stock, return to the boil and reduce slightly.

Heat half of the oil in a frying pan until smoking and season the pieces of cod. Add the butter to the pan, place the cod in meat-side down, then sear the fish over a high heat until golden brown. Turn the fish over and transfer to a pre-heated grill and continue cooking for about 3-4 minutes depending upon the thickness of the fish. Once cooked remove the fish and keep warm.

Heat the remaining oil in a frying pan; when smoking add the chorizo, fry for a few seconds then add the potatoes. Continue frying until the sausage and the potatoes have taken on a good colour. Add the rocket, lightly season with salt and toss this through the sausage and potato until the rocket just starts to wilt.

Divide this mixture between the plates; place a portion of cod on top. Spoon the sauce around and drizzle with truffle oil at the last second.

24 small new potatoes about 550g/20oz

140g/5oz chorizo

75ml/2½fl oz balsamic vinegar

225ml/8fl oz fish stock (see page 23)

75ml/2½fl oz dry white wine

200ml/7fl oz veal stock (see page 33)

30ml/1fl oz olive oil

4 x 175g/6oz of cod, the thicker the better

salt and freshly ground white pepper

25g/1oz unsalted butter

175g/6oz picked and washed leaves of rocket

30ml/1fl oz truffle oil (optional)

Wine Note • Pozuelo Crianza, Yecla Do • Such a robust combination cries out for a rich, deep spicy Rioja, of which this is a great example.

Crab

French: *Crabe* • Italian: *Granchio* • German: *Krabbe* • Spanish: *Cangrejo*

There is a wide variety of crabs available but here in Britain we tend to only be familiar with one, the common or edible crab. Although both sides of the Atlantic have many fish in common, the common crab is not one of them as it is not found on the west of the Atlantic at all. Crabs such as the rock, blue and snow are available stateside and the blue or soft-shelled are the most highly sought after. Other types include the spider, red and shore crab, all of which are edible.

I'd like to concentrate on the edible crab – give me a large fresh Cornish crab over a lobster any day. If you have never eaten a freshly cooked Brixham crab then I suggest you make it a resolution to do so as there is very little that tastes finer. By large, I mean approximately 2.25kg/5lb and cock crabs are the best, although they can be quite expensive, as the yield is so much greater than the smaller ones and the flavour is just so sweet! Cromer crabs are tiny by comparison but the yield per pound is actually very good and they are also much cheaper than the Cornish ones.

Like all shellfish, crabs must be bought alive (do not be tempted to buy them frozen) and the sign of a good crab is that it will feel comparatively heavy for its size. Normally, the larger the crab the better the yield but also the easier it is to clean; cleaning a crab properly can be a very time-consuming job, but don't let that put you off as it is well worth the effort. When buying fresh crab always try to go for the males as they have a larger amount of meat than the females and a sweeter flavour. The females carry a greater amount of brown meat and as their claws are smaller the white meat yield is not so good. To tell the difference between the sexes turn the crab onto its back; the male has a very narrow tail whereas the female's tail is much broader and almost heart-shaped.

It is interesting to note that the 1990 Common Fisheries Policy, Community Grading Notes state that 'Crabs are not subject to specific freshness standards (which is unusual as all other fish and shellfish are). However, only whole crabs and not berried females or soft shelled crabs, may be offered for human consumption.'

Crab, Lemon Grass and Asparagus Broth

Serves 6

Most times when the shells of crabs or lobsters are used they are roasted first to bring out their flavours but producing a stock this way often leaves a slight harshness to the finished article. Here, unroasted, they give a slight oriental feel to the broth.

METHOD Place the shells in a large pan and attack them with the end of a rolling pin, breaking them up quite small.

Peel and roughly chop all of the vegetables, tomatoes, ginger, lemon grass, garlic and fresh herbs, saving a few coriander leaves for garnish.

Heat the oil in a large saucepan and add the vegetables, cover with a lid and sweat down until quite soft. Add the shells, re-cover and continue sweating for a further 5 minutes. Add the dried herbs and spices, the water and the wine. Bring to the boil and simmer very slowly for 2 hours skimming as necessary.

Strain, then pass the resulting stock through muslin. Allow it to go cold and settle then very carefully draw off as much of the liquor as possible leaving behind the sediment, which can be discarded. The resultant stock should be quite, but not perfectly, clear. If the stock boils or simmers too fast during cooking then it will end up being cloudy. Set the liquor over a high heat and reduce till only 1.2 litres/2pts remain.

Peel the asparagus and cut the tips to about 6cm/2½in in length. Cook these in boiling salted water but leave them slightly under-done; refresh in iced water and drain. Cut each spear in two lengthways.

Very finely slice the remaining stalk of lemon grass and add this to the broth. Return this to the boil then add the rice noodles. Place 5 halves of asparagus tips in each soup plate and scatter a few coriander leaves into each. Pour the hot broth and noodles onto the asparagus and coriander.

1.8kg/4lb crab shells

350g/12oz bulb fennel

350g/12oz leek

350g/12oz celery

2 carrots

3 tomatoes

25g/1oz fresh ginger

2 stalks of lemon grass

1 head garlic

good handful of fresh coriander

1 sprig fresh mint

30ml/1fl oz olive oil

2 bay leaves

1tbsp coriander seeds

good pinch saffron

1tbsp black peppercorns

2 star anise

4.5lt/8pts water

½btl dry white wine

To finish:

15 asparagus tips

1 stalk of lemon grass

55g/2oz rice noodles

> **Wine Note** • Four Sisters, Sauvignon/Semillon *(W. Australia)* • This light broth with interesting additions would be mirrored well by a soft blend of light, bright Sauvignon joined by some Semillon to give a gentle fruity richness to the palate. In both cases there is delicacy with style.

Timbale of Crab with Gazpacho and Topped with Parmesan Crisp

Serves 6

5lb cock crab

court bouillon (see page 22)

salt and freshly ground white pepper

Worcester sauce

tabasco

lemon juice

soft white breadcrumbs

55g/2oz coarse grated Parmesan

12 cooked asparagus tips

30ml/1fl oz olive oil

handful of frizzy leaves

300ml/10fl oz gazpacho (see page 23)

If you cook the crab the day you get it and leave it to cool in its cooking liquor, it will keep for a day. Quantities of other ingredients should be judged according to the wetness of the crab's brown meat.

METHOD Bring the court bouillon to the boil and plunge in the crabs, cover and return to the boil. Simmer for about 5 minutes and then remove the pan from the heat and allow to go cold.

When cold, shell the crabs, keeping the brown and the white meat separate. Save the shells and use these for the crab broth (see page 69). Process the brown meat in a food processor until smooth. Season with salt and pepper, a few dashes of Worcester sauce, a splash of Tabasco and a little lemon juice. Add some white breadcrumbs and process again until smooth. You are looking for a consistency similar to that of whipped cream; if it is too wet add a few more crumbs. It should be firm but not dry. Check for seasoning.

Place a 7.5cm/3½in cutter on a sheet of silicone paper on a baking sheet; sprinkle in some of the grated Parmesan until it just thinly coats the base. Carefully remove the cutter and repeat a further 5 times. Carefully place the baking sheet into an oven pre-heated to 200°C/400°F/Gas 6 for about 5 minutes or until golden brown. Remove from the oven, allow to cool slightly and carefully remove the crisps from the tray; place on a flat surface till cold.

Trim the asparagus tips to about 6cm/2½in in length. Quickly cook them in boiling salted water until just cooked, refresh in iced water and drain. Break up the frizzy leaves and lightly season, then toss with the olive oil. Lightly season the white meat with salt and a little pepper; add a squeeze of lemon juice if necessary.

Place a 6cm/2½in cutter in the centre of the plate. Press in the white meat until about half full. Place a spoon or two of brown meat on top of this and level it out. Remove the cutter and place a Parmesan disc on top. Pile a little of the frizzy leaves on top of that, cut each asparagus tip in half and then arrange them on the leaves allowing 4 halves per portion. Spoon a little of the gazpacho around.

Salad of Crab, Pink Grapefruit and Avocado

Serves 6

5lb cock crab

court bouillon (see page 22)

salt and freshly ground white pepper

Worcester sauce

tabasco

lemon juice

soft white breadcrumbs

2 pink grapefruit

2 plum tomatoes

6 basil leaves

45ml/1½fl oz olive oil

115g/4oz mixed salad leaves, e.g. lollo rosso, frizzy, rocket, red oak leaf, little gem, endive, trevisse

1 avocado

Wine Note • Cremant de Bourgogne, Corinne et Thierry Drouin *(Burgundy)* • Normally citrus fruit in a dish needs a bone dry white with plenty of acidity but pink grapefruit tends to be slightly less sharp and the richness of the crab will counteract it. This lovely 'sparkler' offers a full creamy palate balanced by a fresh lemony acidity and as this is a starter it keeps the palate clean for bigger wines to follow.

This is a classic combination of ingredients brought together into a simple to prepare yet colourful salad fit for a summer's day. As with any crab dish I always find it better to cook my own; frozen crab meat is all well and good but it really does not resemble real crab at all. Some of the ingredients do not have quantities listed; this is because it is impossible to tell how wet the brown meat in your crab will be and the seasonings and crumbs will obviously differ from crab to crab.

METHOD Bring the court bouillon to the boil and plunge in the crabs, cover and return to the boil. Simmer for about 5 minutes and then remove the pan from the heat and allow to go cold.

When cold, shell the crabs keeping the brown and the white meat separate. Save the shells and use these for a crab broth (see page 69). Process the brown meat in a food processor until smooth. Season with salt and pepper, a few dashes of Worcester sauce, a splash of Tabasco and a little lemon juice. Add some white breadcrumbs and process again until smooth. You are looking for a consistency similar to that of whipped cream; if it is too wet then add a few more crumbs; it should be firm but not dry. Check for seasoning.

Segment the pink grapefruit and squeeze the core of its juice. Blanch, skin and de-seed the tomatoes, cut the flesh into small neat dice. Shred the basil and mix into the tomato, season with salt and pepper and mix in 15g/½fl oz of the olive oil.

Place a 6cm/2½in cutter just off centre on each plate. Press in the white meat until about half full. Divide the tomato across the top of the white meat and spread to an even layer. Place a quenelle of the brown meat on top of the white. Toss the salad leaves in the remaining oil and season. Build a small salad at the top of each plate beside the crab. To the left side of the crab lay 5 grapefruit segments, cut the avocado into quarters and peel, slice each quarter into 5 slices and brush them with the grapefruit juice. Lay slices of the avocado opposite the grapefruit.

It is best not to cut the avocado until you are ready to serve in order to minimise the chance of it going black.

Dory

French: *Saint-Pierre* • German: *Heringskonig* • Italian: *Pesce San Pietro*
Spanish: *Pez de San Pedro*

Boy, what an ugly fish! Certainly not famed for its good looks, it more than makes up for it with its flavour and texture and is an exceptionally fine fish. What's more it was recently described by one of my customers (on eating it for the first time) as the sexiest fish she had ever eaten. A curious but not altogether bad accolade!

Known throughout Europe as St. Peter's fish (because of the thumb print on its side) it is only known as Dory in the UK. John Dory can be found around the seas of Europe from as far north as Norway to as far south as Morocco. It is not overly abundant around the English Channel and is at its best during the late summer and early autumn.

The rather alarming features of the John Dory have undoubtedly put many people off eating it. It is a grey fish with, when very fresh, a yellowish brown tint and it can range in size from as small as 350g/12oz through to 4.5kg/10lb or more, but these larger fish are becoming very rare these days. Curiously, it is a flat fish that swims upright, so that it presents a very thin profile. I imagine that it must also be quite an accomplished hunter, as it's so thin that it must be difficult for other fish to detect and it has a telescopic jaw which it uses to engulf its prey. It is heavily armoured, with two rows of rather lethal spines on both sides of its body, along its back and on its belly, which are capable of inflicting more than a little damage to unsuspecting hands. The head is very bony and culminates in a rather pointed and sharp rear-facing protrusion just in front of the pectoral fin.

The one bad attribute of the John Dory is the amount of waste you can expect from it. Once filleted the meat will normally only account for about 35% of the body weight which, compared to most fish, is very low indeed, making what is already an expensive fish even more costly. The redeeming factor is that the firm, white, delicate, boneless flesh is an absolute delight to eat. It is the only fish I know of that has six fillets, as each fillet breaks into three natural fingers.

Any recipe using a firm white fish such as sole, turbot or brill could be used equally well with Dory. It also lends itself well to salads.

John Dory with Saffron Mash and Sweet Peppers

Serves 4

225g/8oz red pepper

100ml/3½fl oz dry white wine

45ml/1½fl oz soy sauce

300ml/10fl oz fish stock

175ml/6fl oz veal stock

15ml/½fl oz olive oil

Salt and freshly ground white pepper

350g/12oz John Dory cut into 12 fingers (a 900g/2lb fish should yield this amount of meat)

salt and black pepper

15g/½oz unsalted butter

½ recipe for mash (see page 25)

5g/⅛oz (good pinch) saffron

METHOD Cut the peppers into quarters and remove the seeds. Trim these quarters then cut them into a neat julienne.

In a saucepan bring the white wine, soy and the fish stock to the boil; reduce until only about 100ml/3½fl oz remains. Add the red pepper along with the veal stock. Return to the boil and reduce slightly until it starts to thicken.

In a frying pan, heat the oil then season the fingers of fish. When the oil is smoking add the butter and quickly fry the fish in the hot fat allowing about 30 seconds per side. Remove from the pan and drain.

To reheat the mash first gently heat the cream with the saffron then follow the recipe instructions on page 25. Place a spoonful of the finished mash in the centre of each plate. Carefully place 3 fingers of the dory on the mash. Drain the peppers from the sauce and divide into four equal amounts. Drape these over the fish and pour the sauce around the mash.

Wine Note • Pinotage, Bellingham Estate *(S. Africa)* • This dish sounds quite rich and fruity so a wine of similar character that immediately springs to mind is this full, flavoursome and slightly spicy fellow, made from the native grape Pinotage that is virtually unique to South Africa.

John Dory with a Salad of Oranges and Fresh Basil

Serves 4/8

2 oranges

juice of 1 orange

15ml/½fl oz white wine vinegar

40ml/1½fl oz olive oil

½ head curly endive

24 leaves of fresh basil

salt and freshly ground white pepper

15g/½oz unsalted butter

450g/16oz John Dory cut into 24 fingers

This is a fantastic dish for those warm summer days, suitable as a very light and attractive first course or main course.

METHOD Peel and segment the oranges, squeeze out the core and add the resulting juice to the rest of the juice. Put the orange juice in a saucepan and reduce it by half. Allow to go cold then mix with the vinegar and 30ml/1fl oz of the olive oil.

Wash the endive well and break up the leaves. Add the orange segments and, reserving 4 basil leaves as garnish, tear the rest into the salad. Lightly season with the salt and pepper.

Heat the remaining oil in a frying pan; when hot add the butter. Lightly season the fingers of fish and fry these in the hot fat for about 30 seconds on each side. Remove from the pan and drain.

Divide the salad between the plates and carefully arrange the pieces of fish through it. Pour any excess dressing over and around the salad. Garnish with the saved basil leaves.

Wine Note • Montagny, 1er cru, Louis Latour • Strictly speaking, the citrus element here requires a Sauvignon but this delicious dry white from a world-famous producer has such character that it would grace almost any dish. It has a lovely herbaceous nose that should enhance the basil perfectly and a full-bodied almost nutty style that will appeal to the John Dory perfectly.

Eel

French: *Anguille* • Italian: *Anguilla* • German: *Aal* • Spanish: *Anguila*

Until relatively recently the life of the eel was pretty mysterious. It was in 1922 that a Dr. Johannes Schmidt discovered that the eel starts its life in the northern part of the Sargasso Sea and, much like the salmon or sea trout, it is a migrant from sea to river and then to the sea once more, a journey that takes it halfway across the world and then back again.

The larvae are carried by the prevailing winds and currents not far below the surface of the sea towards the coast of Europe. As they travel across the Atlantic they slowly develop into tiny transparent almost ribbon-like creatures, taking three years to complete their journey. By the time they have made their way to the river of their choice they have reached about 6-7cm/ 2½in in length but are still transparent. At this stage they are known as elvers. Once in the river, the eel grow to adulthood and stay for between 9 and 12 years before setting off across the Atlantic again to spawn. It is thought (although not actually proven) that the eel never returns but dies once it has mated and spawned, making the journey only once in its lifetime.

An eel's colour alters throughout its lifespan but they are usually black or a greenish/black or grey-brown on their backs and sides and a yellowish colour below. Once they are ready to leave the rivers and return to the sea they change to silver. When they reach this stage they are at their fattest and best for eating. One should watch out for them later in the year as it is on the autumn tides that they make their journey back to the breeding grounds.

The eel is extremely rich due to its fatty nature and can be delicious. The drawback is that they really need to be bought alive which presents the problem of having to kill and skin them. This process has to be done almost simultaneously otherwise the skin is almost impossible to remove. The eel can be killed with one sharp blow to the back of the head, then either hold it with a cloth to stop your hand from slipping, or tie a string around its neck and then suspend it from a fastening in the wall. Cut the skin through to the meat around the neck. Ease the skin away all around and turn it back. Grip this with a cloth and tear the skin off in one go. Better still, get your fishmonger to do it for you; he will have much more chance of success.

Matelote of Eel with Button Onions, Bacon and Mushrooms

Serves 4

Matelote, in the words of **Larousse Gastronomic**, *is the 'name given in French cooking to a fish stew made with white or red wine'. Confused? Let me explain. A matelote is almost always made from freshwater fish and more importantly from eel. It can, depending upon the region you are in, be made with either red or white wine. If for instance you were in the Loire then it would almost certainly be made with white wine, in other districts more probably with the local red. It is almost always served with baby onions and invariably with mushrooms. Occasionally it also has an unusual ingredient, the prune! I am told they go surprisingly well together although I have not tried it myself. Classically a matelote should be thickened with beurre manie but as I only rarely use flour in sauces, I use a quality brown stock which I then reduce to thicken. No mention of the eel, be they freshwater or conger eel, would ever be complete without including a matelote.*

METHOD Turn the button mushrooms and cut off their stalks. Peel the onions and garlic. Cover the mirepoix with the red wine and add the garlic, bay leaf and rosemary. Bring this to the boil and simmer till reduced by about half then strain. Cut the bacon into lardons and gently fry until they lightly brown. Season the eel then pour onto it the strained wine and the brown stock. Gently bring this to the boil and simmer for 10 minutes. Add the onions and continue to simmer for a further 10-15 minutes until the eel is just cooked. Add the lardons and mushrooms and simmer again for about 3-4 minutes until the mushrooms are cooked.

If the sauce is a little too thin then remove the eel and garnish from the sauce and arrange on the plates. Bring the sauce to the boil and reduce until it has thickened. Pour this over the eel and garnish then sprinkle the dish with the chopped parsley.

12 button mushrooms

12 button onions

1 crushed clove of garlic

175g/6oz mirepoix (celery, onion, leek, carrot)

425ml/15fl oz red wine

bay leaf

sprig of fresh rosemary

125g/4½oz streaky bacon

1kg/2lb 4 oz fresh eel, skinned and cut into pieces 5-6cm/2-2½in long

salt and freshly ground white pepper

175ml/6fl oz brown stock/veal stock (see page 33)

1tbsp chopped parsley

Wine Note • Beaune 1er cru, Dme des Clos *(Burgundy)* • A wonderfully rich, fruity wine for a rich, wintry meal. Domaine des Clos is a tiny estate of just 3 hectares and the wines they produce are out of this world. The eel will swim very happily with this fine Beaune – but don't use it for cooking!

Bourride of Eel

Serves 4

1kg/2¼lb fresh eel

10 small new potatoes cut in half and turned

4-6 young carrots each to weigh about 85g/3oz

12 small peeled shallots

1.2 litres/2pts of court bouillon (see page 22) omitting the vinegar and the lemon grass

30ml/1fl oz white wine vinegar

1tbsp chopped parsley

Aioli:

2 cloves of garlic

sea salt and freshly ground white pepper

4 egg yolks

225ml/8fl oz olive oil

lemon juice

Traditionally made with a mixture of small fish this very provincial dish is great with eel and when thickened, as it is with aioli, becomes very rich and sumptuously garlicky. It is best served as one would a bouillabaisse, in a large soup tureen in the middle of the table for your guests to tuck into as they wish.

METHOD First make the aioli; this can be made a day in advance if wished. Crush the peeled garlic with a teaspoon of the sea salt. Stir in the egg yolks then gradually whisk in the oil, add the lemon juice and adjust the seasoning.

Cut the eel into pieces 5-6cm/2-2½in long and season.

Turn the potatoes till they are all the same size. Peel the carrots into long cylinders and cut at an angle into 3cm/1½in pieces. Peel the shallots leaving the root intact.

Put the shallots into a pan along with the court bouillon; after about 5 minutes add the turned potatoes and carry on cooking for a further 5 minutes, then add the carrots. When all the vegetables are cooked strain the liquor onto the seasoned eel in another saucepan. Cover the vegetables and keep them warm. Sit the eel over a low heat for about 12-15 minutes or until cooked.

Carefully remove the eel from the pan and keep it warm along with the vegetables.

Pour the cooking liquor back into a saucepan along with the vinegar and return to the boil, then remove the pan from the heat and gradually whisk in the aioli. Check the flavour of the stock for seasoning and correct if necessary.

Add the fish and vegetables to the sauce and allow to reheat over a very low heat for about two minutes. At the last moment add half the chopped parsley to the sauce and stir it in. Transfer to a large tureen and sprinkle the rest of the parsley on top.

Wine Note • Montravel, Moulin Caresse *(Bergerac)* • A fairly crisp dry white is needed here to cut through the richness of the bourride. This is a blend of 80% Sauvignon with 20% Semillon which adds a little more body to the wine and will stand up to the aioli admirably.

Grey Mullet

French: *Munge, Mulet* • Italian: *Cefalo, Muggine* • German: *Meersasche*
Spanish: *Pardete, Cabejudo, Lisa*

Grey mullet is not a widely used fish in the UK but it is highly thought of in France and Spain. There are three main varieties of grey mullet: the common or striped mullet (as it is known in the USA), the thick-lipped and the thin-lipped (none of which are differentiated between in the UK but are in other countries). All are quite similar in appearance and have large heads and very broad bodies yet they appear rather sleek. Their scales are very large and thick and consequently very easy to remove.

It is wise to be aware of the source of any grey mullet that you buy because not only are they bottom-feeding herbivores, but they live in fairly still inshore waters and are therefore prone to the effects of pollution. Harbours, marinas, river outlets, seawater, brackish water and fresh water are all habitats in which they can be found. Fish caught in the open sea are much more likely to be of better quality and have more flavour than those fished closer inland.

Despite this, it is an extremely good fish. It's strong, robust flavour suits meat-based sauces and most bass or gurnard recipes will work well with mullet. The roe can also be used to make taramasalata.

Grey Mullet with Shallots, Girolles and Pancetta

Serves 4

2 x 900g-1.125g/2-2½lb
of grey mullet

15ml/½fl oz olive oil

salt and freshly ground
white pepper

25g/1oz melted butter

a few sea salt crystals

12 shallots

12 girolles

8 thin slices of pancetta;
use dry-cured streaky bacon
if pancetta is not available

175ml/6fl oz fish stock
(see page 23)

125ml/4fl oz red wine

225ml/8fl oz veal stock
(see page 33)

25g/1oz unsalted butter

250g/9oz picked and washed
spinach leaves

Pancetta, an Italian way of dry curing bacon, is so different to any bacon we seem to produce in this country. Good quality deli's should either stock it or be able to get it for you, as should good butchers.

METHOD Scale and fillet the mullet, remove the pin bones then cut each fillet into two, across and at a slight angle. Lightly oil a grilling tray with the olive oil. Season the fillets and lay them on the tray skin-side up. Brush the skin with melted butter and lightly sprinkle with sea salt.

Peel the shallots making sure you keep the root end intact. Scrape the girolles of any dirt and trim off any root; only wash if they are really dirty. Cook the shallots in boiling salted water until almost ready then remove them from the water and allow them to cool.

Combine the fish stock and the wine and bring to the boil, then reduce until almost gone. Meanwhile grill the mullet under a pre-heated grill for about 3-4 minutes or until the fish is just cooked; remove and keep warm. Grill the slices of pancetta slowly until crisp. Once the wine and stock have reduced add the veal stock and return to the boil; reduce until it just starts to thicken then add the shallots; simmer until they are cooked and finally add the girolles; remove the sauce and keep warm.

Heat the butter in a saucepan and when it starts to sizzle add the spinach which should be well drained. Season and cook over a heat until it just starts to go limp. Remove from the pan and drain well.

Arrange the spinach in the centre of the plates. Place two fillets of mullet, one head and one tailpiece, on top of each other on the spinach, then spoon three girolles and three shallots alternately around the fish with a little of the sauce. Dribble a little sauce over the fish and top with two rashers of the cooked pancetta.

Wine Note • Valle de Vistalba, Cabernet Sauvignon *(Argentina)* •
A flavoursome fish with some fairly hefty accompaniments suggest a reasonably powerful red that is not too tannic since this would clash with the sweetness of the shallots. A New World Cabernet Sauvignon is ideal since it has a good full palate to stand up to the pancetta yet the tannins are relatively soft and sweet.

Grey Mullet on Cabbage with Roasted Onions

Serves 4

2 x 900g-1.125g/2-2½lb of grey mullet

15ml/½fl oz olive oil

salt and freshly ground white pepper

25g/1oz melted butter

a few sea salt crystals

225g/8oz leek

oil for deep frying

12 small button onions

400g/14oz young, green cabbage

175ml/6fl oz fish stock (see page 23)

125ml/4fl oz red wine

225ml/8fl oz veal stock (see page 33)

40g/1½oz unsalted butter

Almost every time I use grey mullet it is with a red wine, soy or balsamic based sauce and very often with roasted vegetables of one sort or another – here I use roasted onions. Try adding a few puy lentils to the sauce.

METHOD Scale and fillet the mullet, remove the pin bones then cut each fillet into two, across and at a slight angle. Lightly oil a grilling tray with the olive oil. Season the fillets and lay them on the tray skin-side up. Brush the skin with melted butter and lightly sprinkle with sea salt.

Cut the leek into a fine julienne about 6cm/2½in long and deep fry in oil at 140°C/275°F until just turning brown; drain on kitchen towel and sprinkle with salt.

Peel the button onions and blanch in boiling salted water and refresh, then drain well. Remove the outer leaves from the cabbage and tear them, removing and discarding the central ribs of each leaf.

Combine together the fish stock and red wine and reduce until only about a quarter remains. Meanwhile place the fish under a pre-heated very hot grill for about 3 minutes until the fish has just cooked and the skin has crispened. Once the stock has reduced add the veal stock, return to the boil and reduce slightly until it just starts to thicken.

Heat 25g/1oz of the butter in a saucepan and add the cabbage, season well, cover and cook very quickly over a high heat until just cooked. Heat the remaining butter in a frying pan and roast the onions until golden brown.

Drain the cabbage and place a pile of this in the centre of each plate and place two fillets of mullet, one head and one tailpiece, on top of each other on the cabbage. Spoon the sauce around and place three button onions on the sauce around the fish. Then top the fish with a ball of the deep fried leek.

Wine Note • Hay Shed Hill, Pinot Noir *(W. Australia)* • A big, bold fruity wine to accompany its 'twin' in the food world. The power of this wine will tackle the earthy character of the dish handsomely, with room to spare. Definitely a wine where quality not quantity is the watchword!

Gurnard

French: *(Rouget) Grondin* • Italian: *Capone* • German: *Knurrhahn*
Spanish: *Rubios, Garneos*

What a strange little fish this is, with its heavily armoured head and big eyes. It never grows terribly large – normally not more than about 30 cm/12in and a maximum of about 2kg/4lb 8oz. All four varieties of gurnard make a sort of croaking sound, similar to snoring, both when swimming and on being caught, as though they are protesting, which I am sure they are!

The reddy skin colour above the lateral line of the red gurnard really is quite pretty, almost red mullet-like, and the belly is almost white. The grey gurnard, the most common in British waters, is more grey to greyish brown with lots of small pale spots that occasionally have a red tinge. The fins of the gurnard are probably its most striking feature as they look just like legs protruding from behind the head. They are in fact pectoral fins and are used (just like fingers), to feel for food on the sea bed. Gurnard can be found from Norway to the Mediterranean, although the red variety is not that common in the North Sea.

The other two varieties are the tub gurnard (larger than the grey or red) and the flying gurnard, also known as sea robin, and best-known off the Atlantic coast of America where they are quite spectacular with their wing-like pectoral fins.

I have long predicted that one day the gurnard will 'come of age' and be recognised as a worthwhile fish. I hope so, because I have always liked it. It has a lovely flavour and although a little bony it's a good fish to eat. I normally only use the tails (from the vent down) and roast them whole then make soup with the remainder. This way the problem with the bones is almost eliminated.

Cotriade of Gurnard

Serves 6-8

55g/2oz unsalted butter

3 onions, chopped

1 medium leek, chopped

2 cloves crushed garlic

1kg/2lb 4oz potatoes, peeled and cut into 2cm/¾in dice

1 bay leaf

4 plum tomatoes, skinned, seeded and cut into 2cm/¾in dice

salt and freshly ground white pepper

a few threads of saffron or ½ teaspoon powdered saffron

1 litre/1¾pts fish stock

1kg/2lb 4oz of gutted and trimmed gurnard cut into chunks, saving the heads

juice of half a lemon

1tbsp mixed thyme, parsley and chervil

A Cotriade is in a way similar to a bouillabaisse; in fact it is also known as **Breton bouillabaisse** *and is obviously, as the name suggests, a very old classical French fish stew. It would normally be made with the likes of mackerel, John Dory, bream, hake, conger eel, mullet or gurnard, any one of these or a mixture of them all. We add the fish heads during cooking, to be removed just before serving, to help concentrate the flavour of the fish.*

METHOD Heat a large pan and when it is hot add the butter; once it starts to sizzle add the chopped onions and leek, cover and cook over a medium heat until they are soft and golden, stirring gently from time to time to prevent sticking.

Add the crushed garlic, potatoes, and bay leaf. Mix well and cook for a few moments before adding the tomatoes, salt, pepper, saffron and stock. Cover and simmer for 10-15 minutes until the potatoes are softening. Add the fish and heads and cook gently for a further 8-10 minutes uncovered until the fish is cooked.

Put the fish and potatoes into a dish, discard the heads and squeeze over lemon juice and sprinkle the herbs on top. Check the seasoning then strain the liquid over the fish and potatoes. Serve with crusty French bread as you would a good bouillabaisse.

Wine Note • Domaine de Seriege, vin de pays des Côteaux de Fontcaude •
A fairly robust, rustic-sounding dish that would be too much for many everyday whites yet probably does not merit anything too costly. This is a harmonious blend of Cabernet and Merlot that is both fruity and savoury at the same time. Excellent value and just right for the peasants' table!

Roasted Gurnard on Puy Lentils with Garlic Confit

Serves 2

Red gurnard is one of those fish that is waiting for its time to come. It is possible that it will, in years to come, be as popular as monkfish is today. After all only 15 years ago monkfish could be bought for a song. I can well remember trying to buy it on Folkestone fish market to be told that they did not sell monk – that was only for baiting lines with! How times change. Gurnard is currently really cheap, it is a great fish, a little bony towards the head I grant you but the flesh is quite fine. Go on, treat yourself – see what you think.

METHOD Gut, and chop of the heads of the fish. (Save the heads for soup or fish stock.) Wash the bellies well and pat dry. Using a pair of scissors cut off the fins and the tail.

Wash the lentils well in running water. Peel the onion and put this along with ½ stalk of celery, ¼ of the carrot, the bacon and the ½ clove of garlic in a saucepan with the lentils, cover with about 300ml/10fl oz water. Bring to the boil and simmer until the lentils are cooked, for about 20 minutes. Leave to go cold. Pick out the vegetables and discard, then strain off the liquid.

Peel the celery; cut this and the remaining carrot into small dice.

In a frying pan heat the oil; season the fish inside and out. When the oil is hot add half of the butter. Roll the fish in the hot fat then place in an oven pre-heated to 220°C/425°F/Gas 7 for about 6 minutes. Once cooked remove and keep warm.

In a saucepan bring the white wine and fish stock to the boil. Reduce this until almost gone. Add the veal stock, bring to the boil and reduce slightly. Warm the confit garlic through in its cooking liquor.

Heat the remaining butter and oil in a saucepan and sweat off the diced celery and carrot. Add the lentils, season and heat through. Place a pile of the lentils in the centre of each plate and a gurnard on the lentils. Spoon the sauce around and place five confit garlic cloves on the sauce around the fish with a little spoonful of the liquor with each clove.

2 x 350g/12oz of red gurnard

85g/3oz puy lentils

½ small onion

1½ stalks celery

1 peeled carrot weighing about 115g/4oz

25g/1oz streaky bacon

½ clove garlic

15ml/½fl oz olive oil

1tsp olive oil for heating the lentils

salt and freshly ground white pepper

25g/1oz unsalted butter

60ml/2fl oz dry white wine

150ml/5fl oz fish stock (see page 23)

100ml/3½fl oz veal stock (see page 33)

10 cloves of garlic confit (see page 23)

Wine Note • Château La Nerthe *(Rhône Valley)* • The flagship wine from this excellent producer is rich and deep with exceptional concentration of fruit and a strong backbone to match the robust flavours and dense character of this wintry, satisfying dish.

Roast Gurnard with Grilled Potatoes and Broccoli

Serves 4

METHOD Trim the gurnard of its fins and trim the tail. Boil the potatoes in salted water until just cooked; allow to cool. Trim the broccoli of any excess stalk and blanch in boiling salted water for about 30 seconds then refresh in iced water and drain well.

Cut each potato into 3 slices each at least 5mm/¼in thick. Lightly oil a grilling tray using a little of the oil and place the potato slices and the broccoli florets on it, brush them all with the melted butter and season.

Heat the remaining oil in a roasting pan, season the gurnard tails, add 15g/½oz of the butter and roll the gurnard in this. Transfer to an oven pre-heated to 220°C/425°F/Gas 7 and roast for 10 minutes, turning at least three times during cooking. Once cooked remove and keep warm.

Bring to the boil the fish stock, wine and lemon juice, and reduce by two thirds. While this is reducing place the potatoes and broccoli under a pre-heated grill until nicely browned. Once the stock has reduced then add the cream, reduce slightly and gradually add the remaining butter (which should be cold), whisking continuously until melted. Do not allow the sauce to boil once the butter has melted.

Place the grilled potatoes and broccoli in an alternating circle in the middle of each plate allowing 3 potatoes and 3 broccoli florets per portion. Place a tail of gurnard on top and spoon the sauce around and a little over the fish.

4 tails of gurnard, cut from just below the vent

4 medium-sized new potatoes (about 180g/10oz)

12 florets of broccoli about 25g/1oz each

30ml/1fl oz olive oil

25g/1oz melted butter

salt and freshly ground white pepper

40g/1½oz butter

300ml/10fl oz fish stock (see page 23)

125ml/4fl oz dry white wine

juice of ½ lemon

60ml/2fl oz whipping cream

Wine Note • Linden Estate, Chardonnay *(N.Z.)* • This fishy fellow is often seen on a menu in N.Z. so why not serve him with a wine he'll recognise? As with spinach, Sauvignon is best avoided with broccoli, so a fruity, biscuity Chardonnay seems the obvious choice.

Haddock

French: *Eglefin, St. Pierre, Anon* • Italian: *Asinello* • German: *Schellfisch*
Spanish: *Erlefino*

This rather dour-looking fish, a cousin of the cod, is the Scottish preference for a fish and chip supper. In fact, it seems to be better thought of generally the further north of England you go. There is, as always, a counter argument to this statement – if you are from Yorkshire or Durham then haddock is the accompaniment to chips, whereas if you come from the other side of the Pennines it is cod that takes pride of place. In Iceland the haddock has always been thought of as a much better fish than the cod, as is the case in most of the Scandinavian countries. Without doubt it has a finer flavour than cod, but what it does lack is those thick white moist flakes that make cod so delicious.

Both fish are in fact from the same family (*Gadidae*) and are both classed as ground fish. Like cod, haddock is a deep water shoaling fish and consequently their numbers are giving great cause for concern, as stocks seem to be dwindling year on year. With its mark of the 'thumb print' (similar to that of John Dory) it is sometimes known in France as 'faux St. Pierre'. The haddock never grows as large as the cod, reaching only 40-60cm/16-24in in length or 1.8-2.7kg/4-6lb in weight.

Haddock comes into its own when it is smoked and takes on a delicious and distinctive flavour. It can also be turned into Finnan haddock and Arbroath Smokies. The Finnan was traditionally cold smoked over peat to a lovely golden yellow, although I believe that peat is no longer used. Smokies on the other hand are always hot smoked.

I have concentrated on smoked haddock in this section as any recipe for cod, whiting or hake will suit fresh haddock.

Smoked Haddock and Chive Tagliatelle

Serves 6 (first course)

So simple yet so good, this really is simplicity itself yet you could not wish for better flavours. Either as a first course or a main course, I have had it on my menus now for many years and I still eat it myself at home.

METHOD Bring the water to boil in a large pan with the oil and salt. Once boiling add the tagliatelle, return to the boil and cook for about one minute, drain and refresh, then drain well.

Bring the fish stock and the wine to the boil in a saucepan and reduce by two thirds. Season the smoked haddock with the pepper and add to the stock, add the cream and return to the boil. Reduce till the cream starts to thicken and the fish is cooked.

Add the pasta to the sauce and heat it through; once hot add the cheese and the chopped chives and stir in well, check the seasoning and serve with lots of warm ciabatta.

2.8litres/5pts water

60ml/2fl oz olive oil

salt

25og/9oz tagliatelle

250ml/9fl oz fish stock (see page 23)

100ml/3½fl oz dry white wine

350g/12oz of smoked haddock fillet, boneless and skinned

freshly ground white pepper

350ml/12fl oz whipping cream

55g/2oz freshly grated Parmesan

3tbsp finely chopped chives

Wine Note • Soave Classico Superiore, DOC, Masi *(Italy)* •Masi wines are consistent and this soave is bigger than most, with nuances of almonds and a creamy texture that will complement this smoky, fishy pasta ideally.

Smoked Haddock on Champ with Poached Egg and Grain Mustard Sauce

Serves 2

2 x 140g/5oz of smoked haddock

freshly ground white pepper

175ml/6fl oz fish stock (see page 23)

60ml/2fl oz dry white wine

150ml/5fl oz whipping cream

1 tsp whole grain mustard

2 poached eggs

3 sliced spring onions

175g/6oz mash (see page 25)

If I did not include this recipe in this book there would be so many people who would never forgive me. Don't get me wrong – this is not the only reason for it being here but it is a major one! We had one customer who wanted to have it every time he came and was upset (almost) when it was not on the menu. I have always changed my menus on a daily basis so I could or would never tell him in advance if it would be on or not. Still it meant that he had to try new dishes instead of the same old thing every time, so some good came of it. For you, John, enjoy!

METHOD Make sure all of the pin bones are removed from the haddock and season with the pepper. Combine the stock and the white wine in a pan large enough to take the fish fillets side by side and lay these in the stock. Bring this to a simmer and gently poach for about 3 minutes until cooked. Remove the fish and keep warm and covered. Strain the stock and set over a high heat to reduce by two thirds. Have a pan of hot water ready to reheat the poached eggs in.

Once the stock has reduced add the cream and the mustard and reduce until it just starts to thicken. Place the eggs in the hot water to reheat for about 30 seconds.

Mix the spring onions into the hot mash and place a mound in the centre of each plate. Carefully remove the skin from the fish and arrange a fillet on the mash. Drain the eggs and sit an egg on each piece of fish, then pour the sauce over the egg and around the plate.

Wine Note • Muscadet de Sevre et Maine "sur lie" Château Coing de St. Fiacre *(Loire Valley)* • An uncomplicated dish with simple flavours not too demanding of a wine. Muscadet is always good with fish and this one comes from one of the top houses in the Loire Valley. Having been aged on its lees, it has just a little more character and elegance than the basic cuvée.

Timbale of Arbroath Smokies 'Nicoise'

Serves 4

250g/9oz small new potatoes

salt and freshly ground black pepper

60ml/2fl oz dry white wine

125ml/4fl oz fish stock (see page 23)

8 black peppercorns

sliver of fresh ginger

1 small red chilli roughly chopped

2 cloves fresh garlic finely sliced

200ml/7fl oz whipping cream

juice of ¼ lemon

3 plum tomatoes

85g/3oz French beans

6 quail's eggs

2 Arbroath smokies to weigh about 450g/1lb

45ml/1½fl oz olive oil

handful of curly endive

sprigs of fresh chervil

Wine Note • Carneros Creek Chardonnay *(California)* • This spectacular Chardonnay is complex, full of fruit and sunshine, with more than enough power to work with this rich, flavourful delight.

It is worth taking a little extra time over this dish. The bones can be quite small and it will need a bit of concentration to remove them all successfully. If quail's eggs are unavailable then small hen's eggs would suffice but cut them into quarters or sixths if they are large.

METHOD Turn the new potatoes into small neat pointed barrel shapes. Boil these in salted water and cool.

Combine the wine, fish stock, peppercorns, ginger, chilli and garlic in a saucepan and reduce over a high heat until only about a quarter remains. Add the cream and a little juice of the lemon; reduce slightly until it just starts to thicken. Strain and allow to go cold.

Blanch, skin and seed the tomatoes. Cut the flesh into small neat dice. Top and tail the beans and boil in salted water until just cooked, refresh in iced water and drain. Cut the beans across into about the same size as the tomatoes.

Boil the quail's eggs for 2½ minutes, quickly cool them and peel the shells away gently as the yolks should still be soft; cut each egg in half.

Taking your time, very carefully skin the smokies then gently remove the meat from the bone making sure you do not miss any of the bones. Flake the meat into a bowl and lightly season with fresh black pepper and mix with two thirds of the sauce.

Season the beans and dribble with about a third of the oil and mix well. Do exactly the same with the tomato and this time add a squeeze of the lemon juice. Stand a cutter of about 6cm/2½in diameter and 5cm/2in deep in the centre of each plate; spoon a quarter of the beans into this and press them down. Spoon onto that a quarter of the fish and press this down, then spoon a quarter of the tomato on top pressing this down also. Carefully remove the cutter and repeat on the other plates. Toss the curly endive in a little of the oil and season. Place a small pile of this on top of each timbale. Dribble the remaining sauce around the timbales on the plates. Place three potatoes on each plate evenly spaced and a half quail's egg between each of the potatoes. Garnish with the sprigs of chervil.

Smoked Haddock with Peas

Smoked haddock and peas go together like ducks and water, or in the words of the song, love and marriage and a horse and carriage. What I am trying to say is that they are naturals together. Instead of little gem you could use small heads of cos or romaine lettuce. The bitterness of grilled trevisse, if available, would also work very well with this dish.

METHOD Finely slice the shallot and garlic. Heat 10ml/2tsp of the oil in a saucepan and sweat the shallot and garlic in this for a few seconds, then add half of the peas, seasoning and half of the sugar. Pour in the water and bring to the boil until the peas are cooked. Once cooked liquidise and pass through a strainer. Cook the remaining peas in boiling salted water with the remaining sugar; refresh in iced water once cooked.

Trim the lettuces of any outer and discoloured leaves, wash well and cut them into quarters. Grease a grilling tray with the remaining oil, lay the lettuce quarters on this and brush with the melted butter; season.

Lay the fish in a suitable pan; season with pepper only and add the fish stock and wine and cover. Gently heat this till simmering and cook the haddock for about 3-4 minutes depending upon thickness. Once cooked remove the fish from the pan, cover and keep warm.

Place the lettuce under a pre-heated grill until nicely grilled. They still need to have a crispness left but should be partly browned; this will take about 4 minutes and the lettuce will need turning after about 2 minutes.

Re-heat the mash, warm the sauce through and add the peas.

Place a spoonful of mash just off centre on each plate. Place 3 lettuce quarters next to the mash; carefully skin the fillets of fish. Place a portion of fish part on the mash and part on the lettuce. Spoon the peas and the sauce around.

Serves 4

1 shallot

½ clove garlic

15ml/½fl oz olive oil

225g/8oz fresh shelled peas

salt and freshly ground white pepper

2tsp sugar

300ml/10fl oz water

3 little gem lettuce

40g/1½oz melted butter

4 x 140g/5oz of smoked haddock, pin bones removed

250ml/9fl oz fish stock (see page 23)

60ml/2fl oz dry white wine

450g/1lb finished mash (see page 25)

Wine Note • Muscadet de Sèvre et Maine, Vinifie en Futs de Chêne *(Loire Valley)* • Vinified in oak casks, this is slightly darker in colour than classical Muscadet, with a lightly wooded perfume and very powerful fruit flavours that will balance well with the depth of the pea sauce.

Smoked Haddock Tart

Serves 6

225g/8oz shortcrust pastry (see page 30)

a little flour for rolling the pastry

dried beans for baking

450g/1lb natural smoked haddock

salt and freshly ground white pepper

300ml/10fl oz fish stock (see page 23)

300ml/10fl oz whipping cream

2 eggs

2tbsp chives

Tarts like this one can of course be made with almost anything – look through the fridge, see what's there and pop it into a tart! They make great first courses or main courses, one-course dishes, a snack or a supper dish, they are so versatile. Instead of haddock use crab, trimmings of cod with broccoli, salmon with courgettes or asparagus, sorrel or chives, prawns and mussels, anything that is left over or any sort of trimmings. Use your imagination – it is amazing what you can come up with!

METHOD Pre-heat the oven to 220°C/425°F/Gas 7. Roll out the pastry and line six 11cm/4½in fluted tart cases; allow to rest in the refrigerator for at least 30 minutes. Line the cases with greaseproof paper then fill with baking beans. Bake the cases in the oven for about 15 minutes until they are just starting to colour. Remove from the oven and turn down the heat to 200°C/400°F/Gas 6. Remove the beans and greaseproof paper.

Skin the haddock and remove any bones. Season with salt and pepper then place in a saucepan along with the fish stock, cover with a buttered paper and gently poach the fish until just cooked. Drain the fish from the stock and allow to go cold. Set the stock over a high heat and reduce until almost gone, add 125ml/4fl oz of the cream, bring to the boil and remove from the heat; allow this to go cold. Once cold add this to the remaining cream and the eggs and beat together well; season to taste.

Roughly flake the fish and divide it evenly between the pastry cases, sprinkle with the chopped chives and pour in the egg mix. Transfer to the oven for 15-20 minutes until the egg mix is just set. Serve either straight from the oven or allow to cool and serve just warm.

Wine Note • Hunters Chardonnay (N.Z.) • With smoked haddock there is a choice – to complement with Chardonnay or to contrast with Sauvignon. However, in this case, the addition of cream and pastry suggest that a Chardonnay is the safest bet, rather than cause a fight between the acidity of a Sauvignon and the creamy nature of the filling. Jane Hunter runs a small independent family winery with a tremendous reputation; their Chardonnay is totally matured in French oak and is rich, elegant and delicious.

Hake

French: *Merlu or Merluche* • German: *Seehechte* • Italian: *Nasello*
Spanish: *Merluza*

Hake, a member of the same family as cod and haddock, was seldom seen in this country until recently. Most hake fished by British trawlers went straight to Spain where it is greatly sought after, but then the Spanish were given permission to fish it for themselves in the Irish Box! This means that they don't need ours as much now and as a result the price has dropped and hake has become more widely available in the UK.

So, if it is sought after in Spain, why not here? One of the reasons could be that it is such a soft-fleshed fish that many people may not understand that this is the way it should be. When I say that the flesh is soft I mean very soft – almost like a milky white paste at times. If the fish you buy is unmanageably soft then once filleted and cut into portions, lay these on a tray and cover with cling film and place another tray on top. Leave this for an hour or so and the fish will firm up.

With adult fish taking about 7 years to reach sexual maturity we have to hope that they can continue to survive, but sadly it's looking doubtful. If there was ever a case for making net sizes bigger instead of smaller (which sadly is what is happening) then the hake and all its cousins would survive very well indeed. Once we can get away from eating young fish (in this case they are called *merluchon* in France), the better it will be for all those that remain. *Merluchon* are about half the size of fully mature fish and it is estimated that only 4% of hake reach maturity. I only buy large hake, never smaller than about 2.7kg/6lb, and so, theoretically, well into maturity.

This razor-toothed fish has a charcoal grey back and is available most of the year but probably at its best during the summer months.

Tournedos of Hake with a Courgette Purée and a Sauce of Fresh Squid

Serves 8 – 9

This method works well with other fish such as haddock and cod but is at it's best when using hake. The way the salt in the ham reacts with the soft flaky texture of the fish and brings it together, firming it up, works wonders with hake as it can sometimes be very soft and loose making it difficult to handle. Other herbs, such as basil or even sage, could replace the flat parsley.

METHOD The hake needs to be prepared 12 to 24 hours in advance.

On a sheet of aluminium foil lay out the slices of parma ham to form a sheet about 6cm/2¼in in from each side and about 24cm/9in deep. Lay the parsley onto the ham to cover it from the sides to about half of its depth.

Cut the fillet of hake so that it fits the width of the ham; place the off-cuts down its length to even out the thickness of the fish. Lightly season the fish and roll into a tight cylinder about 7cm/3in in diameter. Place this on one end of the ham and roll it in the ham and some foil. Once rolled tie off the ends. At 1.5cm/⅝in spacings tie a string around the roll as if tying up a fillet. This should give you 18 strings along a roll about 7cm/3in wide by 34cm/14in long. Refrigerate for at least 12 hours.

Cut the roll into tournedos, allowing two strings for each; e.g. cut between every other string. Assuming you started with 18 strings, this will give 9 tournedos.

Clean the squid and cut the body into strips. Cut the tentacles into pieces and reserve.

Cut all but two of the courgettes into quarters lengthways and remove the seed core and discard. Peel and finely slice the shallots. Peel and crush the garlic. In a saucepan heat 30ml/1fl oz of the oil, add the shallots and garlic, cover and sweat for a couple of minutes without browning. Add the courgette and season, cover and cook very quickly over a high heat without colouring, stirring often. The cooking of the courgettes will only take a couple of minutes. Transfer to a food processor immediately and process until smooth. Remove and spread on a tray to cool quickly. Cut the remaining courgette into very small but neat dice.

Heat the remaining oil in a frying pan; when hot add 15g/½oz of the butter, lightly season the tournedos and place them cut-side down in the

1.8-2kg/4-4½lb hake fillet skinned and pin boned

125g/4½oz thinly sliced parma ham or similar

140g/5oz flat parsley leaves

salt and freshly ground white pepper

2 small squid about 85-115g/3-4oz each

1.3kg/3lb courgettes

4 shallots

1 clove garlic

45ml/1½fl oz olive oil

85g/3oz unsalted butter

125ml/4fl oz dry white wine

425ml/15fl oz fish stock (see page 23)

250ml/9fl oz whipping cream

Wine Note • Hay Shed Hill, Chardonnay *(Western Australia)* • Lots of different nuances here, with the underlying flavour of the squid sauce adding yet another dimension. Quite a big wine is needed and a rich, oaked Chardonnay would seem to fit the bill. Hay Shed Hill use hand-selected parcels of fruit from low-yielding vines to make this full-bodied wine, which is fermented and aged in French oak, giving tremendous character and length.

pan and bake in a hot oven for 4 minutes. Turn and return to the oven for a further 2-3 minutes. The fish should now be lightly browned on both sides. Allow to rest in a warm place.

In a saucepan bring the wine and fish stock to the boil and reduce until only a third remains. Add the cream, return to the boil and gradually add 55g/2oz of the butter whisking continuously until melted. Add the strips of squid and the diced courgette and keep warm.

Warm the courgette purée through with the addition of a little cream. In a small pan heat the remaining butter; when sizzling add the reserved tentacles and season. Fry these very quickly and once they turn purple remove them from the pan.

Place a spoonful of the purée in the centre of each plate. Place a tournedos on this then spoon the sauce around. Top the tournedos with a little of the sautéed tentacles.

Fillet of Hake with a Tomato and Fennel Broth

Serves 4

4 x 140-175g/5-6oz pieces of hake fillet

400g/14oz plum tomatoes

½ onion

½ clove garlic

225g/8oz fennel

45ml/1½fl oz olive oil

60ml/2fl oz dry white wine

1tbsp tomato purée

175ml/6fl oz fish stock (see page 23)

salt and freshly ground white pepper

25g/1oz unsalted butter

20 leaves fresh basil

METHOD Blanch, peel and seed the tomatoes. Roughly chop the flesh. Peel and thinly slice the onion and crush the garlic. Trim the fennel and cut into thin wedges. Heat 30ml/1fl oz of the oil in a saucepan and sweat off the onion and garlic without colouring for a minute; add the fennel, cover with a lid and continue to sweat until the fennel just starts to soften. Add the white wine and reduce until gone, stir in the purée and add the stock, bring to the boil and simmer for 5 minutes. Add the tomato and simmer for a further 3 minutes. Check the seasoning.

Heat the remaining oil in a frying pan. When hot, season the hake, add the butter to the pan and fry the hake for 2 minutes, meat-side down, very quickly, browning it well. Once well browned turn the fish on to the skin side and cook for a further 2 minutes.

Roughly tear the basil leaves and fold them into the broth. Spoon this in the centre of each plate and place a fillet of the fish on top.

Wine Note • Berberana, Gran Reserva *(Spain)* • This needs a fairly powerful red and what better than a top quality Rioja. Bodegas Berberana have an excellent reputation, well reflected in this complex wine with well-integrated oak and lots of character, made from classic regional grape varieties.

Halibut

French: *Fletan* • Spanish: *Halibut* • German: *Heilbutt* • Italian: *Halibut*

This elongated, diamond-shaped fish is often regarded as the king of the flat fish. With its rather pointed head and very narrow tail it is almost impossible to mistake it for any other fish, except perhaps the Greenland halibut, which is very similar to look at but different to eat, as it has an inferior texture and flavour. The two main differences to the eye are that the lateral line in the Greenland halibut is almost straight, whereas true halibut has a definite kink around the pectoral fin. The other is that the Greenland is blackish grey to brown on the dark side and the true halibut is a dark olive green.

The halibut is certainly the largest of the flat fish. It can grow to enormous sizes: once in a fish market in Reykjavik I saw one weighing 100kg/225lb, and its backbone when filleted was almost as thick as my leg (it made the most wonderfully flavoured and jellied stock). The fish, I would guess, was about 1.8metres/6 feet long! They have been recorded much bigger than that though, up to and occasionally beyond 250kg/560lb, although this size would be extremely rare, especially these days. Although the texture of halibut is quite distinct (meaty but still quite soft) it does have a tendency to be a little on the dry side.

The normal range of sizes of halibut is from 5-7kg/12-15lb – any smaller than this and they are known as chicken halibut and are often cooked whole. When buying halibut try to buy middle cuts as the tail does not lend itself to very many recipes. Often halibut is sold cut into tronchon (a cross cut of flat fish on the bone) as cooking it on the bone can help to keep it moist (as I have already mentioned it can be a little dry, especially the larger fish). The Greenland halibut is invariably sold cross-filleted like plaice, as its flesh is much thinner.

The halibut is one of many fish being farmed these days. It will never be quite as tasty as those fished in the wild, but if it helps conserve stocks and keep prices down it has to be a good thing.

Poached Halibut on a Salad of White Beans

Serves 4

4 x 175g/6oz fillets of halibut cut from a thick fish

salt and freshly ground white pepper

White bean salad:

175g/6oz white beans

1 small carrot, peeled

½ medium onion finely chopped

1 stick celery washed

1 leek white only washed

2 cloves garlic peeled

55g/2oz bacon

60ml/2fl oz sesame seed oil

Court bouillon:

1 onion

1 leek, white only

3 sticks celery

3 sticks lemon grass

3 cloves garlic

15g/½oz ginger

2 jalapeno chillies

2 star anise

15g/½oz white peppercorns

150ml/5fl oz rice wine vinegar

25g/1oz sea salt

15g/½oz coriander seeds

1.7 litres/3pt water

Although this dish can be served either hot or cold I much prefer it at room temperature, cooked then allowed to cool without the use of a refrigerator, and served while it is still just ever so slightly warm. I know that this is frowned upon by all environmental health officers but any food, once cold, e.g. subjected to the refrigerator, loses most of its flavours. It is a delicate dish anyway and any food straight from the cold of the refrigerator is always bland.

METHOD Soak the beans 24 hours before needed in lots of cold water. Drain the beans and place in a saucepan along with all the white bean salad vegetables, garlic and bacon. Only the onion need be chopped; the rest should remain whole. Cover well with water and bring to the boil. Allow to simmer until cooked. Once cooked leave to cool then drain off the liquid. Cut the vegetables into small dice and return them to the beans. Cut the bacon into small dice, add to the beans, season and mix with the sesame oil.

Roughly chop the vegetables for the court bouillon. Thinly slice the lemon grass. Peel and roughly chop the garlic, slice the ginger and roughly cut up the chillies. Place all of these along with the remaining ingredients and the water into a saucepan and bring to the boil. Simmer for 5 minutes, allow to go cold then strain.

For the cucumber salad, first peel the cucumber. Cut this into slices about 3mm/⅛inch thick then into strips. Split the chilli down the middle and remove the seeds, then finely chop the flesh. Mix this with the other ingredients and pour over the cucumber, seasoning with a little freshly ground white pepper.

Bring the court bouillon to the boil. Season the fish with salt and freshly ground pepper. Place the fish in a pan lightly greased with a little sesame oil, and pour the stock over making sure it is covered. Sit this on a very gentle heat for about 2-3 minutes depending upon its thickness, remove from the heat and allow to finish cooking as it cools down.

Arrange a circle of the cucumber on each plate. Spoon the beans into the centre of the cucumber and place a fillet of fish on top. Spoon the juice from the cucumber over and around the fish.

Cucumber Salad:

225g/8oz piece of cucumber

1 jalapeno chilli

60ml/2fl oz rice wine vinegar

½tsp sugar

100ml/3½fl oz court bouillon

1 plum tomato, blanched, skinned and seeded, cut into a small dice

60ml/2fl oz sesame seed oil

Wine Note • Linden Estate, Sauvignon Blanc *(New Zealand)* • A delicate dish but with some lively contrasting Eastern elements. Thai flavours undoubtedly work best with either a rosé wine or with a crisp dry white. Sauvignon Blanc is the ideal grape variety, particularly the ripe, gooseberry fruit style from New Zealand that will stand up to a fair amount of chilli.

Grilled Halibut with a Sweet Pepper Cream and Tapenade

Serves 2

METHOD Heat the frying oil to 160°C/325°F, plunge in the peppers and fry till the skin starts to blister. Plunge into iced water and cut them in half. Once cool enough to handle peel off the skin and remove the seeds. Cut the flesh into strips about 1cm/½in wide.

Grease a grilling tray with the olive oil, season the undersides of the fish and lay them on the tray presentation-side uppermost. Brush with the melted butter. Place the fish under a hot grill for about 4-6 minutes depending upon the thickness.

Combine the wine and the fish stock in a saucepan and bring to the boil, reduce by three-quarters. Add the cream, return to the boil then add the strips of peppers with a little salt and pepper. Continue to boil until the sauce starts to thicken then gradually add the cold butter shaking the pan continuously until it has all melted; check the seasoning.

Divide the peppers evenly between the plates and spoon the sauce around. Place a fillet of halibut on the top of the peppers and dribble the coriander oil around the sauce. Place a teaspoon of the tapenade on top of each fillet of fish.

app. 1 litre/1¾pts oil for frying

450g/1lb sweet red peppers

15ml/½fl oz olive oil

2 x 140g/5oz of fully trimmed halibut

salt and freshly ground white pepper

15g/½oz melted butter

60ml/2fl oz dry white wine

175ml/6fl oz fish stock (see page 23)

85ml/3fl oz whipping cream

25g/1oz cold unsalted butter

2tsp coriander oil

tapenade (see page 31)

Wine Note • Mondavi, White Zinfandel *(California)* • A lovely, summery wine that is full of fruit, flavour and sunshine – rather like this tasty combination. The wine is pink in colour and made from red grapes – don't ask why it's called white! It is crisp and subtle with a hint of spice.

Fillet of Halibut in a Mussel, Spring Onion and Marjoram Broth

Serves 2

350g/12oz mussels

1 shallot finely chopped

200ml/7fl oz fish stock (see page 23)

60ml/2fl oz dry white wine

3 spring onions

1 tomato

2 x 140g/5oz of fully trimmed halibut

salt and freshly ground white pepper

225g/8oz new potatoes cut in 15mm/¾in dice

60ml/2fl oz whipping cream

15g/½oz unsalted butter

250g/9oz spinach picked of its stalk and well washed

20 marjoram leaves

METHOD Thoroughly clean the mussels pulling off the beard and discarding any that are broken or open. Leave them standing in cold water for 10 minutes, change the water and stand again for at least 10 minutes. Place the chopped shallot in a saucepan along with the fish stock and white wine; bring this to the boil. As soon as it boils drain the mussels from the water and add to the stock, cover with a lid and return to the boil, then cook the mussels for about 3-4 minutes or until they are all open. Turn the mussels into a colander to drain.

Once drained pick the meat from the shells. Pass the stock through a fine strainer or muslin into a saucepan. Bring the stock to the boil and reduce down until only 200ml/7fl oz remains then allow to cool.

Trim the spring onions of any discoloured leaves and cut into pieces of about 5mm/¼in. Blanch, skin and deseed the tomato then cut the flesh into dice similar to the size of the onions.

Lightly season the underside of the halibut fillets and place them with the stock in a pan large enough to hold them without overlapping. Cover with paper and gently bring to the boil; just as the liquid starts to tremble lower the heat to prevent it from actually boiling and keep hot for about 1 minute. Gently remove the fish from the stock, cover and keep warm.

Return the stock to the boil along with the potatoes, simmer until the potatoes are just cooked then add the cream, the mussels and the spring onions; check the seasoning. Return to the boil and then keep warm. Heat the butter in a saucepan then very quickly cook the spinach with a little seasoning, stirring as it cooks. Once cooked squeeze out all of the excess liquid and place a mound of the spinach in the centre of each plate. Add the tomato and the marjoram to the sauce and spoon the garnish around the spinach. Place a fillet of the fish on each mound and spoon the broth over and around the fish.

Wine Note • Dashwood Sauvignon Blanc *(NZ)* • The clean, fresh flavour in this archetypal NZ Sauvignon perfectly mirrors the light, bright nature of this heavenly halibut dish.

Tronchon of Halibut with Spinach and Wild Mushrooms

Serves 4

25g/1oz puy lentils

1 peeled clove garlic

½ stick celery

½ medium onion

175g/6oz mixed wild mushrooms, e.g. chanterelles, girolles, oyster, trompet

140g/5oz spinach

2 tomatoes

8 baby leeks

salt and freshly ground white pepper

4 x 250g/9oz tronchon of halibut

30ml/1fl oz olive oil

25g/1oz unsalted butter

125ml/4fl oz red wine

225ml/8fl oz fish stock (see page 23)

175ml/6fl oz veal or brown chicken stock (see page 33)

1 finely chopped shallot

splash Madeira

Here I cook the fish as a tronchon, which is a cross cut of flat fish, normally longer than it is wide and always on the bone. Although I would not normally serve a fish on the bone, cooking halibut this way will keep the meat moist.

METHOD Wash the puy lentils and combine them in a pan with the garlic, celery and onion; cover with water and bring to the boil, simmering until cooked, then cool, discard the garnish and drain the lentils. Pick through the mushrooms removing any roots and twigs etc., wash then drain them well. Pick the spinach of its stalks then wash it in at least three changes of water and drain well. Blanch, skin and de-seed the tomatoes, cut the flesh into small dice. Trim the leeks of any root and any unusable outer leaves, cut them to about 15cm/6in in length and wash them well. Blanch in boiling salted water until they are just starting to give then refresh in iced water and drain.

Preheat the oven to 230°C/450°F/Gas 8. Season the halibut on all sides. Heat 15ml/½fl oz of the oil in a roasting pan and once smoking add 15g/½oz of the butter. Place the halibut tronchon in on one of the meat sides, allow to brown lightly and roast in the oven for 4 minutes. Turn onto the other side and return to the oven to continue roasting for a further 4 minutes. Remove from the oven and keep warm. While the halibut is roasting reduce the red wine and fish stock by three quarters. Once reduced add the veal stock, return to the boil and keep warm.

Using the remaining oil grease a grilling tray, roll the leeks in this oil and season them, then place them under a very hot grill until they just start to brown. Heat a frying pan and add the remaining butter; over a high heat add the mushrooms, season and add the shallots, toss for a few seconds, add the splash of Madeira and the spinach leaves, toss this all together until the spinach goes limp.

Return the halibut to the oven for a minute to reheat. Divide the spinach and mushrooms into four equal amounts and place a pile in the centre of each plate. Place a tronchon of halibut on top. Add the puy lentils to the sauce and warm it through. Cross two leeks on the top of each piece of halibut then spoon a little of the sauce over the fish and the remainder around; scatter with the tomato dice.

Wine Note • Morgon, Côte du Py, Thomas la Chevalière *(Beaujolais)* • Rich, deep flavours here suggest a wine of similar character and a generous Morgon immediately springs to mind. This one is typically full of rich, ripe fruit flavours and will work particularly well with the earthy mushrooms and lentils.

Herring

French: *Hareng* • Italian: *Aringa* • German: *Hering* • Spanish: *Arenque*
Norwegian, Danish, Icelandic: *Sild*

What a remarkable little fish the herring is! Eaten in almost every country in the northern hemisphere, it has been pickled, smoked, salted and preserved in every conceivable way, sustaining whole generations of people from Denmark to Wales and from Iceland to Canada.

There have been important herring fisheries all over the UK too, from Scotland down to Northumberland, the home of the Craster Kipper which, along with the Manx kipper from the Isle of Man, is thought to be the best kipper produced. Norfolk (and Great Yarmouth in particular) has always been famous for its herring. It has an important herring fishery too and is the home of the bloater. The bloater is a herring which has been brined for a short time and then cold smoked whole, whereas the kipper is simply split and smoked.

Even way back in medieval times herring was preserved. A method was developed to preserve this pungent, heavily salted fish for the longest possible time and did little for the flavour. These strong-smelling fish were once used to lay a false trail to break hounds off a scent, which is how the term 'red herring' (meaning to divert someone from the matter in hand) came into being.

The huge herring fleets of the last century and the earlier part of this one have now gone, as have the majority of the herring sadly – like so many other species. The herring catch in the North Sea, the most badly affected fishery, halved between 1950 and 1960. Great Yarmouth alone had over a thousand boats running at the turn of this century but the days of the quay-side covered with swills (baskets) overflowing with herring are over. The demise of industry inevitably meant the closure of the huge onshore trade too which depended upon the catch.

The demise of the herring industry has also meant that people have lost their taste for herring in the UK, although it is still highly regarded in many continental countries. The Germans alone have hundreds of recipes for curing herring. Restaurant customers in Britain would probably turn their noses up at the thought of herring on the menu, but there is still a large market for rollmops and sweet cured herrings. Fresh herring though should not become a thing of the past because it is a great fish.

Sweet Pickled Herrings with Crushed Potatoes

Serves 8

4 herrings

sea salt and freshly ground white pepper

app. 48 leaves of tarragon

55g/2oz carrot

½ small onion

115g/4oz cooking apple

1 clove crushed garlic

2tbsp whole grain mustard

175ml/6fl oz white wine vinegar

100ml/3½fl oz water

25g/1oz brown sugar

2 bay leaves

½tsp caraway seeds

15ml/½fl oz olive oil

650g/1lb 7oz new potatoes

55g/2oz unsalted butter

Cucumber Salad:

225g/8oz piece of cucumber

1 jalapeno chilli

60ml/2fl oz rice wine vinegar

½tsp sugar

Almost every recipe ever written for herrings includes vinegar, mustard and often potato and apples; this one is no exception to the rule. For this first course I make a sweet pickle using cooking apples; the herring is then slow baked in it and served cold on hot crushed new potatoes. I have always liked the combination of hot with cold especially if the textures are right. This dish is best served the day after making to allow it to chill thoroughly before serving. I have topped it with a cucumber salad which I think goes well but is very much an optional extra and should be made almost immediately before serving.

METHOD Fillet the herrings and remove as much bone as possible. Lay the fillets out and liberally season the meat side with the sea salt and the pepper. Sprinkle the fillets with the tarragon leaves then roll each one tightly and skewer them in position using a cocktail stick.

Peel and finely dice the carrot, onion and cooking apple. Mix these together with the crushed garlic, mustard, vinegar, water, sugar, bay leaves and caraway seeds. Lightly grease an ovenproof dish with the oil then stand the rolled fillets of herring in this. Pour in the pickle mixture and even it out. Place the fish in an oven pre-heated to 150°C/300°F/Gas 2 for 50 minutes. Half way through the cooking turn the fillets over and return to the oven. Once cooked allow the herring to go completely cold. Boil the new potatoes in their skins in salted water; once cooked allow to go cold then peel. Crush the potatoes and mix with the melted butter and seasoning.

For the cucumber salad, first peel the cucumber. Cut this into slices about 3mm/⅛inch thick and then into strips. Split the chilli down the middle and remove the seeds, then finely chop the flesh. Mix this with the other ingredients and pour over the cucumber, seasoning with a little freshly ground white pepper.

To serve, heat a frying pan until it just starts to smoke, add the crushed potatoes, and brown them really well. Remove the cocktail sticks from the herrings and cut each one into two. Place a mound of the potato in the centre of each plate and place two halves of the herring on top of this. Spoon the garnish over and around then pile a little of the cucumber on top of the fish.

Wine Note • Manzanilla La Gitana Sherry • Vinegar and wine are natural enemies. For this tart dish try the intense flavour of a sublime sherry.

Tomato Baked Herrings

METHOD Fillet the herrings and remove as much bone as possible. Lay the fillets out and liberally season the meat side with the sea salt and the pepper. Roll the fillets tightly starting at the head end and skewer them in place using a cocktail stick.

Blanch the tomatoes and remove their seeds; cut the flesh into rough dice. Finely slice the shallots and crush the garlic. Split the chilli in two and remove the seeds, then very finely chop the flesh.

Heat two thirds of the oil in a saucepan and gently cook the shallots and garlic till they just start to soften. Then add the tomato and chilli and stir in the tomato purée. Add the vinegar, sugar and fish stock and allow to simmer, stirring occasionally, for about 15 minutes.

Using the remaining oil grease an ovenproof dish then stand the fillets of herring in it, pour the tomato sauce over and bake in an oven pre-heated to 150°C/300°F/Gas 2 for 50 minutes.

Once cooked serve either hot or cold.

6 herrings

sea salt and freshly ground white pepper

6 plum tomatoes

3 shallots

1 clove garlic

1 small red chilli

30ml/1fl oz olive oil

1tbsp tomato purée

125ml/4fl oz white wine vinegar

½ tsp sugar

175ml/6fl oz fish stock (see page 23)

Wine Note • Muscadet, Coing de St. Fiacre • A really crisp dry white is needed here to cut through the intense flavour of both herring and tomato. This very good quality Muscadet comes from one of the top houses in the Loire. Alternatively a good fino sherry would make an interesting alternative.

Grilled Herrings with a Hazelnut Crust, Roast Apple and Horseradish Cream

Serves 4

175ml/6fl oz whipping cream

25g/1oz finely grated fresh horseradish

¼ lemon

salt and freshly ground white pepper

4 herrings

2tbsp whole grain mustard

55g/2oz ground hazelnuts

115g/4oz fresh white breadcrumbs

15g/½oz chopped parsley and chopped dill

15ml/½fl oz olive oil

1 granny smith or golden delicious apple

15g/½oz unsalted butter

175g/6oz baby spinach leaves

300ml/10 fl oz olive oil

55g/2oz any fresh herb

My good friend Shaun, from whom this recipe came, has always been a lover of, shall we say, the more ordinary or cheaper foods, seeing in them merits that others would blindly pass by. I told him there were to be some recipes for herring in this book (there were none in the last one!) and he supplied me with this one. When I test-cooked the other two herring recipes he sampled them and, I believe, pronounced that they were okay!

METHOD   Begin by making a batch of herb oil by finely chopping 55g/2oz of fresh herbs in a food processor and then gradually pouring in 300ml/10fl oz of olive oil. Put to one side. Next whip the cream and mix in the grated horseradish, a squeeze of lemon juice and seasoning. Leave to stand in the refrigerator for a couple of hours.

Fillet the herrings and remove as much bone as possible then rinse and dry the fish. Lay the fillets out and season them. Spread each fillet on the meat side with a little of the grain mustard. Mix the ground hazelnuts with the breadcrumbs and the herbs then lightly season. Generously coat each fillet with the crumb mix. Using the olive oil lightly grease a grilling tray and lay the fillets on this, crumb-side uppermost.

Cut the apple into 12 pieces and turn these, removing the skin and seeds. Heat the butter in a frying pan and when sizzling add the apple and fry, browning it lightly; once browned remove from the pan and keep warm.

Place the fish under a pre-heated grill for 4 minutes or until cooked. Dress the spinach leaves with a little of the herb oil and season. Pile some leaves in the centre of each plate, and cross two of the herring fillets on each salad. Top each one with a quenelle of the horseradish cream, drizzle the remaining oil around the salad and place three pieces of apple on each plate around the salad.

Wine Note • Sauvignon Blanc, Chevalier de Berticot *(S.W. France)* •
An aromatic very fruity Sauvignon made from mature vines and just right for cutting through the crust and matching the 'tart' nature of the herring.

Langoustine

French: *Langoustine* • German: *Kaisergranat* • Italian: *Scampi*
Spanish: *Cigala, Langostina*

Although langoustine is not the English name for this magnificent shellfish it is the one that is most commonly used within the catering industry to mean the Dublin Bay Prawn. They are also known simply as prawns, as Norway Lobster and of course scampi, although please do not confuse them with the frozen breaded lumps (which I presume to be a fish of some sort). In Iceland if you ask for lobster this is what you will be served. Technically the langoustine is a member of the prawn family but out of respect I have given them their own chapter.

It is strange today to think that langoustine were discarded by British fishermen until the 1950s and now Scotland, which is where most of our langoustine come from, has developed a thriving industry around them.

It is important to try to buy your langoustine while they are still alive – difficult I know but not impossible. You will never see them running around like a lobster and they will, at best, only barely move but unless they come to you alive then their freshness cannot be guaranteed. Their keeping quality even while alive is poor at best and diminishes rapidly once they are dead.

They are undoubtedly at their best when they are prepared very simply so never try to be too clever with them. Roasted or grilled and served with good quality mayonnaise or aioli they are delicious, but here are a few recipes that complement them well without going over the top!

Langoustines with Poached Egg and a Tomato Butter

Serves 4

400g/14oz red potatoes

85g/3oz unsalted butter

½ small onion finely chopped

25g/1oz melted butter

salt and freshly ground white pepper

12 large langoustines

2 plum tomatoes

15ml/½fl oz olive oil

12fl oz tomato sauce (see page 33)

4 poached eggs

few sprigs of fresh chervil

This makes a fantastic first course if you only have a few langoustines, but if you have more there is no reason why it could not be turned into a main course! When poaching the eggs try doing it the restaurant way; set a deep pan of water to boil rapidly with a touch of vinegar in it to help set the whites. Crack the eggs into individual cups and place them in the water one at a time. The deeper the pan the better; as the egg tumbles down through the water it turns the white around the yolk and, if the water is deep enough, it will return to the surface without ever having touched the bottom. Once cooked (the yolks should still be very soft just as the whites are set) then plunge the eggs into iced water. They can be kept for a couple of days like this; to use just pop them back into hot water for a minute to reheat.

METHOD Peel the potatoes and parboil them in salted water – they should have started cooking but still be very firm; drain and allow to cool. Once cool enough to handle grate them into a bowl. Heat 15g/½oz of the butter in a pan and gently fry the chopped onion without colouring until soft. Mix the onions, the melted butter and seasoning into the potatoes and form them into four small cakes about 7.5cm/3in across and 2cm/¾in deep.

Plunge the langoustines into boiling salted water for 45 seconds then allow to cool. Shell the tails reserving the shells for another recipe.

Blanch, skin and de-seed the tomatoes, then cut the flesh into a 1cm/½in dice. Heat the oil in a frying pan and add the potato cakes, gently frying these until golden brown on both sides. Meanwhile heat 15g/½oz of the butter in another frying pan and quickly cook the langoustines in this for 1½ minutes; remove and keep warm.

Bring the tomato sauce to the boil and just before boiling gradually whisk in 55g/2oz of the butter, whisking continuously until all the butter has melted. Keep the sauce hot but do not allow it to boil.

Reheat the poached eggs for one minute in hot water. Place a potato cake in the centre of each plate, drain the eggs and place an egg on each potato cake. Position three langoustines around each cake; add the tomato dice to the sauce then spoon the sauce over the egg and the langoustines. Garnish with a few sprigs of fresh chervil.

Wine Note • Puligny Montrachet, 1er cru, Hameau de Blagny, Domaine Prosper Maufoux *(Burgundy)* •
A classic wine for a classic dish. White Burgundy is a must here and this superbly rich wine is full of complex characteristics that are a combination of floral, nutty and biscuity flavours. Simply stunning!

Lobster

French: *Homard* • Italian: *Astice* • German: *Hummer* • Spanish: *Bogavante*

This is probably the one shellfish that is known the world over as they are extensively fished. The American or Canadian varieties are slightly different in colour to the European. The European lobster is a rich blue-black, turning to white underneath; the American is more of a russet brown. Although the colour of a lobster varies according to its habitat, they all have one thing in common and that is that they turn bright red once cooked.

It is quite ironic that the lobster should now be so expensive as during the 17th and 18th centuries it was so common it was almost considered to be 'junk food'. When caught in great quantities or stranded on the shore after severe storms, the lobster was used as a fertiliser or given to widows and orphans, servants and prisoners as food. In Massachusetts a law was passed forbidding it to be served more than twice a week, as a daily lobster dinner was considered cruel punishment! These days it tends to be kept for romantic occasions, high days and holidays.

Lobster are at their best during the summer months and, more often than not, the most expensive of all shellfish. The meat of the cock crab is often thought to be the tastiest you will find, but the meat of the female lobster just before she lays her eggs is superior even to this. So how do you sex a lobster? Well there are two main ways. Firstly, the tail of the female is much broader and straighter than that of the male, whose tail tapers slightly. Secondly, when you turn the lobster upside down, the first two legs on the tail, nearest the carapace, of the female are very spindly, whereas those of the male are very heavy and thick.

When buying lobster it should, like all crustaceans, be alive and the livelier the better! It should also feel heavy for its size. Always allow 450g/1lb per person as a main course and save the shell! It makes great stock for soups, sauces and risottos.

Lobster with Pulses

I first served this dish back in 1989 when I had my ill-fated restaurant in London's Knightsbridge. It was a great dish then and it still is; the restaurant was pretty good too, but we were just the victims of extremely bad timing! Still, can't be expected to get it right all the time!

METHOD Bring the bouillon to the boil and once boiling plunge the lobsters in; return to the boil and simmer for 3 minutes. Remove them and allow to cool.

Once cool enough to handle carefully remove the meat from the shells. Split the tails in two lengthways and remove the intestinal tract. Place the meat in an ovenproof dish and add a little of the bouillon and cover.

In a saucepan combine the fish stock and the wine with 100ml/3½fl oz of the strained court bouillon. Bring this to the boil and reduce by two thirds. Add the pulses and the sweetcorn along with the cream. Return to the boil and reduce slightly until it just starts to thicken. Place the lobster in an oven pre-heated to 180°C/350°F/Gas 4 for two minutes to reheat.

Meanwhile heat the butter in a pan and add the spinach; season and cook very quickly until it becomes limp. Drain well.

Place a mound of the spinach in the centre of each plate then arrange the lobster meat on top of this placing the smaller pieces on the bottom then the two halves of the tail and top it off with the claws. Spoon the sauce and garnish around.

Serves 2

app. 4.5 litres/8pts court bouillon (see page 22)

2 x 450g/1lb lobsters

225ml/8fl oz fish stock (see page 23)

75ml/2½fl oz dry white wine

175g/6oz cooked mixed pulses, e.g. chick peas, haricot blanc, flageolet, puy lentils, black eyed beans

55g/2oz sweetcorn kernels

125ml/4fl oz whipping cream

15g/½oz unsalted butter

175g/6oz picked and washed spinach

salt and freshly ground white pepper

Wine Note • Savigny Les Beaune, Blanc, Ch. Genot Boulanger • You could force yourself to drink champagne although it would certainly have to be vintage in this case to have sufficient body to balance the pulses (the food not yours!). However, a good quality white Burgundy, such as this prime example from a top producer (of which very little reaches the U.K.), would probably be more appropriate and more at home with the casserole.

Lobster and Chicken Sausage with a Spring Onion Purée

8 sausages

1.2 litres/2pts court bouillon (see page 22)

1 x 650g/1½lb live lobster

15g/½oz chopped chives

1tbsp olive oil

25g/1oz butter

Mousseline:

2 x 175g/6oz breasts of chicken

10g/¼oz salt

1 egg white

150ml/¼pt whipping cream

25ml/1fl oz dry sherry

freshly ground white pepper

Sauce:

25g/1oz unsalted butter

2 bunches spring onions, roughly chopped

150ml/5fl oz whipping cream

To serve:

sprigs of fresh dill

There are probably about four dishes that others would call my signature dishes – ones that I have been doing for years and years – and this is one of them. I probably started making it in 1984; in fact I seem to remember that it was for our first New Year's Eve dinner at Restaurant Seventy-Four in Canterbury.

METHOD To make the mousseline, chop the chicken breasts into small pieces, place in a blender or food processor with the salt, and blend to a smooth paste. Add the egg white and process again until it stiffens. Rub the mixture through a fine sieve into a bowl set on crushed ice. Gradually add two-thirds of the cream, mix in well, then add the sherry and season with a little salt and pepper as required. Test the mousse by dropping a little of the mixture into simmering water until it is cooked. If the texture is too rubbery or firm, add more cream and test again until the desired consistency is reached. Place in the refrigerator until needed.

Bring the court bouillon to the boil, plunge the lobster in, bring back to the boil and continue boiling for 2 minutes. Remove the pan from the heat and allow the lobster to cool in the stock. When it is cold, remove the lobster meat from the shell (saving the shells to make soup or sauce for another recipe), and dice the meat into 5mm/¼inch cubes. Fold the meat and the chives into the mousseline. Using the cling film as a sausage skin, form the mixture into 8 individual sausages and tie off the ends. Leave to rest in the refrigerator until needed; they will keep in this form for about 4 hours.

To make the sauce, melt the butter in a saucepan, add the spring onions, season, cover with a lid and sweat them until cooked – about 3-4 minutes. Then place the cooked onions in a liquidiser and process so that they are chopped but not too finely. Return them to the saucepan, stir in the cream and reheat.

To serve drop the sausages, still in their cling film skins, into boiling water and poach for 10 minutes. When cooked, gently remove the film, heat the oil and butter in a frying pan, and gently roll the sausages in the hot fat until brown.

Place a spoonful of the sauce in the middle of each plate and sit a sausage on top. Garnish with a few sprigs of dill.

Once cooked the sausages can be kept for up to three days in the refrigerator. After poaching, drop them into iced water to cool them rapidly. To reheat, drop them into boiling water and simmer for 2-3 minutes.

Wine Note • Hay Shed Hill 'Pitchfork Pink' *(Australia)* • Originally made in a hay shed, this stunning rosé is bursting with fruit and the addition of a little Muscat to the principal grape variety of Cabernet Sauvignon adds a touch of sweetness on the finish that is just right with the creamy mousse and lobster.

Poached Lobster in an Oriental Broth

Serves 2

METHOD Bring the court bouillon to the boil. Plunge in the lobsters, return to the boil for 2 minutes, remove from the heat and allow to cool.

Trim the baby pak choi and blanch these for a few seconds in boiling salted water until they go limp, refresh in iced water and drain. Trim the spring onions and cut them into pieces at an angle. Remove the stalks from the mushrooms and cut the caps into 3 slices.

Carefully remove the lobster meat from the shells, saving the shells to make a soup or sauce. Cover the meat and put to one side.

Place the water, soy and vinegar into a saucepan. Finely slice the chilli and add this to the water along with the mushrooms, garlic and ginger. Bring this to the boil; once boiling add the noodles and simmer for about three minutes until the noodles are cooked.

Place the lobster in another saucepan along with the pak choi, the spring onions and peas. Pour the hot stock over the lobster, pour in the sesame oil and return to a low heat for a minute until the lobster is heated through.

Just before serving tear the basil leaves and add them to the stock. Carefully arrange into individual soup bowls.

court bouillon (see page 22) sufficient to cover lobsters

2 x 550g/1¼lb live lobsters

2 baby pak choi

2 spring onions

3 shiitake mushrooms

400ml/14fl oz water

2tsp dark soy sauce

4tsp rice wine vinegar

1 small hot red chilli

½ small clove of garlic cut into a fine julienne

10g/¼oz ginger cut into a fine julienne

15g/½oz rice noodles

25g/1oz cooked fresh peas

4 basil leaves

2tsp sesame oil

Wine Note • Joseph Perrier, Rosé Champagne • Lobster loves champagne and Thai food is very happy with anything sparkling, especially rosé. This dish contains lots of different oriental flavours but none of them are too fiery so the champagne, which is perfumed, fruity and slightly spicy, reflects the style of the food perfectly.

Lobster with Fresh Vanilla

Serves 2

appr. 4.5 litres/8pts court bouillon (see page 22)

2 x 450g/1lb lobsters

175g/6oz middle cut of leek

15g/½oz unsalted butter

1 fresh vanilla pod

2 x ½ star anise

2 sprigs fresh mint

sea salt and freshly ground black pepper

60ml/2fl oz Sauternes

175ml/6fl oz fish stock (see page 23)

Lobster goes really well with fresh vanilla. It is a combination I have used many times in many different ways, and here it is combined with mint (another great accompaniment) then cooked 'en papillote'.

METHOD Bring the bouillon to the boil then plunge the lobster in, cook over a high heat for 1 minute to set the meat and remove from the pan and allow to cool.

Trim the leek and cut into 16-20 rounds each about 1cm/½in thick. Once the lobster has cooled sufficiently carefully remove the meat from the shell. Split the tail in half lengthways and remove the intestinal tract.

Cut two sheets of greaseproof paper or foil about 35cm/14in square. Smear the butter in the middle of the paper over an area about 15cm/6in wide by 23cm/9in deep. Lay the slices of leek on one half of this buttered area, slightly overlapping each round. Arrange the lobster on this with the smaller pieces from the legs on the bottom, the two halves of tail next then the two claws on top. Split the vanilla pod in half across its length, then split each half in two down their length; place two halves on each lobster along with half a star anise and a sprig of the mint. Season and then start to seal the bag. Fold the greaseproof paper over the top of the lobster so that the edges meet and, starting at one end, fold over the edge tightly two thirds of the way round, mix the wine and the stock together and pour half into one bag. Finish off sealing the bag, checking that it is tightly folded. Pour the remaining liquid into the other bag and seal as before.

Place the bags on an oven tray and put them in an oven pre-heated to 230°C/450°F/Gas 8 for 7 minutes. If sealed correctly, the bag will inflate like a pillow.

Either serve the bags as they are and let your guests open their own or alternatively open them in the kitchen before serving.

Wine Note • Charles de Cazanove, Champagne • Lobster and champagne – a marriage made in heaven. This particular house produce a delicious good value N.V. that is light and biscuity for a richer, more full-bodied vintage that is quite delicious. If you want to go really mad try their 'Stradivarius' – a supreme, deluxe champagne that is subtle, fragrant and 'sheer music'!

Lobster with Fresh Peas

Serves 2

app. 4.5 litres/8pts court
bouillon (see page 22)

2 x 450g/1lb lobsters

50g/1¾oz unsalted butter

55g/2oz chopped shallots

½ clove garlic crushed

55g/2oz leeks roughly
chopped

175ml/6fl oz fish stock
(see page 23)

140g/5oz fresh peas

salt and freshly ground
white pepper

½tsp sugar

5 mint leaves

85ml/3fl oz whipping cream

I have always thought that lobster is a great bedfellow of both peas and of mint, and we all know how well peas and mint go together. Here I poach the lobster but I am sure it would work equally as well if the lobster were to be roasted instead.

METHOD Bring the bouillon to the boil and once boiling plunge the lobsters in; return to the boil and simmer for 3 minutes. Remove the lobster and allow it to cool.

Once cool enough to handle carefully remove the meat from the shells. Split the tails in two lengthways and remove the intestinal tract. Place the meat in an ovenproof dish and add a little of the bouillon and cover.

In a saucepan heat 40g/¾oz of the butter; as it starts to sizzle add the shallots and garlic, cover the pan and sweat for a few minutes without colouring then add the chopped leek, cover and sweat for a further minute. Add the stock and bring to the boil, add the peas, season with salt and pepper and the sugar, then cover and cook over a high heat for 3 minutes until the peas are just cooked. Shred the mint leaves and add them to the peas then transfer the peas and stock to a food processor and process for a couple of short bursts to just start to break the peas up but not so long as to purée them; return to the saucepan.

Bring 150ml/5fl oz of the bouillon to the boil and reduce this by two thirds, add the cream and return to the boil, reducing until it just starts to thicken. Place the lobster in an oven pre-heated to 180°C/350°F/Gas 4 for two minutes to reheat. Meanwhile return the peas to the stove to reheat.

Place circle of the peas in the centre of each plate then arrange the lobster meat on top of this placing the smaller pieces on the bottom then the two halves of the tail then top it off with the claws. Spoon the sauce over and around.

Wine Note • Chassagne-Montrachet, 1ᵉʳ cru, Genot Boulanger *(Burgundy)* • Lobster always demands quality and, if not champagne, then it has to be good white Burgundy. This is a gem from a top house that exports only a small proportion of their excellent production. The wine has a deep, yeasty nose with almond hints and a very full, rich, fruity palate with plenty of body to match the meaty lobster and peas.

Mackerel

French: *Maquereau* • Italian: *Maccarello* • German: *Makrele* • Spanish: *Caballa*

What a fish! Say mackerel and everyone knows what you are talking about. It is cheap, nutritious, plentiful and its only drawback is that it has a rather strong odour that has a tendency to linger, especially in confined spaces.

The humble mackerel is actually a member of the more exotic Tuna family. They're all in the same genus *(Scombridae)* – tuna, bonito, mackerel, Spanish mackerel, painted mackerel, and King mackerel – yet what a price difference between the mackerel and the tuna! All fish in this family have the same tails – very long, thin and almost coming to a point before culminating in a very pronounced 'V' shaped fin. They are powerful swimmers and their shape indicates that they are well adapted to gliding rapidly through the water.

Mackerel is a sleek, incredibly colourful fish. The French word for pimp is 'maquereau' and it's said that the fish received its name because of its bright, almost gaudy colouring. When fresh it has brilliant greeny-blue metallic sides, with black wavy lines and a white/silver belly, and it's one of the most handsome of all the Atlantic fishes.

Mackerel is a shoaling fish and as a result it has suffered heavily from over-fishing in certain areas. The big mackerel fishing fleets of the south coast, especially Cornwall where they were once the backbone of the local fishing industry, are largely gone and those that are left are subject to strict controls. Mackerel are also what is known as Pelagic, which means that they are oil rich and swim in shoals near the surface. Ask any yachtsman which fish he manages to catch on a line and it is always the mackerel.

Their long spawning season, from spring to as late as the end of summer, brings these fish into shallower waters, making it easier to catch them. During the winter they tend to retreat to deeper waters, going into a state of near hibernation until the spring returns. Mackerel of 55cm (almost 2ft) and over have been known, but the normal marketable size would be from about 25-35cm/10-11in weighing from 350g/12oz to 900g/2lb.

Although the mackerel is incredibly versatile and can be served hot smoked or even raw as sushi, I prefer to just grill a fillet, add a squeeze of fresh lemon juice and serve with a green salad.

Grilled Fillet of Mackerel with Polenta and Stewed Tomatoes

Serves 4

5 tomatoes

1 onion

1 clove of garlic

3tbsp olive oil

1tsp sugar

1dsp red wine vinegar

½tsp tomato purée

¼ polenta recipe
(see page 27)

25g/1oz melted butter

salt and pepper

2 mackerel

4dsp pesto
(see page 26)

Mackerel is very much a favourite fish of mine but it is not often used and has been much maligned. Combined here with polenta it makes a very pretty first course or a good main course. The pesto in the dish could be replaced with coriander oil if preferred.

METHOD Blanch and deseed the tomatoes. Cut each tomato into eight pieces. Peel and finely slice the onion. Crush the clove of garlic. Heat 1tbsp of the oil in a saucepan, add the onion and the garlic and gently cook with the pan covered until the onion softens but without browning. Add the tomato, red wine vinegar, sugar and the tomato purée and season. Stir in well and allow to stew slowly until the mixture dries out a little. It needs to cook slowly for about 20 minutes.

Cut the polenta into rounds of about 7.5cm/3in diameter. Place these onto a greased tray and brush the tops with a little of the melted butter.

Fillet and pin bone the mackerel. Score the skin of each fillet and season on the meat side. Place the fillets skin-side up on an oiled tray. Brush the skin with the remaining melted butter and season lightly.

Place the mackerel and the polenta under a hot grill; when the mackerel has cooked its skin should be crisp and golden brown. The polenta should also brown lightly.

Place a round of polenta in the middle of each plate, spoon the stewed tomato onto the polenta. Lay a fillet of mackerel on top and spoon the pesto around.

Wine Note • Bianco di Custoza, D.O.C., Cavalchina *(Italy)* • Both mackerel and tomatoes require a crisp, dry white with a reasonably high level of acidity. The clean, lemony characteristics of this particular Italian are ideal with this dish; the wine has plenty of body yet remains fresh and zesty on the finish.

Warm Pickled Mackerel with a Salad of Pink Fir Apple Potatoes Quail's Eggs and Cucumber

Serves 4

6-7cm/2½in (app. 115g/4oz) piece of cucumber, peeled, core discarded and the flesh cut into a fine and long julienne

15ml/1tbsp rice wine vinegar

4 x 115g/4oz fillets of mackerel

15g/½oz grain mustard

30ml/1fl oz olive oil

1tbsp chopped mixed herbs

6 hard boiled quail's eggs peeled and cut in half

Pickle:

1 stick celery

1 stalk of lemon grass

½ medium onion

2 cloves garlic

15g/½oz fresh ginger

1 litre/1¾pts water

1 star anise

15g/½oz black peppercorns

2tsp mustard seeds

1tsp coriander seeds

1tsp cumin seeds

150ml/5fl oz white wine vinegar

15g/¼oz sea salt

Thank goodness mackerel has found favour in restaurants at last. For too long it has been seen as cheap and not worthy of a place on any menu. It really does deserve the new standing it seems to have found for itself. Cooking it in pickle, as here, leaves the skin with a slight blue tinge reminiscent of Trout au Bleu. There's nothing clever about it – the vinegar in the poaching liquor gives the skin the colour but it only works with really fresh fish. Pink fir apples are a type of salad potato absolutely perfect for this job; unfortunately they are only around in the late summer so at other times you could try Francines – these red-skinned potatoes will suffice but they are not as good. Failing that then any other new potato would do. This dish is designed as a first course; allow two smaller fillets of mackerel as a main course but there should be no need to increase any of the other ingredients.

METHOD Start by making the pickle as this will keep for quite a few days once made. Cut all of the vegetables up small, and put them into the water along with the rest of the ingredients. Bring to the boil and simmer for 5 minutes. Allow to go cold and then strain.

Boil the potatoes for the salad and cool. Once cold either cut them into slices or cubes. Finely slice the red onion, peel and slice the celery across at a slight angle. Mix the vegetables together, season with salt and freshly ground white pepper, add the oil and toss.

Lightly season the cucumber and toss in the rice wine vinegar.

Remove the line of pin bones that run the length of each fillet of mackerel. Score through the skin diagonally and season the fish on both sides. Split the pickle into two batches. Put 250ml/9fl oz in one pan for the sauce, bring to the boil and reduce by half. Bring the remainder to the boil for the stock. Place the fillets of mackerel out flat, with the skin side up, in a deep pan or tray. Pour the boiling stock over the fish and allow to sit over a low heat for 4 minutes. Once the sauce has reduced add the grain mustard and the olive oil and return to the boil for 30 seconds.

Place a pile of the potatoes in the middle of each plate and lay a fillet of fish on top. Add the herbs to the sauce and spoon over and around the fish. Garnish the dish with the halves of quail's eggs. Place a pile of the pickled cucumber on top of each of the fillets of fish.

> **Wine Note** • Ninth Island, Chardonnay *(Tasmania)* • Something of a dilemma here since a crisp, dry wine is needed to complement the dressing although Chardonnay is generally the best grape variety to drink with anything containing eggs. This cool climate, unwooded wine is citrusy and delicate with enough fruit and body to give the best of both worlds – freshness and character.

Potato salad:

450g/1lb pink fir apple potatoes

½ medium red onion

2 sticks celery

salt and freshly ground white pepper

100ml/3½fl oz olive oil

Mackerel 'en Papillote'

Serves 8

Although this dish is designed for the barbecue it will work equally well in the oven. If you want to serve it as a main course increase the amount of fish in each parcel. The great thing about cooking in this way is the intense aroma that hits you as soon as the bag is opened.

METHOD Fillet the mackerel and remove the line of pin bones. Cut each fillet into two. Peel and cut the garlic and ginger into a fine julienne. Slice the spring onions through at a slight angle and wash and drain them well. Pick the coriander of its leaves.

Use a piece of tin foil 25cm x 20cm/10in x 8in per bag if for small barbecue portions and 45cm x 30cm/18in x 12in if you are preparing main course portions. Pour 1tbsp of the oil onto one half of the foil. Lay a half fillet of mackerel on this, lightly season with salt and pepper, place a little of the garlic and ginger on the fish and top with a couple of leaves of coriander then some of the spring onions. Fold the foil over so the edges meet. Tightly seal the bag by folding the edges over and crimping them; do this only two thirds of the way around. Pour 1tbsp of white wine into each bag and finish sealing them.

Place them on the barbecue and cook until the bag fully inflates. If cooking in the oven pre-heat it to 220°C/425°F/gas 7. Once blown up like a pillow the fish will be cooked. If cooking in the oven the same applies.

2 x 550g/1¼lb of mackerel

2 cloves garlic

25g/1oz fresh ginger

2 spring onions

2 sprigs fresh coriander

120ml/4fl oz olive oil

salt and freshly ground white pepper

120ml/4fl oz dry white wine

> **Wine Note** • Quincy, Dme de la Commanderie *(Loire Valley)* • Lovely crisp, fresh flavours demand a light, bright wine with plenty of acidity. Sauvignon Blanc is an obvious choice and this Quincy has a really tongue-tingling acidity with an intense aromatic quality that will agree readily with the ginger here.

Monkfish

French: *Lotte, Baudroie* • Italian: *Rana* • German: *Seeteufel* • Spanish: *Rape*

I've described John Dory as ugly but this is the most bizarre of all fish and listed in *North Atlantic Seafood* (by Alan Davidson) under the heading of 'Miscellaneous Uncouth Fish', which is very apt indeed! Monkfish is also known as angler fish in the UK and sea devil in Germany. Monkfish I don't understand, but angler fish is easy. If you have seen the fish whole then it's not difficult to understand how it got its name, as it has a sort of antenna that acts as a fishing rod. Sea devil is easy too – just look at it!

It is also known in some areas as bellyfish or goosefish because of its habit of stuffing itself with too much food. One was reported measuring 65cm/26in and contained a codling of some 58cm/23in! The reason for this is quite simply the enormous mouth that it possesses – so big in fact that its head weighs in at over 50% of the total body weight. It is unusual to see whole monkfish offered for sale as normally the head has been removed, but recently I've noticed more whole fish on the market.

The skin, which is black/charcoal grey with a white belly and almost jelly-like, is easily removed just by pulling it away, but this leaves behind at least two other layers which need to be cut away from the meat. It is one of the easiest fish to prepare if it comes to you with its head removed as it only has one bone running down the centre of its body.

It is only in the last decade or so that Monkfish has been prized for its flesh. There was a time when it would be thrown back or used to bait hooks! Its popularity probably came about initially because it was so cheap and plentiful. In the past it has been passed off as scampi and even lobster by the unscrupulous, but this wouldn't happen now as the price has rocketed. It lives both inshore as well as down deep (up to 300 metres/1,000 feet below).

The meat, which is very white and firm, makes this an excellent fish for roasting. Small monk roasted whole on the bone is often known as **Gigot de Lotte** or 'leg' of monkfish. It is useful for mousselines and soups too as the flesh will not break up. The enormous head also contains the cheeks, which are excellent. Unfortunately they are not often found for sale as they tend to be cut only if they are large enough and the fishermen have time.

Daube of Monkfish with Lardons and Button Mushrooms

Serves 4

I first served this dish some 18 or so years ago and it is featured, or at least its predecessor is featured, in my first book. It has evolved since then and I now use monkfish cheeks (I doubt if they were available in the UK back in the late seventies or early eighties and if they were, I was blissfully unaware); then it was braised with bacon in red wine, so there is not really much difference.

METHOD Cut the cheeks if too large into about 5cm/2in pieces. Peel the onions being careful to keep the root end intact otherwise they will fall apart. If possible, 'turn' each mushroom and cut the stalks level with the caps. Cut the bacon into lardons about 5mm/¼in x 2.5cm/1in. Blanch the bacon in boiling salted water for a couple of seconds and drain well then fry them in about 15ml/1tbsp of the oil until nicely browned.

Combine the red wine with the port and reduce until almost gone. Add the fish stock and reduce again until only about a third remains. Add the veal stock and bring to the boil. Dry the monk cheeks really well and season. Heat the remaining oil in a frying pan until smoking, add the cheeks and fry very quickly till sealed and lightly browned. Drain and add to the sauce. Heat the sauce until it just starts to tremble, cover and place in an oven pre-heated to 200°C/400°F/Gas 6 until cooked; it should take about 4 minutes. Once cooked remove the fish and cover.

Set the sauce over a high heat and add the onions; boil the sauce reducing it as the onions cook and when they are almost cooked add the mushrooms. Once the entire garnish is cooked – the onions should still retain a little bite – and the sauce has reduced to thicken slightly, add the bacon and return the monkfish to the sauce. Allow the fish to warm through in the sauce for a minute over a very low heat. Serve with a spoon of mash (see page 25) as one would for a classic 'Daube de Boeuf'.

900g/2lb monkfish cheeks trimmed

20 small button onions

20 small button mushrooms

85g/3oz piece of smoked streaky bacon

salt and freshly ground white pepper

45ml/1½fl oz olive oil

175ml/6fl oz red wine

100ml/3½fl oz port

225ml/8fl oz fish stock (see page 23)

175ml/6fl oz veal stock (see page 33)

To serve:

mash (see page 25)

Wine Note • Chateau Gloria 1988 *(Bordeaux)* • A quality claret with plenty of backbone is the only answer to accompany such a 'meaty' meal.

Roast Monkfish on a Leek and Bacon Mash, with a Sauce of Red Kidney Beans

Serves 4

115g/4oz centre of leek

40g/1½oz unsalted butter

salt and freshly ground white pepper

175g/6oz streaky bacon

45ml/1½fl oz olive oil

125ml/4fl oz red wine

225ml/8fl oz fish stock (see page 23)

225ml/8fl oz veal stock (see page 33)

175g/6oz red kidney beans

4 x 175g/6oz of monkfish tail

½ recipe for mash (see page 25)

Monkfish is one of the many fish that will take either a delicate flavour or one that is so robust it blows your socks off. It is great on mash and the bacon and leeks are perfect partners for it.

METHOD Wash the leek well and cut up small. Heat 15g/½oz of the butter in a small pan; add the leek, season, and cover and sweat for about 2 minutes until just cooked. Remove and allow to cool. Cut the bacon into small lardons and blanch for 3 seconds in boiling water; drain well. In a frying pan heat 15ml/½fl oz of the oil until just smoking, add the lardons and fry until just browned, drain and cool.

Reduce the red wine over a high heat until almost gone; add the fish stock and reduce by two thirds. Add the veal stock and the kidney beans, return to the boil and reduce slightly; keep warm.

In a frying pan heat the remaining oil until just smoking, add the last of the butter, season the fish and sear in the hot fat on all sides until golden brown. Transfer to a very hot oven pre-heated to 230°C/450°F/Gas 8 for about 2-3 minutes depending upon the thickness of the fish. Once cooked remove from the pan and keep warm.

Heat the mash together with the leeks and the bacon.

Place a spoonful of the mash in the centre of each plate and a piece of the fish on top. Spoon the sauce around.

Wine Note • Carneros Creek, Estate Grown, Pinot Noir *(California)* • The texture of the beans and the rich flavours of the sauce in this dish really need a wine that has enough character and plenty of rich fruit to stand up to its boldness. This deep, classic Pinot Noir is reminiscent of the very finest quality wines of Burgundy, with mouth-filling fruit, many layers of flavour and a good, long finish.

Fricassee of Monkfish with Mushrooms, Thyme and Bacon

Serves 4

700g/1lb 9oz monkfish tail fully trimmed

28 small tight button mushrooms

10g/½oz unsalted butter

juice of ½ lemon

55g/2oz streaky bacon

15ml/½fl oz oil

350ml/12fl oz fish stock (see page 23)

100ml/3½fl oz dry white wine

salt and freshly ground white pepper

225ml/8fl oz whipping cream

30ml/1fl oz Pernod

2tsp picked thyme leaves

This is not a new dish: it was way back in the middle of the seventies when I first cooked something similar and that was **Fricassee de Lotte Amoureuse** *while I was at the Dorchester with Anton Mosimann. This is a slightly different version but when a dish works, it really works!*

METHOD Cut the monkfish into dice of about 3.5cm/1½in to give about 7 pieces per portion, 28 in total.

'Turn' the mushrooms and cut the stalks square to the caps then wash them well. Place these in a saucepan with the butter and the lemon juice, cover and bring to the boil; cook rapidly for a few seconds until the mushrooms are cooked. Remove from the heat and allow to cool.

Cut the bacon into lardons and plunge these into boiling water for a second then drain well. Heat the oil in a frying pan then fry the bacon in this until just browned; drain well.

Combine the fish stock and white wine in a saucepan. Season the monkfish then place it in the stock, cover and bring to the boil. Just as the liquid starts to tremble transfer the pan to an oven pre-heated to 220°C/425°F/Gas 7 for three minutes. Remove the fish from the stock, cover and keep warm. Bring the stock to the boil and reduce by three quarters. Once reduced add the cream, mushrooms and bacon, return to the boil and reduce until it just starts to thicken. Add the Pernod, return to the boil, add the monkfish and the picked thyme leaves and remove from the heat, allowing the fish to warm through in the sauce for a minute before serving.

Best served with a rice pilaff.

Wine Note • Domaine Azo, Petit Chablis • Unusually this Petit Chablis is made from 50-year-old vines which add great character and intensity to the wine – just what is needed with this many-flavoured dish.

Pesto Grilled Darne of Monkfish with Roasted Aubergines, Spinach and Tomato Vinaigrette

Serves 4

The term 'darne' refers to a round fish cut across and cooked on the bone. Although monkfish is not normally referred to as a round fish it is probably closer to being round than it is flat; the same cut in a flat fish is called a 'tronçon'. The trouble with this cut is that you end up with all the bones on the plate – not a good idea to my mind. Normally if it is not edible then I would not serve it and bones definitely fall into this category, but monkfish just have one bone down the middle; there are no rib bones or little pin bones shooting off at all angles.

Most of my dishes come about for a reason; this time it was because the 3lb monkfish I ordered from my fishmonger ended up being nearer 10lb! So the original dish I intended to make went out of the window to be replaced with this one and, even if I say so myself, it worked very well.

350g/12oz fresh spinach

2 medium aubergines

125ml/4fl oz olive oil

salt and freshly ground white pepper

4 x 225g/8oz darnes of monkfish cut from a large fish

40g/1oz melted butter

75ml/2½fl oz pesto (see page 26)

40g/1oz unsalted butter

1 quantity of tomato vinaigrette (see page 32)

METHOD Pick the spinach of its stalks and wash the leaves well, in at least three changes of water; drain well. Cut each aubergine into half lengthways and then each half into three lengthways; cut away the main core of seeds. Heat a frying pan with 100ml/3½fl oz of the olive oil and when hot turn the aubergines in the oil so they are fully coated in it, season and brown them really well over a high heat, allowing the flesh to caramelise and crispen slightly. Once cooked keep them warm.

Lightly grease a grilling tray with the remaining oil, lay the monkfish on the tray, brush with the melted butter and season. Place under a very hot grill for about 3 minutes, turning after 2 minutes, until almost cooked. Brush the fish with the pesto and return to the grill for a further minute. Meanwhile heat the butter in a saucepan and add the spinach and season. Quickly cook the spinach, stirring occasionally, then drain well. Gently warm the vinaigrette through.

Place three pieces of aubergine in the centre of each plate in an overlapping triangle. Place a pile of spinach in the middle of the aubergine then a darne of monkfish on the spinach pesto-side up. Spoon the warmed vinaigrette around.

Wine Note • Regaleali Rosso *(Sicily)* • A rich, chewy red with plenty of persistence will match the meaty characteristic of the fish as well as the robust flavours of the accompaniments. Pesto in a simple pasta dish would enjoy the company of the crisp, dry white Regaleali but the red is more fleshy and suitable for this particular dish.

Monkfish with Braised Endives and Puy Lentils

Serves 2

I love the richness of this dish, not only the flavours but the colours too; it really reminds me of winter evenings. The endive adds a touch of bitterness to the dish, which complements it well.

METHOD Trim the monkfish of any dark meat.

Wash the lentils and put in a pan with at least 3 times their volume of water; add to this the garlic, onion and celery; season with a little freshly ground pepper. Bring to the boil and simmer for about 12-15 minutes until the lentils are just cooked. Allow them to cool. Once cold remove and discard the vegetables and drain off the liquid.

Trim the endives of any discoloured leaves. Combine the red wine, port and stock together in a saucepan. Add the endive, cover and bring to the boil, then transfer to an oven pre-heated to 180°C/350°F/Gas 4 for 25 minutes. Once cooked remove the endives from the sauce, cover them and keep warm.

Heat the oil in a roasting or frying pan and season the monkfish. Once the oil is hot add the butter and sear the monkfish on all sides, browning it well. Transfer to the oven and roast for about 4 minutes, turning once. When cooked remove and keep warm.

Reduce the sauce down by half; by now it should be very rich, sticky and glossy. Return the endives to this and allow to warm through on a very low heat. Place two of the endives in the centre of each plate and put a piece of fish on top. Add the lentils to the sauce and allow to warm through for a few seconds. Spoon the sauce around.

2 pieces of filleted monkfish each weighing 140-175g/5-6oz

15g/½oz puy lentils

1 peeled clove of garlic

½ peeled small onion

½ stick of celery

salt and freshly ground white pepper

6 small Belgium endives about 350g/12oz (or 3 larger ones cut in half)

60ml/2fl oz red wine

60ml/2fl oz port

125ml/4fl oz veal stock (see page 33)

30ml/1fl oz olive oil

15g/½oz unsalted butter

Wine Note • Château Hauchat, Fronsac *(Bordeaux)* • Such a weighty combination requires a powerful wine yet not too much sophistication. This Fronsac is made from a selection of 30-year-old vines and benefits from 18 months ageing in oak barrels. Both wine and fish are really 'meaty'.

Mussels

French: *Moule* • Italian: *Cozza* • German: *Miesmuschel* • Spanish: *Mejillon*

The quality of mussels seems to get better each year thanks to advances in production and purification methods. I, for one, am very grateful to the man who decided mussels would sell better if they were pre-washed and had their beards and any barnacles removed. Still be careful when using them, as just because they are coming to you cleaned these days, this does not mean that they are perfectly clean! Because of the way mussels feed they are always very sandy and need washing in many changes of water. I always like to wash them in at least three changes of fresh, cold water, leaving them sitting in each change of water for at least 5 minutes.

Everyone must be familiar with the dark blue shells of the mussel and think of them primarily in connection with the classic dish Moules Marinieres, but they can be used in many other ways, both hot and cold.

As with any shellfish, mussels must be bought alive. Once dead they deteriorate rapidly and can become quite toxic. By law mussels must be passed through an UV (ultraviolet) filtration system and have a certificate to prove it. They will be tightly shut and if open should close as soon as they are touched. They should also feel comparatively heavy for their size and sound full if you tap the shell. Always discard any that have damaged or broken shells – if in doubt throw it out! If they are to be kept for a couple of days then cover them with wet newspaper and top with a heavy weight before placing them in the refrigerator.

Although mussels can be picked from most beaches it is not advisable to do so unless you are confident that the water they are in is pure as they are very susceptible to diseases. Go to some of the more remote beaches in Scotland and Ireland and the mussels you find will be fine. I have picked mussels from the seashore in Iceland, which is as remote as you can get. You'll notice when shelling or eating mussels that some of them are pale and almost white, whereas others are a bright yellow or orange. The pale ones are the males and the bright orange ones the females!

Gnocchi, Mussel and Asparagus Broth

Serves 6

Gnocchi is very easy to make yet one rarely sees it these days, even in Italian restaurants. Coupled here with mussels it makes a great starter and the addition of a little saffron changes its complexion totally. Gnocchi is best cooked in small amounts.

METHOD Peel the potatoes and cook them in boiling salted water along with one clove of garlic (also peeled). Once cooked drain and dry them off. Pass them through a ricer or mouli. Add the egg yolk, 55g/2oz of the flour and a few turns of the pepper mill then knead together well. Flour the work surface and your hands with the flour that remains and roll the potato mix out into a long sausage about the thickness of your thumb. Cut this into pieces about 2cm/¾in long. You should get between 35 and 40 pieces. Roll each one on the floured surface using a fork and press the fork into each one to make a depression. Lay them onto a floured tray so that they are not touching each other.

Thoroughly clean the mussels, pulling off the beards and discarding any that are broken or open. Leave them standing in cold water for 10 minutes, change the water and stand again for at least 10 minutes. Crush the remaining ½ clove of garlic and place in a saucepan along with the shallots, fish stock and white wine; bring this to the boil. As soon as it boils drain the mussels and add them to the stock, cover with a lid and return to the boil. Cook the mussels for about 3-4 minutes or until they are all open. Turn the mussels into a colander to drain.

Once drained, pick the meat from the shells. Pass the stock through a fine strainer or muslin into a saucepan. Bring the stock to the boil and reduce down until only 450ml/1pt remains. Add the cream and the saffron and return to the boil, reducing again slightly.

Cook the gnocchi in boiling salted water for 5 minutes and drain carefully. Return the mussels to the sauce to warm through. Place about 6 gnocchi on each plate and 5 cooked asparagus tips, spoon the mussels evenly into the bowls and divide out the stock between them. Scatter with the chives cut into 2cm/¾in lengths.

450g/1lb **Desiree potatoes**

1½ cloves garlic

I egg yolk

salt and freshly ground white pepper

115g/4oz plain flour

1kg/2lb 4oz live mussels

2 shallots finely chopped

200ml/7fl oz fish stock (see page 23)

150ml/5fl oz dry white wine

350ml/12fl oz whipping cream

good pinch of saffron (optional)

30 cooked asparagus tips about 6cm/2½in long

small bunch of chives

Wine Note • Bin 222 Chardonnay, Wyndham Estate *(Australia)* • Chardonnay is the best mate for any dairy-related dish and this is an ideal case to demonstrate the point. The tropical peachy fruit of this wine has a touch of soft oak that makes it hard to beat for sheer 'drinkability' and slips down very easily with the rich, saucy broth.

Lightly Curried Mussel Broth

**1kg/2lb 4oz fresh
live mussels**

10 small new potatoes

8 spring onions

1 medium onion

2 stalks of celery

1 stick lemon grass

85g/3oz fennel

2 cloves garlic

3 good sprigs fresh coriander

1 bay leaf

½tsp cumin seeds

1 star anise

125ml/4fl oz dry white wine

**600ml/1pt fish stock
(see page 23)**

¾tsp curry powder

good pinch saffron

75ml/2½fl oz whipping cream

This is an interesting way of eating mussels with the hint of curry giving just a little nuance of something different. Curry goes so well with mussels that you might try adding a spoonful or two when cooking moules marinière.

METHOD Scrape the mussels of any barnacles, remove the beards and wash the mussels in at least three changes of fresh cold water.

Cut each new potato in half and turn each half into small barrel shapes giving 20 pieces in total. Trim the spring onions of any root and unusable outer leaves and cut each onion into three pieces at a slight angle.

Roughly chop all the remaining vegetables and garlic, and place them in a saucepan along with the coriander, bay leaf, cumin, star anise, wine, stock and curry powder. Cover and bring this to the boil; simmer for 5 minutes. Plunge in the mussels, cover and return to the boil. Continue boiling until the mussels have all opened. Tip them into a colander to allow the liquor to drain off and the mussels to cool. Once the mussels are cool enough to handle, remove them from their shells; discard the vegetables and shells. Strain the liquor through a fine strainer or preferably through muslin then return the liquor to a saucepan along with the saffron and the new potatoes. Bring to the boil and simmer until the potatoes are cooked; meanwhile remove the mussel meat from the shells.

When ready to serve add the mussels and the cream to the liquor, return to the boil and add the spring onions, then divide it out equally between your soup plates.

Wine Note • Verdelho, Capel Vale *(W. Australia)* • Rules for curry normally suggest an aromatic white or a fruity red. However, rules are made to be broken and the inclusion of saffron and spring onions here with just a hint of curry mean it's worth experimenting with this deliciously zingy, fresh, fruity wine that would be pleased to partner almost any lightly spicy dish.

Mussels in a Tomato and Herb Broth

Serves 4

1kg/2lb 4oz mussels

2 plum tomatoes

2 sprigs fresh parsley

1 sprig fresh thyme

1 bay leaf

150ml/5fl oz dry white wine

55g/2oz chopped shallots

100ml/3½fl oz tomato essence (see page 32)

freshly ground white pepper

75ml/2½fl oz whipping cream

1tbsp chopped mixed herbs, e.g. chervil, dill, chives, parsley and tarragon

Basically the same as the French classic 'moules marinière' except with the addition of tomatoes giving a slightly different twist to the dish.

METHOD Wash the mussels in at least three changes of water and remove barnacles and beards. Blanch, skin and de-seed the tomatoes, then dice the flesh.

Place the sprigs of herbs, the bay leaf, white wine, shallots and tomato sauce in a large saucepan and bring to the boil. Once boiling add the mussels and some freshly ground white pepper. Cover with a tight-fitting lid and cook over a high heat until all of the mussels have opened (discard any that remain closed). Remove the mussels from the stock and divide out between the serving plates.

Strain the liquor and return it to the boil with the cream; add the tomato dice and the chopped herbs and pour over the mussels.

Wine Note • Muscadet de Sèvre et Maine "sur lie" Ch. Coing de St. Fiacre *(Loire)* • Moules and Muscadet are perfect partners and the crisp 'green' nature of the wine will also compliment the tomato element extremely well.

Oysters

French: *Huitre* • German: *Auster* • Italian: *Ostrica* • Spanish: *Ostra*

Oysters were once so plentiful that they were considered to be the food of the poor and used to bulk out other ingredients. The Victorians added them to dishes such as steak and kidney pudding or Lancashire hot pot. Nowadays they are an expensive delicacy only to be eaten in luxurious surroundings, on special occasions and at certain times of the year. This is particularly true of the native, which is the most expensive of the oysters mainly because they need five years to develop before they are ready to be eaten as opposed to their cousins, the Pacific or rock oysters, who take just three years. Oysters are normally referred to by the name of the region they are from, e.g. Royal Whitstable, Colchester and Helford.

The two types of oyster are easily distinguishable from each other. The native has a smooth, round shell and its meat tends to be rounder and plumper with a slightly sweeter and more complex flavour than the Pacific. The shell of the Pacific is elongated and deeply grooved and the meat, like the shell, is very elongated. Pacific or Rock oysters are available all year round and are much cheaper and therefore more accessible. Unfortunately if it is pearls you are seeking then they will not be found in either the native or the Pacific, but in an Oriental species, so head east!

During the warmer months of the year, the oyster's breeding season, the young native develops partly inside the mother oyster, so if you do eat them in the summer then you are putting paid to future stocks. The oysters also turn an unappetising milky colour, due to the spawning, but they are not harmful in any way – in fact the French like to eat them this way. Once the colder weather comes along and the spawning season is over then they really come into their own, becoming much rounder and juicier than before. The summer months are when the Pacific and Rock oysters are at their best, although they will also go slightly milky.

The same rules apply for oysters as for mussels – make sure you buy them alive and store in newspaper in the refrigerator. When cooking them, keep the cooking period to a bare minimum or they will go tough and leathery.

Oyster, Celery and Potato Ragout

Serves 4

12 oysters

115g/4oz celery

½ clove garlic crushed

2 shallots finely sliced

8 cardamom pods crushed

½tsp coriander seeds

½tsp black peppercorns

1 bay leaf

juice of ¼ lemon

sprig of parsley

125ml/4fl oz white wine

600ml/1pt fish stock (see page 23)

225g/8oz new potatoes

100ml/3½fl oz whipping cream

175g/6oz puff pastry (see page 27)

1 egg yolk

1tbsp milk

12 leaves flat parsley

Wine Note • Macon Blanc Villages, Dme du Vieux Puits, Drouin *(Burgundy)* • Oysters are at home with Champagne or Chablis but for this informal combination a good quality Macon is perfectly acceptable. This is a bright, zesty wine to suit the oysters, with a soft palate and lingering finish to suit the pastry topping.

This is a great dish for a dinner party as it can all be made well before hand and just 10 minutes before you are ready to sit down, pop it in the oven; nothing more to do then except take it to the table. Another good thing, as it is encased in pastry it will stay hot for a lot longer than most dishes. Then when you break into the pastry there is the waft of oysters and sea as the steam and aromas escape. It works either as a first course or a fish course but do be careful what you serve to follow, as with all oyster dishes, it is very rich. Filo will work just as well as puff pastry; instead of egg wash just brush the filo with melted butter.

METHOD Shell the oysters and reserve the juice separately: there should be about 125-175ml/4-6fl oz. Pass it through a fine strainer or muslin. Peel the celery and save the peelings for the stock and the leaves as garnish. Cut the celery into batons 3.5cm/1½in long. Put any celery trimmings along with the peelings into a saucepan with the oyster juices, garlic, shallots, cardamom, coriander seeds, peppercorns, bay leaf, lemon juice, parsley, wine and fish stock. Bring this to the boil and simmer gently for 20 minutes then strain and squeeze all the juice from the vegetables.

Peel the potatoes and cut them into 1cm/½in dice; cook these along with the celery batons in the strained stock. Once cooked add the cream and reduce with the stock till 425ml/15fl oz remains then allow to cool. Roll out the pastry to a thickness of 3mm/⅛in; cut out three discs large enough to fit over a soup cup and have a 1cm/½in overhang. Beat the egg yolk with the spoonful of milk and brush around the edge of the soup cups. Divide the celery and the potato between the cups and put three oysters into each one along with a few celery leaves and three parsley leaves.

Place a pastry disc over each cup pulling it tightly and trim the edges. Lightly score a criss-cross pattern on the top and brush with the egg wash. Leave to rest in the refrigerator for at least 30 minutes.

Once well-rested, place in an oven pre-heated to 220°C/425°F/Gas 7 for 15 minutes or until it is golden brown and the pastry has puffed up. Serve immediately.

Perch

French: *Perche* • German: *Barsch* • Italian: *Percha* • Spanish: *Perca*

For centuries the perch has had its praises sung. Izaak Walton described the perch in *The Compleat Angler* (1653) as being a 'bold biting fish' and thought it to be 'so good and wholesome that physicians should allow it to be eaten by wounded men'.

This, the prettiest of the freshwater coarse fish, is easily recognisable because of its double dorsal fin; the first of these has sharp spines, so be careful to handle them with gloves on. Its striped grey-green back and its orange tinted fins make it rather colourful. Feeding on larvae, freshwater shrimps and small fish as well as insects and worms means that the perch tends not to be as muddy tasting as some freshwater fish. Whilst trolling a loch in Scotland for trout a few years ago I was able to catch only perch, but unfortunately none of them were large enough to eat. I was quite surprised that such small fish (only about 115-175g/4-6oz) were taking such large lures. Although they are found in rivers and lakes all over the country it is unusual to see them offered for sale.

They are rarely to be found weighing much more than 450g/1lb and are often smaller. It is also an extremely difficult fish to scale, and this is best done as soon as it is caught, after it has been dipped in boiling water for a minute or two to assist the process. They can, however, be cooked with the scales on.

Serves 2

4 fillets of perch each
85-115g/3-4oz

15ml/½fl oz olive oil

15g/½oz melted butter

salt and freshly ground
white pepper

1 plum tomato, blanched,
skinned and seeded

1 shallot, finely chopped

125ml/4fl oz Noilly Prat

300ml/10fl oz fish stock
(see page 23)

15ml/½fl oz white
wine vinegar

125ml/4fl oz whipping cream

2tbsp fresh tarragon leaves

20g/¾oz unsalted butter

Perch with Tarragon

Most freshwater fish are not as fishy as other fish and therefore need careful flavour enhancing. They will not normally take to such robust sauces as their seawater cousins. This recipe is a simple derivation of the Troisgros classic salmon with sorrel. It is a lesson for us all in simplicity.

METHOD Season the fillets of perch on the meat side; using the oil lightly grease a grilling tray and lay the fillets skin-side up. Brush the skin with the melted butter then season with salt.

Cut the tomato into 1cm/½in dice. Combine the shallot, Noilly, stock and vinegar together in a saucepan and bring to the boil. Reduce this until it is almost gone. Meanwhile cook the fish under a preheated grill for 3-4 minutes until just cooked. Add the cream to the sauce and return to the boil, reducing until it just starts to thicken. Add the tarragon leaves and gradually add the butter shaking the pan continuously until it has melted. Check the seasoning and add the tomato dice. Pour the sauce onto the plates and place two fillets of perch on top.

Wine Note • Orvieto Classico, Domenico Brugnoli *(Italy)* • A delicate wine for a delicate dish. This is a light, crisp wine with a suggestion of fresh grapefruit on the palate that will cope happily with the hint of vinegar in the sauce. An unoaked Chardonnay would be a good alternative here.

Perch Braised in Cider

As I mention in the introduction, perch can be difficult to scale and, although not always practical, this is best done as soon as it is caught. The other way is to plunge the whole fish into boiling water to which you've added the juice of a lemon, leave for a few seconds then remove. Both the scales and the skin should now peel off easily, a bit like blanching a tomato. Do take care when handling perch as it has some very sharp spines, particularly on the dorsal fin, and on the gill covers; it also has very sharp teeth!

METHOD If not already scaled, prepare the fish as above. Butter a flameproof dish large enough to hold the perch. Add the shallot, tomato and apple. Season the fish with salt and pepper and arrange on top of the shallot mixture. Pour in half the cider, the wine and the fish stock. On top of the stove, bring the cooking liquid to a simmer. Cover the dish with buttered, greaseproof paper and bake in a pre-heated oven at 180°C/350°F/Gas 4 for 15 minutes, or until the perch are cooked. Remove the fish to four warmed plates and keep warm.

Pour the liquid into a saucepan, add the cream and reduce over a moderately high heat until it coats a spoon. Beat in the butter, cut into pieces, the mustard, and the rest of the cider along with the Calvados. Taste for seasoning and add salt and pepper if necessary. Spoon the sauce over the fish and sprinkle with the chopped tarragon. Serve immediately with new potatoes.

4 perch, each to weigh at least 450g/1lb

55g/2oz unsalted butter

1 finely chopped shallot

250g/8oz tomatoes, peeled, seeded and diced

1 large, tart, cooking apple, peeled, cored and diced

salt and freshly ground pepper

125ml/4fl oz dry cider

60ml/2fl oz dry white wine

225ml/8fl oz fish stock (see page 23)

125ml/4fl oz whipping cream

1tsp Dijon mustard

60ml/2fl oz Calvados

2 tablespoons fresh tarragon leaves, chopped

> **Wine Note** • Sancerre, Les Beauregards, Domaine Gitton *(Loire)* • Once again there is no alternative but to put Sauvignon with this dish because of the acidity coming from the cider braising liquid; anything else would pick a fight ... and lose. The wines of the Gitton family are of irresistible and consistent quality, based on traditional wine-making methods and plenty of T.L.C.

Plaice

French: *Plie* • Spanish: *Pltija* • German: *Scholle* • Italian: *Passera*

What is it about the poor plaice? People either love it or hate it. Personally I love it, but that may of course be because all the ones I have eaten have been really fresh, and if they are not fresh they lose all flavour and turn into something not unlike a piece of soggy paper. The plaice is an extremely easy fish to recognise as the dark or upper side is a rich brown dotted with bright orange spots. I say 'bright' orange spots as this is exactly how they should be, and these spots are a very good indicator as to its freshness.

They are and always have been a very important species of flat fish with many ports such as Lowestoft (I have heard it called the plaice capital of the world) valuing them above any other fish.

The plaice, along with many other fish, is preferred small on the continent whereas we in the UK seem to like them on the larger size. I have seen some over 50cm/20in long and they can grow even bigger than that, although the normal size is about 400-550g/14oz-1lb 4oz. What this means, for example, is that fishermen will sell the smaller fish in Holland for a good price, and the larger fish here in the UK for a lower price – often much lower than we can sell our own fish at. In fact more than once while I have been talking to a merchant, a lorry has pulled up and offered a consignment of larger fish for far less than they were being sold not five minutes earlier on the dock side. The problem with this is that the small fish are in my opinion far too young to have been caught in the first place. It may be legal but that doesn't make it right. Plaice is an important fish to the fishing industry, but if fish are continually taken when they are small how long can they survive?

Plaice belong to the same family as flounder, dabs and lemon sole, any of which could be used as a substitute in the following recipes. Grilling and frying are probably the best ways to cook plaice but whichever method you choose it should be done very quickly and poaching is rarely successful.

Tomato Crostini Topped with Grilled Plaice and Tapenade

Serves 4

This makes a great lunch dish or starter; it is colourful and light to eat, great for lunch in the garden on a summer's day. Simple to make and quick to cook, nothing could be easier.

METHOD Dribble 60ml/2fl oz of the oil over the French bread and season. Place them on a baking sheet in an oven pre-heated to 180°C/350°F/Gas 4 until they are golden brown and crisp, then increase the heat of the oven slightly to 200°C/400°F/Gas 6. Lightly grease a grilling tray with a little olive oil, lay the fillets of fish on it, brush with the melted butter and season. Slice the tomatoes and lay a tomato on each crostini, lightly season and dribble with remaining olive oil.

Place the crostini in the oven to lightly cook the tomato, for about two minutes. Grill the plaice under a hot grill for about 1-1½ minutes.

Lay a fillet of plaice over the tomato crostini and top with a spoonful of tapenade. Serve immediately.

4 slices of French bread, cut at an angle and about 1cm/½in thick

75ml/2½fl oz olive oil

salt and freshly ground white pepper

4 x 55-85g/2-3oz skinned fillets of plaice

25g/1oz melted butter

4 plum tomatoes

4tbsp tapenade (see page 31)

> **Wine Note** • Barbera d'Alba, D.O.C. Nicolello • Earthy, simple flavours demand a wine with plenty of backbone and enough 'bite' to match the tapenade yet without losing the subtlety preferred by the delicate plaice. This Italian red is quite robust and spicy but the fruit is sufficiently concentrated to give a deliciously rich, approachable style.

Plaice in a Lobster and Vegetable Bisque

Serves 2

85g/3oz courgettes

1 shallot

55g/2oz leek

55g/2oz fennel

55g/2oz celery

55g/2oz carrot

½ blanched, skinned and seeded plum tomato

6 fillets of plaice

salt and freshly ground white pepper

225ml/8fl oz lobster sauce (see page 24)

25g/1oz unsalted butter

15ml/½fl oz cream

15g/½oz wild rice cooked

Using an ingredient like lobster bisque adds a little luxury to what is normally thought of as a very ordinary fish. The addition of the vegetables and especially the wild rice give not only a splash of colour but also an extra texture in the form of a little bite to the dish, which is necessary, as plaice is essentially a very soft fleshed fish.

METHOD Cut all the vegetables into very fine dice using only the outside green of the courgette; these can all be mixed together with the exception of the tomato.

Season the undersides of the plaice fillets then fold them over to form neat fillets about 7.5-10cm/3-4in long. Place these in a saucepan with the lobster stock; cover with a buttered paper and gently heat until the liquid starts to tremble. Transfer to an oven pre-heated to 220°C/425°F/Gas 7 for about 3 minutes or until the fish is just cooked. Remove the fish from the bisque and keep warm. Set the lobster bisque to reduce by a third. In a separate pan heat 15g/½oz of the butter; as it starts to sizzle add the vegetables with the exception of the tomato, lightly season them then cover with a lid and sweat without colouring for two minutes.

Once the stock has reduced add the cream and pour over the vegetables; return to the boil and reduce slightly, then gradually add the butter, shaking the pan continuously until it has melted. Strain the vegetables out of the sauce then add the rice and tomato to the sauce and keep warm.

Spoon the vegetables into the centre of each plate to form a bed. Arrange the fillets of plaice on top then spoon the sauce over and around.

> **Wine Note** • Montravel 'Sur Lie' Moulin Caresse *(Bergerac)* • A big rich, dry wine aged in oak barrels, which is exactly what this powerful dish needs. Dry enough for the fish and tomato yet full enough for the body of the nutty wild rice.

Grilled Fillets of Plaice with Peas Bonne Femme

Serves 4

225g/8oz fresh shelled peas

85g/3oz streaky bacon

15ml/½fl oz olive oil

2 heads of little gem lettuce
(175g/6oz app.)

2 shallots

12 single fillets of plaice
each about 55g-85g/2-3oz

salt and freshly ground
white pepper

25g/1oz melted butter

300ml/10fl oz fish stock
(see page 23)

60ml/2fl oz dry white wine

175ml/6fl oz whipping cream

15g/½oz unsalted butter

24 leaves fresh basil

I know it is not right to mix languages like this and I am the last one to use the French if I can use English, but sometimes it just has to be done! Without the words bonne femme then the explanation of the dish would take almost as much space as the recipe does. The description for bonne femme in **Le Repertoire de la Cuisine** *is peas cooked in the French way (with small button onions and shredded lettuces, with butter, sugar and salt, cover with very little water and cook quickly), with pieces of cooked bacon. See what I mean?*

METHOD Boil the peas in salted water with a touch of sugar until just cooked (remember they will cook further in the sauce). Refresh in iced water then drain well. Cut the bacon into lardons then blanch for a couple of seconds in boiling water and drain well. Wash the heads of lettuce and shred them finely. Peel and very finely slice the shallots.

With the oil, lightly grease a grilling tray. Season the underside of each fillet of fish and lay them on the tray. Brush with the melted butter. Combine together the fish stock and the wine; reduce by half over a high heat. Add the cream, return to the boil and reduce slightly.

Heat the butter in a saucepan, add the shallots and bacon and gently fry these for a minute without colouring; add the lettuce and continue to gently fry until the lettuce has wilted. Pour in the cream sauce, return to the boil and reduce until just thickened.

Grill the fillets of fish under a very hot grill for about 1-1½ minutes so they are just cooked.

At the last minute tear the basil leaves quite small and stir into the sauce. Divide the sauce and garnish across the plates and lay the fillets of plaice on top.

Wine Note • Vina Esmeralda, Torres *(Spain)* • A deliciously fragrant blend of Muscat and Gewürztraminer that is rather like this dish – an interesting variation on a traditional theme.

Deep Fried Plaice with Mustard and Red Tomato Chutney

Serves 4

This is a slightly unusual way of serving a deep-fried fish, turning what is normally a fairly bland fish into something a little more special. The tomato chutney replaces the ubiquitous tomato ketchup so common with fried foods in Britain.

METHOD First make the batter: sift the flour and the pinch of salt into a bowl making a well in the centre. Put the egg yolk, oil and beer into the well and mix to a smooth batter. Add the chopped dill, cover and refrigerator for at least 30 minutes.

Trim the fillets of plaice and lightly season them then spread each fillet on one side with a thin coating of the grain mustard.

Heat the oil to about 180°C/350°F, dust the fillets of fish in the flour and shake off the excess then dip them in the batter. Deep-fry them for about 4 minutes or until crisp and golden brown. Serve on a puddle of the tomato chutney either cold or warmed through.

85g/3oz plain flour

pinch of salt

1 egg yolk

2tsp oil

100ml/3½fl oz beer

15g/½oz chopped dill

8 fillets of plaice each about 100g/3½oz in weight or 12 if they are smaller

salt and freshly ground white pepper

40g/1½oz grain mustard

oil for deep frying

a little flour for coating

225-280g/8-10oz red tomato chutney (see page 28)

> **Wine Note** • Hay Shed Hill, Sauvignon Blanc *(W. Australia)* • It has to be Sauvignon to contrast with the rich batter and it has to be a full-bodied one to cope with the tomato chutney. Look no further than this stunner from the famous winery where wines were originally made in the hay shed. It is so fresh and lively there is almost a 'spritz' on the tongue, which will keep the palate clean.

Prawns

French: *Crevette* • German: *Krabbe, Garnele* • Italian: *Gambero*
Spanish: *Gamba, Camaron*

Under the heading of prawns I have grouped together the deep-water (or northern prawn) along with the common prawn, the warm water prawn and the shrimp, and I have given the Dublin Bay prawn (or langoustine) it's own section.

For many years I rarely served prawns, as I have been waging war against those who, whenever they go out for dinner, only want prawn cocktail, then steak & chips followed by gateau, but at least now I feel a little more able to acknowledge the existence of the prawn!

There are many types of warm water prawn which almost always come to us frozen, as we do not have warm enough water in this part of the world. They will never taste as good as they would where they were originally caught but they can be tasty all the same. Prawns are now being farmed fairly extensively in some countries but they need extremely careful management. As with all frozen products, be very selective when choosing prawns, as that great invention of the frozen food industry 'the glaze' can be deceptive. Like the scallop, the prawn under a thick glaze can look fantastic but once defrosted it turns limp and flaccid and loses most of its flavour.

Brown shrimps, often known as Morecambe Bay shrimps over here, are found in sandy areas from the Mediterranean to Norway. They used to be fished extensively but due to the cost of labour it is now a declining industry. Most shrimps on sale today probably come from Holland.

I still have to confess that I've only ever used the brown shrimp (for potted shrimps – that Lancastrian classic) and tiger prawns. Although there is nothing wrong with the various cooked prawns you can buy, I still have no intention of providing a recipe for prawn cocktail (which if made properly can be very good). Nor, I am sure, do you need me to tell you to eat large cooked prawns with some good quality mayonnaise, lemon and brown bread, with possibly a salad and a good bottle of Chablis.

Marinated Hot Smoked Prawns

Serves 4

You will need a home smoker for this; if you do not have one, then they are easily made. All you need are two biscuit tins, or similar tins of the same size, one with a lid. Punch holes in the base of one, put some wood chips in the base of the other and sit the one with holes on top. Then all you need is a wire rack to fit inside, pop the lid on and there you have your own smoker.

METHOD Shell the prawns, leaving on the shell at the tail end; de-vein them then season with salt and cover in the Thai spice mix for at least 12 hours, preferably in a stainless steel or plastic container.

To make the dressing: whisk together the oil, vinegar, lime juice, Tabasco and mustard powder, season with the salt, pepper and sugar as needed then stir in the capers and coriander.

Drain the prawns from the marinade. Place 2-3 tablespoons of oak chips and a splash of water into the smoker. Put on the lid and set over a low heat to smoke. Once the smoke is rising place the prawns in and cook for about 15 minutes depending on the size of the prawns.

Dress the salad leaves with a little of the dressing and divide between the plates. Place the prawns around the salad and drizzle the remaining dressing on top.

16-20 large tiger prawns

8tbsp Thai spice mix (see page 31)

140g/5oz mixed salad leaves (frizzy, oak leaf, lollo rosso, gem, rocket etc.)

Dressing (optional):

150ml/5fl oz olive oil

60ml/2fl oz cider vinegar

juice of 2 limes

few drops of Tabasco

1tsp mustard powder

salt and freshly ground black pepper

1tsp sugar

1tbsp drained capers

1tbsp chopped coriander

Wine Note • Pouilly Fumé, Dme Gitton *(Loire)* • Remember, always fizzy pink or a crisp Sauvignon with Thai food. A second appearance of this terrific Pouilly fumé whose flinty, smoky character will easily identify with these smoky spicy prawns.

Oriental Shrimp Broth

Serves 4

115g/4oz leek

115g/4oz onion

2 sticks celery

1 stick lemon grass

2 slivers of fresh ginger

2 cloves garlic

15ml/½fl oz olive oil

350g/12oz shrimp or prawn shells

1 jalapeno chilli

125ml/4fl oz dry white wine

1 litre/2pt fish stock (see page 23)

225ml/8fl oz tomato sauce (see page 33)

2 bay leaves

1 star anise

½ head little gem lettuce

2 spring onions

55g/2oz red pepper

100ml/3½fl oz whipping cream

55g/2oz rice noodles

16 leaves fresh coriander

salt and freshly ground white pepper

The best time to make this is after you have just made the potted shrimps on page 163 because although it would taste wonderful made from whole shrimps it is equally good made only with the shells after peeling the shrimp. It is almost a free meal!

METHOD Roughly chop the leek, onion and celery, lemon grass, ginger and garlic. Heat the oil in a saucepan; when hot add these vegetables, cover with a lid and gently sweat down without colouring for 5 minutes until soft. Add the shrimp shells, cover and continue to sweat for a further 5 minutes without colouring. Add the chilli, the wine, fish stock, tomato sauce, bay leaves and star anise. Bring to the boil and then simmer for 30 minutes then strain through a fine strainer or muslin.

Finely shred the lettuce, slice the spring onions and cut the red pepper into a fine julienne. Add the red pepper and the cream to the broth and return to the boil. When it comes to the boil, break the noodles up and add to the broth along with the spring onions then remove it from the heat; allow it to stand for a minute to cook the noodles. Divide the lettuce equally between the soup plates and add four leaves of coriander to each plate. Check the seasoning, spoon the hot soup over the lettuce and serve immediately.

> **Wine Note** • Pitchfork White *(W. Australia)* • The irresistible, irrepressible Pitchfork White would be at home with almost anything but definitely shows its best character with any food showing oriental influence. Always remember, Sauvignon Blanc or a blend where it predominates is the best accompaniment for Thai-style dishes, otherwise fizzy pink …or beer!

Paella

Serves 2

Paella is great for using up all those little bits and pieces of leftovers, be they fish, meat or vegetables. I have included it in this section as the main ingredient of this one is prawns and, anyway, no matter what you do end up putting in it I think it should always have at least some prawns. Many recipes are written with the idea that you are about to have the whole street popping in for some and are often difficult to scale down. Not so this one as it is only for two, enough for an average-sized frying pan. Let's face it, how many people have a paella pan?

METHOD Remove the heads from the prawns and save for another recipe. Clean the squid and cut into thin rings. Cut the other fish into 2.5cm/1in pieces. Slice the chorizo sausage into half moons, de-bone and skin the chicken thighs and cut these into slivers. Finely chop the onion, remove the seeds from the pepper and cut it into strips. Slice the courgette into half moons.

Heat the oil in a paella pan or large frying pan, fry the prawns for a few seconds on each side then remove; fry the squid also for a few seconds and remove, then add the chicken, seal this and remove. Add the onion, peppers and garlic and fry again for a few seconds; add the chorizo and continue frying then add the fish and the chicken back to the pan. Add the rice and stir in well then add the saffron and the stock, stir through, season and add the bay leaf and finally the peas. Cover the pan and simmer over a very low heat for 15 minutes. The rice will have soaked up all of the liquid by then. Take to the table in the pan in which it has been cooked.

10-12 raw tiger prawns

1 small squid about 115g/4oz

85g/3oz firm fish such as monkfish or brill

55g/2oz chorizo sausage

2 chicken thighs

½ small onion

½ medium red pepper

85g/3oz courgette

30ml/1fl oz olive oil

1 clove crushed garlic

175g/6oz arborio or similar rice

pinch saffron

300ml/½pt fish stock (see page 23)

1 bay leaf

55g/2oz peas

Wine Note • Santa Digna, Cabernet Sauvignon Rosé *(Chile)* • Pink with paella is not a bad maxim to follow and normally the drier the better although the predominance of prawns in this particular version suggests something with a little nearer off-dry on the taste bud scale. This lovely strawberry coloured wine is perfect with all seafood and shellfish as it has a delicate citrusy background to follow up the fruity first impression.

Pithivier of Prawns

12 tiger prawns

15ml/½fl oz olive oil

15g/½oz unsalted butter

salt and freshly ground
white pepper

2tsp chopped coriander

450g/1lb puff pastry
(see page 27)

4-6 large spinach leaves

1 egg yolk beaten with
1tbsp of milk

55g/2oz mirepoix (leek,
celery, onion, fennel)

1 plum tomato
roughly chopped

1tbsp Thai spice mix
(see page 31)

350ml/12fl oz fish stock
(see page 23)

150ml/5fl oz whipping cream

Mousseline:

175g/6oz whiting fillet
skinned and boned

½tsp salt

½ egg white

100ml/3½fl oz whipping
cream

This is a very elegant starter, not overly difficult to make but it will take some time. First the pastry needs to be made at least one day in advance; the mousse could also be made a day before you need it. Then once the whole is assembled it needs to rest. I specify whiting in the recipe for the mousse but it must be fresh; if it has been previously frozen then it will not work. Do not try to substitute it with another flaky fish but you could use any of the firm fish, e.g. brill, turbot, monk, sole, even salmon.

METHOD Place the fish in a food processor along with the salt and blend until smooth. Add the egg white and continue to blend until the mixture stiffens. Transfer to a bowl and gradually add the cream stirring it in well. Allow to chill in the refrigerator for at least 20 minutes.

Shell and de-vein the prawns, saving the shells; heat the oil in a frying pan, and when hot add half of the butter and then the prawns. Season and fry these in the fat until just cooked through, for about 3-4 minutes. Tip out onto kitchen paper to drain and allow to cool. Cut the prawns into pieces and add these along with the chopped coriander to the mousse mix and stir in well.

Roll out the pastry to 3mm/⅛in thick. Cut out 4 x 12.5cm/5in circles and 4 x 15cm/6in circles. Lay these on a floured baking sheet and leave to rest in the refrigerator.

Remove the stalks from the spinach and wash the leaves well. Blanch in boiling salted water for a couple of seconds then refresh in iced water and dry well.

To assemble the pithiviers, lay a spinach leaf over each of the smaller circles of pastry and divide the mousse mix equally onto each leaf. Fold the spinach leaf over to completely encase the mousse. Ensure that there is a gap of at least 5mm/¼in between the edge of the pastry and the spinach all the way round. Egg wash the exposed pastry then lay the larger circle over the top. Press the edges down to form a seal and, using the back of a small knife, push the edges into a neat scallop shape. Score curved lines on the top of each pithivier radiating out from the centre. Place on a greased baking sheet, brush with egg wash and chill for a minimum of 30 minutes.

Once well chilled, cook in an oven pre-heated to 200°C/400°F/Gas 6 for 15 minutes or until golden brown.

Meanwhile heat the remaining oil in a saucepan and add the mirepoix of vegetables and the diced tomato; sweat these off for a minute without colouring then add the prawn shells and sweat for a further minute. Add the Thai spice mix stirring it in well. Add the fish stock and bring to the boil. Reduce this over a high heat until only half remains. Strain though a fine strainer and add the cream; reduce until it just starts to thicken.

To serve, place a pithivier in the centre of each plate and dribble the sauce around.

Wine Note • Macon Lugny, Les Genièvres, Louis Latour (*Burgundy*) • This is undoubtedly a candidate for white Burgundy but without going mad! Macon Lugny is tremendous value for money, it is rich and buttery with plenty of fruit and has elements to match all the ingredients in this dish.

Potted Shrimps

Serves 4

Potted shrimps is about as English as it gets! Originally from Lancashire and probably made with shrimps from Morecambe Bay they have been popular since the 18th century. They would once have been pounded to a paste with possibly some whole prawns for added texture and they have always been served with thin slices of brown bread and butter and a mound of watercress. Although it is fiddly to do and, yes, you can buy them ready potted, they will always taste better if you make them yourself. Buy the shrimps in the shells and use the shells for the oriental shrimp broth on page 160.

METHOD Warm the butter through with all of the ingredients except the shrimps, then remove the butter from the heat and allow to cool. When the butter comes to about blood temperature add the shrimps and mix through, seasoning with salt and pepper. Allow to cool stirring occasionally until the butter starts to set then press the shrimps into small ramekins. Allow to set in the fridge; the addition of the oil will ensure that they will not set as hard as if it were all butter. Serve on a mound of watercress with brown bread and butter.

600g/1lb 5oz cooked brown shrimps in their shells or 250g/9oz shelled

70g/2½oz butter

¼tsp ground mace

pinch of ginger

¼tsp cayenne pepper

15ml/½fl oz lemon juice

15ml/½fl oz olive oil

salt and freshly ground black pepper

Wine Note • Who needs wine when the traditional beverage would be tea?

Red Mullet

French: *Rouget de roche* • German: *Rotbarbe, Meerbarbe* • Italian: *Triglia*
Spanish: *Salmonete de roca* • USA: *Goatfish*

As red mullet is widely known and served in the Mediterranean most people assume that it is from warmer climes. This is of course true, as it is found in the warmer waters of the Mediterranean as well as off the coast of Spain and Portugal. It is, however, also to be found much further north, in fact as far north as southern Norway and, perhaps surprisingly, in British waters.

I can understand why it is not readily thought of as a fish native to British shores as it is so striking to look at. There are two main varieties of red mullet available to buy. The one that tends to venture north to the waters of Britain and Ireland is a beautiful pinky-red with stripes of yellow running along the length of its body, fading to almost white on the belly. The red mullet always has two barbels under its chin and its scales are very large and loose.The other type, more often found in the Mediterranean and not quite as nice a fish as our local one, has a much redder and more mottled skin and lacks the bright yellow bands.

The best fish to buy is always one that has all of its scales intact. This means it has not been thrown around in a trawl net but fished fairly close in by a day boat. Red mullet do suffer if badly stored and handled and they also do not stay fresh for very long. As a guide, make sure the eyes and skin are bright and if the belly is at all split do not buy it. A red mullet will not be terribly large – the normal size is around 225-400g/8-14oz but fish up to 900g/2lb can occasionally be found. My suggestion would be to look for one that weighs approximately 450g-550g/16-20oz, allowing one fillet per person.

Although it can be poached it is best grilled or gently shallow fried and is complimented well by fresh herbs such as basil; it also goes well with summer vegetables such as peas, broad beans, tomatoes and artichokes.

Red Mullet on Cous Cous with a Tomato and Basil Butter

Serves 4

METHOD Put the cous cous in a bowl and season well. Bring the fish stock to the boil and pour this over the cous cous. Allow to soak in and go cold. Once cold, stir in the olive oil.

Score the skin of the fish. Season the fillets on the meat side with both pepper and salt. Lay them meat side down on a grilling tray, which has been lightly greased with the oil. Brush the skin with the melted butter and season lightly with salt. Place these under a preheated grill for about 5-6 minutes. Once cooked, remove to a warm place to rest.

In a saucepan bring the fish stock and white wine to the boil, reducing this until only about 4 tablespoons of the liquor remain. Add the cream, return to the boil, then gradually add the chilled diced butter to the sauce a little at a time, whisking continuously until all the butter has melted. Do not allow the sauce to boil once the butter has been added. Add the diced tomato and the basil leaves to the sauce and allow to warm through.

Melt the rest of the butter in a pan and add the cous cous. Gently heat this through and check the seasoning.

Place a pile of the cous cous in the centre of each plate and place a fillet of the mullet on top. Spoon the sauce around the cous cous.

> **Wine Note** • Cousino Macul, Chardonnay *(Chile)* • The ingredients here suggest a Mediterranean style of dish, but why not travel a little further afield and try a Chilean wine? The reds have been popular for some time but their white wines are now much more consistent in both quality and style. This unoaked Chardonnay is surprisingly rich and creamy, with a fruity character that will mirror the basil and tomato nicely.

2 x 450g/16oz of red mullet (scaled, filleted and pinned)

salt and freshly ground white pepper

a little olive oil for greasing the grilling tray

25g/1oz melted unsalted butter

For the cous cous:

115g/4oz cous cous

salt and freshly ground white pepper

175ml/6fl oz fish stock (see page 23)

25ml/1fl oz olive oil

25g/1oz unsalted butter

For the sauce:

125ml/4fl oz dry white wine

425ml/¾pt fish stock

60ml/2fl oz whipping cream

175g/6oz unsalted butter, diced and well chilled

3 plum tomatoes, blanched, skinned, de-seeded and cut into small dice

12 fresh basil leaves

Red Mullet on a Tomato and Basil Tart

Serves 4

175g/6oz puff pastry (see page 27)

40ml/1½fl oz olive oil

sea salt and freshly ground white pepper

4 plum tomatoes

2 spring onions

8 leaves fresh basil

4 x 85g/3oz fillets of red mullet

15g/½oz melted butter

55g/2oz frizzy

115g/4oz tapenade (see page 31)

4tbsp pesto (see page 26)

Why is it that every recipe for red mullet seems to have either tomato or basil or both with it? Could it be because they go so well together? I love this dish; it is easy to make and is great for lunch on a summer's day.

METHOD Roll out the puff pastry into an oblong 18cm/7in wide x 30cm/12in long and only about 2mm/⅛in thick; prick it all over then cut it into four oblongs each 7.5cm/3in wide. Leave these to rest in the refrigerator for at least 30 minutes. Using a small amount of the olive oil lightly brush each piece of pastry then sprinkle quite generously with the sea salt. Bake the pastry oblongs in an oven pre-heated to 220°C/425°F/Gas 6 for 15 minutes until nicely browned. If, once the pastry is cooked, it has puffed up too much then using a palette knife or fish slice just press it down to flatten it out.

Thinly slice each tomato and lay a tomato out on each piece of pastry down its full length. Cut the spring onions into rounds and sprinkle these on the tomatoes; tear the leaves of basil and sprinkle these also over the tomatoes. Season with the salt and pepper and drizzle with a little of the olive oil.

Lightly grease a grilling tray with some of the oil and lay the fillets of fish on it skin side up having first seasoned them on the meat side. Brush the skin side with the melted butter then season.

Place the fish under a preheated grill for 4-5 minutes to cook and return the pastries to the oven for 5 minutes to cook the tomatoes.

Lightly season and toss the frizzy in the remaining olive oil. Place a tomato tart in the centre of each plate, then a little of the frizzy across the tomato; lay a fillet of mullet on this. Top with a spoonful of the tapenade and drizzle the pesto around.

Wine Note • Dashwood , Sauvignon Blanc *(N.Z.)* • This time, to make allowance for the tomato and other ingredients, a dashing Sauvignon seems like a good idea. From the South Island, Dashwood is consistently one of the best N.Z. Sauvignons around, full of zippy gooseberry fruit, with lashings of acidity to cleanse the palate.

Red Mullet with Crushed Potatoes

Serves 4

I have been serving crushed potatoes in one form or another for years now; it really freshens them up and makes an interesting accompaniment to the red mullet. The balsamic sauce could be replaced with pesto or herb oil if wished, but for me I like the walnut oil in the sauce which contrasts well with both the potato and the balsamic vinegar.

METHOD Cook the potatoes without peeling in salted water then once cooked allow to cool. When cool enough to handle peel them of their skins then crush them. Blanch, skin and de-seed the tomatoes and cut the flesh into 1cm/½in dice. Mix the tomato, 25g/1oz of the melted butter, the olives and the basil into the potatoes and season them well.

Using the olive oil grease a grilling tray; season the fillets of mullet on the meat side then place them skin-side up on the grilling tray. Brush the skin with the remaining butter and sprinkle with salt. Place the mullet under a preheated grill for 4-5 minutes until just cooked.

Bring the fish stock and the balsamic to the boil and reduce by three quarters; add the veal stock and return to the boil; add the walnut oil then keep the sauce warm. Heat a frying pan and add the potato mix; gently fry this off colouring it only lightly and check its seasoning. Return the fish to the grill once more for a further minute just to reheat slightly and re-crispen the skin. Place a 6cm/2½in cutter in the middle of each plate and spoon the potato into these gently pressing it down. Remove the cutter and lay a fillet of the fish over the potato, then spoon the sauce around.

Top with a little deep fried julienne of leek.

350g/12oz new potatoes

2 plum tomatoes

40g/1½oz melted butter

25g/1oz pitted black olives, roughly chopped

12 leaves of fresh basil, torn into small pieces

15ml/½fl oz olive oil

4 x 85g/3oz fillets of red mullet

salt and freshly ground white pepper

125ml/4fl oz fish stock (see page 23)

15ml/½fl oz balsamic vinegar

60ml/2fl oz veal stock (see page 33)

15ml/½fl oz walnut oil

Wine Note • Fleur de Carneros, Pinot Noir *(California)* • This Californian wine has a light, fruity, sunny nature that is the perfect partner for this gentle dish. The colour will match well too!

Salmon

French: *Saumon* • Italian: *Salmone* • German: *Lachs* • Spanish: *Salmon*

Cooks and fishermen alike have written much about wild salmon over the years. It is often only a dream for the fisherman and for the cook it has gone from being an everyday food to a luxury. One thing is for sure, the Atlantic salmon is in serious decline, as any salmon fisherman will verify.

Netting has been curbed in many rivers, if not stopped altogether, but the results have been disappointing. It was thought that the numbers of fish entering the rivers would rise dramatically once these nets had been removed, but sadly this has not happened. Rivers are still polluted, although some that were positively toxic now have salmon returning to them, albeit in small numbers.

Farming has played a large part in the downfall of salmon and their ability to breed. Soil disturbance causes soil to enter the rivers as silt and block up the gravel in which the salmon lay their eggs. Undoubtedly though, one of the biggest causes of the decline of the wild salmon has been our greed. Since the discovery in the 1970s of a considerable feeding ground in the North Atlantic, fishing fleets have been decimating the stocks long before they have an opportunity to return to the rivers of their birth to perpetuate the species. A new worry is that the truly wild salmon will disappear even sooner than anticipated due to escapees from fish farms. These former internees are now breeding with what little wild stocks are left, leaving behind a hybrid that could very well take over.

Farming has made cheap salmon available to all but farmed fish still pose a problem to both the health conscious and the welfare friendly. Some dubious substances are used in farming these fish, from chemicals to control the sea lice to antibiotics and colourants to give the fish its characteristic 'pink' hue. But I am also happy to say that I have had some very good quality farmed salmon. I once was able to use fish farmed off Benbecula in the Outer Hebrides and they were tremendous, simply because they were kept in a strong tidal flow and therefore were able to build up natural muscle.

Farmed fish are available all year round but wild salmon can only be found between January and October.

Salmon Salad 'Niçoise'

Serves 2

We have all come across salad niçoise, a traditional Italian dish normally made with tuna. This is more or less the same only it uses salmon, pesto and yoghurt dressing. It is a great way of using trimmings of salmon or any salmon left over from a fish that has been cooked whole. It makes a great starter or a light lunch dish for a summer's day eaten with a loaf of warm and crisp ciabatta – what could be better?

METHOD Bring the bouillon to the boil. Lightly season the salmon and pour the boiling bouillon on top; allow to go cold; once cold the salmon should be cooked but pink in the centre and very moist.

Turn the new potatoes into small pointed barrel shapes about 3.5cm/1.5in long allowing 5 potatoes per portion. Cook these and refresh.

Boil the quail's eggs for 2½ minutes; this should leave them with soft yolks; shell and cut each egg in two. Cut each cherry tomato in two.

Divide the salad leaves between two bowls and equally divide the salmon between the bowls. Put half the beans, half the olives and half the potatoes into each bowl, lightly season, pour in the oil and toss well.

Spoon a circle of pesto around the edge of each of the plates. Carefully pile the salad in the centre. Alternatively arrange the tomatoes and the half quail's eggs around the salad and on the pesto. Drizzle the yoghurt dressing over the salad then sprinkle with the Parmesan and the chives.

600ml/1pt court bouillon (see page 22)

175g/6oz fully trimmed salmon

salt and freshly ground white pepper

225g/8oz new potatoes

6 quail's eggs

6 cherry tomatoes

2 handfuls of mixed salad leaves: frizzy, endive, lolla, red oak leaf, trevisse, little gem

40g/1½oz cooked French beans cut in half

55g/2oz black olives

15ml/½fl oz olive oil

60ml/2fl oz pesto (see page 26)

60ml/2fl oz yoghurt dressing (see page 28)

10g/¼oz shaved Parmesan

few chives cut to 2.5cm/1in

Wine Note • Catarina, Vinho Regional, Terras do Sado • Pretend you're on holiday and enjoy this wonderfully individual white made from native grape varieties with a hint of Chardonnay. You'll find it rich enough for the 'Niçoise' and crisp enough for the salad.

Poached Fillet of Salmon in a Nage of Green Vegetables

Serves 2

1 small courgette

55g/2oz leaf spinach

25g/1oz French beans, topped and tailed

15g/½oz mangetout, topped and tailed

50g/1¾oz broccoli florets

25g/1oz shelled fresh peas

10 asparagus tips

sufficient court bouillon to cover the salmon (see page 22)

60ml/2fl oz dry white wine

175ml/6fl oz fish stock (see page 23)

2 x 140g/5oz salmon fillets trimmed of all skin, dark meat and bone

salt and freshly ground white pepper

125ml/4fl oz whipping cream

few sprigs of fresh chervil (optional)

Perfect for that summer's day, even better if you grow your own vegetables. Although the total quantity of vegetables seems a lot it really is only a little of each type.

METHOD Cut the courgette into 10 wedges about 5cm/2in long and turn them into neat pointed barrel shapes. Pick the spinach of its stalks and wash in at least 3 changes of water.

Blanch all the vegetables separately and refresh in iced water and drain, with the exception of the spinach, which should just be drained well.

Bring the bouillon to the boil. Combine the wine and the fish stock together in a saucepan and bring to the boil; reduce this over a high heat until only about a third remains.

Season the salmon portions and lay them in a tray or pan and pour the stock over them. Cover with foil or greaseproof paper and set over a low heat to poach for about 3 minutes.

Once the stock has reduced add the cream and return to the boil. Divide the sauce between two pans and divide the vegetables into them making sure each portion is equal. Divide the spinach between the pans and gently heat – do not allow to boil – until the spinach is cooked.

Spoon the sauce and vegetables onto the serving plates and drain the salmon from the bouillon. Place a portion of the fish on the vegetables on each plate. Scatter the chervil on top.

> **Wine Note** • Gewürztraminer, Dme Runner • We all drink Chablis with salmon but why not try a spicy Alsatian for a change? You'll be pleasantly surprised by the success of the combination.

Tournedos of Salmon in a Tomato and Basil Essence

Serves 4

This is quite a complicated dish to master but it is well worth the effort. Preparing salmon this way gives it a totally new presentation and the tomato essence is just so intense it is almost overpowering. Vine ripened plum tomatoes are best for this as they have the sweetest and best flavour.

fillet of salmon cut from the middle of a side weighing about 900g/2lb; it should be about 20-23cm/8-9in long

salt and freshly ground white pepper

3 plum tomatoes

10 asparagus tips

10 French beans

350g/12oz leaf spinach

sufficient court bouillon to cover the salmon (see page 22)

425ml/15fl oz tomato essence (see page 32)

12 basil leaves

METHOD Skin the fillet of salmon and very carefully remove the dark meat. Season the fish on the bone side and roll into a cylinder shape with the skin side outermost. Lay this on a sheet of cling film and roll it very tightly, tying off the ends. You should now have a roll of about 18cm/7in long and 6cm/2½in wide. Roll this in foil then using string tie the cylinder at intervals of 2cm/¾in to make a cylinder 18cm/7in long with 8 strings tied around. Leave this to stand in the refrigerator overnight. It will in fact keep easily for three days like this.

Blanch and skin the tomatoes, cut them into quarters and remove the seeds; cut each quarter into half. Cut the asparagus tips to 6cm/2½in in length and blanch in boiling salted water; refreshing them in iced water, cut them in half lengthways. Top and tail the French beans and blanch these also. Cut them in half lengthways. Pick the spinach of its leaves and wash in at least three changes of water.

Cut the salmon into four pieces allowing two strings per portion and discarding the ends. Bring the bouillon to a simmer and place the salmon tournedos in. Cook over a low heat not allowing the bouillon to boil, for 8 minutes. Remove, cover and keep warm.

While the salmon is cooking put the spinach into a pan with 60ml/2fl oz of the tomato essence; season and cook very quickly over a high heat until the spinach starts to wilt. Strain and discard the stock.

Place a pile of the spinach in the centre of each plate. Bring the rest of the tomato essence to a simmer. Gently re-heat the asparagus and French beans in the essence, and then arrange these and the tomato fingers around the spinach and place the basil leaves on this. Carefully unwrap each tournedos and place one on each pile of spinach. Pour the tomato essence over the fish and on the garnish.

> **Wine Note** • Hay Shed Hill, Pitchfork White *(Australian)* • Here's a tricky one: tomatoes love Sauvignon, spinach hates it! This tremendous wine is a blend of Chardonnay, Chenin, Semillon and Sauvignon that keeps everyone happy. 'So fresh it needs slapping!' says the producer.

Serves 4

175ml/6fl oz fish stock
(see page 23)

125ml/4fl oz dry white wine

½ clove garlic

225g/8fl oz whipping cream

60ml/2fl oz natural yoghurt

1tbsp finely chopped chives

salt and freshly ground
white pepper

⅙ head frizzy

30ml/1fl oz olive oil

2 muffins

a little butter

225g/8oz thinly sliced
smoked salmon

4 poached eggs

4tsp caviar

Smoked Salmon with Poached Egg and Caviar

Good God, how ostentatious can one get! Great first course that will impress almost anyone as long as the salmon is of good quality, because let's face it, there is smoked salmon then there's smoked salmon! The trick is getting a good sauce to serve with it. Even without the caviar it is a good starter that is extremely simple.

METHOD Combine the fish stock and white wine together in a saucepan, peel the garlic and add to the stock, bring this to the boil and reduce by two thirds. Add the cream and return to the boil. Once it boils remove the garlic and discard and allow the sauce to go cold. Once the sauce is cold mix in the yoghurt and the chives and check it for seasoning.

Wash the frizzy well and break it into a bowl, season and toss with the olive oil. Cut the muffins in two and toast both halves on both sides. Lightly butter the halves and place one in the centre of each plate.

Drape the smoked salmon on the muffins arranging it so as to give it a little height and leaving a hollow in the centre. Place a mound of the salad into the centre of each muffin in a nice mound and place a poached egg on top of this.

Spoon the sauce over the egg and around the salmon and finish with a teaspoon of caviar on the top of each egg.

Wine Note • Domaine Azo, Chablis 1ᵉʳ Cru • Quite simply, a stunning classic wine to partner a dish of equal class and style.

Seared Salmon with a Watercress, Bacon and Potato Salad

Serves 2

Great on a summer's day, this quick and easy salmon dish is fantastic when eaten **al fresco.**

METHOD Remove any skin, dark meat and pin bones from the salmon.

Cook the new potatoes in their skins in salted water until almost cooked then refresh and peel. Cut them into thick slices. Cut the bacon into lardons; blanch for a second in boiling water, refresh and drain. Fry them until crisp in 15ml/½fl oz of the oil.

Drop the egg into boiling water and cook for 4 minutes. Cool in cold water then carefully peel. Using a fork mash up the egg, mix in the mustard, vinegar and 30ml/1fl oz of the oil and seasoning to make a dressing.

Pick the watercress of its heavier stalks, wash and drain well.

Season the fillets of salmon then heat half of the remaining oil in a frying pan until smoking; add half of the butter then sear the salmon in the hot pan on the presentation side until well browned; turn the fish over and continue cooking for about 1 minute. When cooked the salmon will still be pink in the centre. Remove and allow the fish to rest in a warm place.

Heat the remaining oil in a frying pan until smoking, then add the last of the butter. Season the potatoes and fry these until golden brown turning them carefully so as not to break them up.

Lightly season the watercress and toss this together with the bacon and the dressing. Carefully add the potatoes and then arrange the salad on the plates. Place a fillet of salmon on top.

2 x 175g/6oz fillets of salmon

175g/6oz new potatoes

85g/3oz streaky bacon

60ml/2fl oz oil

1 egg

1tsp wholegrain mustard

1tbsp white wine vinegar

75ml/2½fl oz olive oil

salt and freshly ground white pepper

85g/3oz watercress

25g/1oz unsalted butter

Wine Note • Hay Shed Hill, Semillon *(W. Australia)* • You haven't lived until you've tried this fabulous wood-matured wine. It's intense oaky aromas and fresh lively palate is just right with this summery dish that includes the 'gutsy' elements of seared salmon and bacon. What a combination!

Seared Smoked Salmon with Grilled Spring Onions

Serves 4

12 spring onions

30ml/1fl oz olive oil

115g/4oz picked rocket leaves

salt and freshly ground white pepper

4 slices of smoked salmon each weighing 85g/3oz and 5mm/½ thick

lemon vinaigrette (see page 25)

Cooked smoked salmon is not everyone's favourite. If it is not good quality salmon or if it is overcooked it can end up tasting a little kipper-like and it is too expensive for that scenario. Searing smoked salmon became fashionable during the later part of the nineties; I quite like it although I am sure it is destined to be just a fad. It is important to cut the salmon thickly; if it is too thin then it will overcook very quickly. Baby leeks will work here just as well as spring onions if preferred.

METHOD Using a little of the oil lightly grease a grilling tray, roll the spring onions on this to coat them in oil and season. Grill under a medium heat until lightly browned on both sides.

Toss the rocket leaves in the olive oil and season. Arrange a neat salad of these in the centre of each plate.

Heat a frying pan, preferably non stick, until very hot; season the salmon slices with a little freshly ground pepper then place them in the pan two at a time so as not to lose the heat. Pressing them down with the back of a palette knife, brown them really well but only cook them on the one side. Transfer them to the salad, seared side up. Lay 3 spring onions over the fish and spoon the lemon vinaigrette around.

Wine Note • Cuvée Royale Brut, Joseph Perrier • Yet another perfect couple – champagne and smoked salmon. Joseph Perrier Cuvée Royale is definitely a cut above and has more body and character than you would normally expect to find in non-vintage champagne. It has a delightfully subtle floral perfume with hints of vanilla and spice on the palate. The added 'weight' will match the more intense flavour of smoked salmon caused by searing as well as coping with the spring onions, which could dominate lesser wines.

Scallops

French: *Coquille St. Jacques* • German: *Jakobsmuschellen, Kammuschel*
Italian: *Ventaglio* • Spanish: *Viera*

To me the scallop is the best shellfish available as it is so versatile, sweet and succulent with a fantastic texture. Unfortunately this tends to only apply to fresh scallops and even then not to all of them. Beware, as some scallops are not what they seem. If you buy them pre-shelled they may have been frozen and defrosted and then sold as fresh, or if they are sold as fresh they may also have been pre-soaked.

The scallop is a very obliging little creature. If you cut the meat from the shell, pop it into cold water and let it sit there for around 22 hours it will almost double its size. After that time it will start to lose the water it has soaked up and return gradually to its original size. When you come to cook it, it will lose its water as it cooks and then shrivel up to almost nothing. So if you see big plump, almost pure white scallops, don't buy them. If you see plump off-white, almost pale orange meat then do buy them, as this is the colour fresh scallops should be.

Buying fresh diver-caught scallops really is the best way. They are almost always larger and in far better condition than those which have been dredged. The best scallops come from the west coast of Scotland where divers carefully hand pick each one and bring them to shore all year round. As you take them from the shell they will still be alive, they will be cleaner and therefore easier to use, firm and with a flavour so sweet and nutty it could not fail to convert even the most dubious. Sear them, lightly seasoned and straight from the shell in a little butter for just a few seconds and enjoy!

The scallop lives in its semi-circular, ribbed, fan-shaped shell; the upper shell is flat and the lower one convex, and inside the meat is a firm orange/cream colour with a bright orange and cream coloured roe attached. They are mostly hermaphrodites with the roe containing both the female (orange) and the male (cream) testis. The whole thing is surrounded with a frill or skirt of a thousand eyes – well more like fifty actually. When cleaning scallops always save the skirt as it makes wonderful stock.

Fricassee of Scallops in a Pimento Butter

Serves 4

10 scallops weighing about 350g/12oz

1 courgette, app. 18-20cm/7-8in long and weighing around 225g/8oz

12 small new potatoes, app. 450g/1lb

115g/4oz piece of leek cut 7.5cm/3in long from the centre of the leek

½ recipe for Sauce Jacqueline (see page 29)

60ml/2fl oz whipping cream

salt and freshly ground white pepper

2 tbsp. chopped chives

15g/½oz unsalted butter

You don't have to believe me but to my mind this has to be the sexiest sauce I have ever tasted – pretty bold statement that! It is loosely based around Sauce Jacqueline as made by Louis Outhier and it is absolutely fantastic! Careful how much of it you eat though as it is amazingly rich. Stick to these quantities as a first course and follow it with something light.

METHOD Remove the roes then cut each scallop into two pieces.

Cut the courgette into 4 pieces 5cm/2in long then each of these into six. Turn each one into a small barrel shape to give 24 pieces altogether. Cut each potato in half and turn these also. Cook the potatoes in boiling salted water then refresh and drain. Cut the leek into a very fine julienne.

Bring the stock from the sauce recipe up to a gentle boil along with the cream and add the courgettes; simmer until they are almost cooked, for about 1 minute.

Lightly season the scallop meat and the roes and add to the sauce along with the potatoes. Return the sauce almost to the boil then stand it over a very low heat to cook the scallops gently for 2 minutes. Carefully remove the scallops and the garnish and divide them out between the plates. Add the chives to the sauce then gradually add the butter from the sauce recipe a little at a time, whisking continuously until it has all melted. Do not allow the sauce to boil or get too hot, as it will split.

Heat the unsalted butter in a saucepan and add the leek julienne; season and cook gently until just limp and cooked yet retaining a hint of crispness. Spoon the sauce over the scallops and garnish then place a pile of leeks in the middle of each dish.

> **Wine Note** • Meursault, Louis Latour *(Burgundy)* • Rich and buttery can only mean one thing – Chardonnay. This time, though, we will stick to France and Burgundy since the dish is a starter and the wine at this stage of a meal needs sufficient body to match the first course without over-powering the palate for the rest of the meal. The House of Latour needs no introduction and this is a superb example of their craft.

Seared Scallops with Cracked Wheat and Sauce Vierge

Serves 4

85ml/3fl oz fish stock
(see page 23)

115g/4oz cracked
bulgar wheat

salt and freshly ground
white pepper

45ml/1½fl oz olive oil

2 heads little gem lettuce

sauce vierge (see page 30)

20 scallops

15g/½oz unsalted butter

This dish has appeared on my menus recently more times than I care to think. It is not only delicious but it is also dead easy, especially on a busy Saturday night. Sauce vierge is such a natural accompaniment to scallops – they go so well together. If you are not a cracked wheat lover or if it is not available then use cous cous instead. The number of scallops you use depends upon their size. I am allowing 5 scallops per portion but they would only be medium-sized ones. Why be mean?

METHOD Bring the fish stock to the boil, season the cracked wheat and add to the stock once it boils; return to the boil then transfer to a bowl to cool. Once cooled, stir in 15ml/½fl oz of the oil.

Break up the little gem lettuce removing any outer leaves then wash and drain well. Place these in a bowl with the cracked wheat and half of the vierge dressing, season lightly and toss well.

Season the scallops, heat the remaining oil in a frying pan, and when hot add the last of the butter. Very quickly sear the scallops in this over a high heat, cooking for only about 30 seconds on each side.

Arrange the leaves on the serving plates, place five cooked scallops on top and spoon the remaining dressing over.

Wine Note • Pelorus, Cloudy Bay *(N.Z.)* • Not easily available but a stunning glass of sparkling wine from 'down under' that would be just perfect with this light, bright summery-sounding dish – both to be taken on a palm-fringed beach surrounded by an ocean-lapped bay!

Scallops Baked under Filo Pastry

This dish is an adaptation of one that we served at a charity auction many years ago. Kam Po Butt (I do hope that is spelled right!), the then chef of Memories of China, came and cooked one of the courses – scallops baked in their shells with soy, ginger and spring onions. I have taken that basic idea and changed it slightly by adding the filo topping. This keeps all of the flavours in while cooking; and once the lid is broken the waft of the freshly cooked scallop juices is mouth-watering.

METHOD Thoroughly clean and wash the scallops leaving them attached to the cupped half of the shell. Trim the onions of any outer leaves and root then thinly slice them into rounds, and sprinkle these onto the scallops. Very finely slice the chilli and peel and cut the ginger into a fine julienne; sprinkle both of these over the scallops. Mix together the soy, oil and vinegar; evenly spoon this over the scallops. Lightly season the scallops with a touch of the sea salt (not too much as the soy can be very salty) and the black pepper. Lay a leaf of basil over each one.

To make the filo lids first cut the pastry into squares a little larger than the scallop shells. For each shell, lightly brush a square of pastry with the melted butter, lay another square on top and brush that too with the butter, then lay another on top of that. Dampen the edges of the shells with a little water then lay the pastry over the shell. Press down around the edges and cut away any excess pastry. Do the same with the rest of the scallops. Using the larger pieces of the excess pastry fold three or four pieces together to form a rosette and place in the middle of each shell. Lightly brush the rosettes and the pastry with the melted butter then sprinkle with a little of the sea salt. These can be kept in the refrigerator for a few hours until needed if necessary.

Bake in an oven pre-heated to 230°C/450°F/Gas 8 for 10 minutes until the pastry is golden brown then serve immediately.

Serves 4

12 scallops in their shells

5 spring onions

1 small hot chilli

15g/½oz fresh ginger

30ml/1fl oz dark soy sauce

15ml/½fl oz sesame oil

15ml/½fl oz rice wine vinegar

sea salt and freshly ground black pepper

12 fresh basil leaves

175g/6oz filo pastry

55g/2oz melted butter

Wine Note • Pitchfork White, Hay Shed Hill *(W. Australia)* • To accompany a dish with its variety of flavours and slightly oriental feel, this wine being a blend of Sauvignon, Semillon, Chardonnay and Chenin will give a real burst of fruit and sunshine in the mouth and is just about perfect with this kind of food.

Serves 4

Scallop and Saffron Soup

12 scallops

salt and freshly ground white pepper

600ml/20fl oz fish stock (see page 23)

1 crushed clove of garlic

15g/½oz unsalted butter

1 medium carrot, finely diced

1 small leek, finely diced

1 stick celery, finely diced

25g/1oz shallot, finely chopped

1tbsp Pernod

pinch of saffron

few sprigs of fresh chervil

This simple, colourful soup combining the flavour of the scallops with the scent of saffron and a hint of Pernod is one I have always liked – it is so fresh and vibrant. The only drawback is the expense of the scallops.

METHOD Shell, clean and wash the scallops; dry well. Remove the roes from 4 of the scallops and save the white meat to one side. Roughly cut the rest of the scallop meat, including the roes, into small pieces and season. Place the scallop meat into a saucepan with the fish stock and garlic and poach for two minutes. When cooked, place in a food processor or blender and blend till smooth, then pass through a strainer.

Heat the butter in a saucepan and once sizzling, add the diced vegetables and fry gently without colouring for about 30 seconds. Add the Pernod, followed by the scallop mixture and the saffron, and mix well. Bring to the boil and simmer for about 4 minutes; the vegetables should still be a little crisp.

Thinly slice the saved white meat; each scallop should yield about 5 slices. Place these slices into the soup plates, stir the soup well to mix the garnish through evenly then pour the soup over the scallops. The heat of the soup will be enough to cook the slices, as they are very thin. Garnish with sprigs of chervil on top of the soup.

Wine Note • Vouvray, Domaine de Vaufuget *(Loire)* • The delicate flavour of scallops has been enhanced with aromatic saffron and Pernod, which would suggest a slightly less dry white than might first be considered. The Chenin Blanc grapes here have been affected by 'noble rot' (which is a good thing!) that gives a definitely off dry, almost medium style with a honeyed flavour balanced by typical Loire acidity on the finish.

Scallop Sausage with a Nage of Asparagus

Water asparagus works much better than the everyday kind but it is difficult to get hold of and has a fairly short season. You can, if you wish, add a firm white fish to the scallops: up to half the amount as you have in scallop meat will make the scallops go further and it will also make the mousse a lot firmer and easier to handle.

METHOD Ensure that the scallops are well cleaned and washed; dry thoroughly. Remove the roes and cut these into 1cm/½in dice. Place the white meat in a food processor along with the salt and blend until smooth. Add the egg white and blend again to mix it in thoroughly. Rub this mixture through a sieve into a bowl set on crushed ice. Gradually add two thirds of the cream, and then stir in the vermouth and a little ground pepper. Now test the mousse by dropping a small amount into a pan of water that is just off the boil. Once cooked test its consistency: if it is very rubbery then add a little more cream and test again until you are satisfied with the final texture. Fold into this the chopped chives and the diced roes. Using cling film as a sausage skin, form the mixture into 6 individual sausages and tie off the ends. Bring a pan of water, large enough to take the sausages comfortably, to the boil. Drop the sausages in and poach them for 8 minutes but do not allow the water to return to the boil. Once cooked transfer them to iced water. Once cold they will keep for up to 3 days in the refrigerator.

Peel the asparagus tips and cut them to 5cm/2in in length, boil them in salted water until just cooked then refresh them in iced water and drain. Blanch, skin and de-seed the tomatoes; cut them into fingers. Bring the stock and the vermouth to the boil and reduce by half. While the sauce is reducing drop the sausages into a pan of almost boiling water for one minute to reheat. Once hot carefully remove the cling film, heat the oil in a frying pan and add the butter; when sizzling add the sausages and gently roll them in the fat until they are lightly browned.

Add the sweet corn and the cream to the reduced stock then return it to the boil. Add the asparagus tips, tomato fingers and the chives and allow to warm through. Divide the sauce and garnish between the plates and place a sausage on top.

6 sausages

Mousseline:

8-9 (225g/9oz) fresh scallops

1tsp salt and freshly ground white pepper

1 egg white

300ml/½pt whipping cream

40ml/1½fl oz dry vermouth

3tsp chopped chives

Nage:

30 thin asparagus tips

2 plum tomatoes

350ml/12fl oz fish stock (see page 23)

150ml/5fl oz dry vermouth

15ml/½fl oz olive oil

15g/½oz unsalted butter

140g/5oz sweetcorn kernels

150ml/5fl oz whipping cream

1tbsp chopped chives

Wine Note • Château Canteloup, Graves de Vayres *(Bordeaux)* • This dish calls for something slightly less dry than a straight Sauvignon. We have the perfect answer in this wonderfully aromatic white Graves that is a blend of Sauvignon, Semillon and Muscadelle, resulting in an off-dry, almost honeyed style with a lovely fresh finish.

Seared Scallops with Roast Cashew Nuts and Apple Crisps

Serves 4

2tsp sugar

juice of 1 lemon

200ml/7fl oz water

2 eating apples
(granny smiths probably
work the best)

175ml/6fl oz olive oil

40g/1½oz unsalted butter

100g/3½oz plain cashew nuts

salt and freshly ground
white pepper

85g/3oz mashed potato

55ml/2fl oz plain yoghurt

75ml/2½fl oz fish stock
(see page 23)

½ clove garlic

55ml/2fl oz whipping cream

½ head curly endive

20 scallops

few chives cut to
4cm/1½inches

Fruit and vegetable crisps have become a bit of a trendy item over the last few years. They are very simple to make and very tasty. When cooking the scallops it is important not to put too many in the pan at once. If the pan cools down too much then the scallops will end up boiling instead of searing. When frying scallops it is important to get the juices to caramelise on the outside.

METHOD Dissolve the sugar in the lemon juice and water. Peel and thinly slice the apples into the lemon mix. Lay the apple slices out on a sheet of silicone or greaseproof paper and place in an oven heated to 140°C/275°F/Gas 1 for at least 3 hours. After one hour turn the apple slices over. Remove the crisps from the oven; they will still feel soft at this point. Allow them to cool and as they do so they will become crisp.

Heat 50ml/1fl oz of the oil in a frying pan; when hot add half of the butter then the cashew nuts. Roast the nuts in the hot fat and as they are just starting to brown remove them to a kitchen towel and salt lightly. Do not let them brown too far, as once they come out of the fat they will continue browning.

Combine the potato, yoghurt, stock and garlic in a food processor or liquidiser. Blend together and gradually add 100ml/3½fl oz of the oil then the cream, and season to taste. If too thick then add more stock to the required consistency. Pick and wash the endive and drain well.

Season the scallops; heat the remaining oil in a frying pan and when hot add the last of the butter. Very quickly sear the scallops over a high heat, cooking for only about 30 seconds on each side.

Toss the lettuce with the cashew nuts and about half of the potato dressing. Arrange this on the plates. Share the scallops out evenly between the salads and interleave the apple crisps throughout. Dribble over the remaining dressing and scatter with the chives.

Wine Note • Brown Brothers, Dry Muscat *(Australia)* • Nuts can be unfriendly towards wine but this wonderfully aromatic, fragrant and slightly spicy example has enough character to cope with both the cashew and caramel flavours here. It retains a crispness on the finish to complement the tart apples.

Skate, Ray

French: *Pocheteau, Raie bouclée* • Italian: *Moro, Razza spinosa*
German: *Glattroche, Keulenrochen* • Spanish: *Noriega, Raya de clavos*

Skate, scat, blue skate, dinnan, ray and roker are all names for skate and ray. Once cut and skinned you would find it virtually impossible to tell if it was skate, thornback ray, blonde ray, sand ray or any of the fish known commonly as skate. The true skate has a long snout compared to the ray as well as a smoother skin, and the thornback skate, considered to be the best for eating, has coarse prickles which in adulthood develop into spines. The thornback is the most abundant of the rays in British waters and it is likely to be the one on your plate.

Technically they are boneless fish; that is to say although they have a skeleton it is not one of bone but of cartilage and they are also free of the fine pin bones that can be found in other fish.

The one problem with skate is the smell and taste of ammonia, which once it sets in makes the fish inedible. Skate should be bought and used when it has no smell at all, and it should have a light rosy pink colouring to the flesh and look bright and fresh. If it does not answer to this description then do not use it. The ammonia is due to the breakdown of urea in the blood, but if the fish is properly bled when caught this minimises the problem. I do not think I have ever seen a whole skate for sale; it is always sold as wings making it very economical to buy and much easier to use.

Pressed Terrine of Skate

Serves 18

2kg/4lb 8oz of skate wings, skinned both sides

salt and freshly ground white pepper

app. 1 litre/1¾pt court bouillon (see page 22)

4 plum tomatoes

115g/4oz cucumber

12 small gherkins

3 limes

85g/3oz capers

15g/½oz green peppercorns

25g/1oz chopped chives

15-18 large spinach leaves

This is a very simple terrine to make compared to most. The more fish you can pack in the less jelly will be needed and therefore it will be nicer to eat. The only note of caution I would sound is that the fish should be really fresh; if there is any hint of ammonia then do not use for this dish. Great for a summer's **al fresco** *luncheon party.*

METHOD Season and poach the skate wings in just enough of the court bouillon to cover them scantily for about 10-15 minutes depending upon their thickness. The fish is ready when the flesh pulls away from the bone without too much difficulty. Drain the fish from the stock then carefully peel the meat off the bones, cover and cool. Return the bones to half of the stock and allow these to cook for a further 10 minutes over a very low heat. Strain through a very fine sieve or muslin and allow it to cool.

Blanch, skin and de-seed the tomatoes then cut them into 1cm/½in dice; cut the cucumber into similar-sized dice discarding the central core of seeds. Chop the gherkins and segment the limes. Mix all these ingredients together along with the capers, peppercorns and chives. Wash and drain the spinach leaves then blanch them in boiling salted water, refresh in iced water and drain well; pat them dry between two cloths.

Line a 28cm/11in terrine mould with cling film allowing an overlap of at least 7.5cm/3in all round. Line this with the spinach leaves allowing an overhang of at least 5cm/2in all the way around and being careful not to leave any gaps between the leaves. Put two tablespoons of the court bouillon in the bottom of the terrine then cover the base with a thin layer of the skate meat. Sprinkle this with some of the vegetable mixture and two tablespoons of the court bouillon. Top this with another layer of the skate and a further layer of the vegetable mixture then a further two spoons of the liquor. Continue to build up the terrine like this until it is full, making sure to press each layer down well; try to aim to finish the terrine with a layer of fish. Once the terrine is full, fold over the overhanging spinach then fold over the overhanging cling film to completely seal the dish. Place a weight on top – the best thing is an identical terrine mould filled with water; alternatively cut a piece of wood or stiff cardboard the same size as the terrine, wrap in foil or film then lay this on top and sit some medium-sized tins on it. Leave in the refrigerator overnight to set.

To serve: unmould the terrine; if it does not slip straight out then dip it in hot water for a few seconds just to slightly warm the outside. Using a sharp knife and with the cling film still wrapped around cut the terrine into slices. Remove the cling film after cutting – this will help to hold it together if it is a little soft.

Serve with a light vinaigrette, a yoghurt dressing (page 28) or sauce vierge (page 30) and a salad of French beans or baby spinach leaves.

> **Wine Note** • Domaine de la Riquette, Blanc *(Bordeaux)* • Such a fresh, clean dish needs something dry, crisp and fairly light so as not to overpower the delicate fish. A youthful white Bordeaux is the obvious answer; this one is terrific value and perfect for 'al fresco' dining.

Skate Braised with Onions and Cider

Serves 2

This is a rustic peasant-style dish, more suited to serving straight from the pan in which it is cooked rather than trying to be too pretty with it.

METHOD Peel and very finely slice the onions. Heat the oil in a saucepan with a tight-fitting lid and add the onions; season with salt and pepper and cover the pan. Allow to sweat over a low heat for 20-30 minutes, stirring occasionally. Be careful when lifting the lid to stir the onions that you hold the lid over the pan so any juices run back into it. When the onions are really soft add the cider, the garlic and the sugar, cook very slowly still covered for a further 20 minutes then add half of the thyme leaves.

Season the skate wings and place them in the pan pushing them into the onions so they are covered; replace the lid and cook very slowly for a further 4-5 minutes.

Follow the recipe for mash on page 25 then place a spoon of the mash onto each plate. Carefully lift the skate from the pan placing it on the mash and spooning the onions over and around, then sprinkle with the remaining thyme.

400g/14oz onions

30ml/1fl oz olive oil

salt and freshly ground white pepper

300ml/10fl oz dry cider

1 clove crushed garlic

25g/1oz sugar

2tsp fresh thyme leaves

450g/1lb skate wing

¼ recipe for mash (see page 25)

Wine Note • Pinot Grigio, La Delfina *(Italy)* • Skate alone would be happy with almost any crisp dry white; the addition of onions means a touch more care is needed and this Pinot Grigio has just that little extra fruitiness that will enhance the sweetness of the onions.

Sole: DOVER & LEMON

French: Dover, *Sole,* Lemon, *Sole Limande* German: Dover, *Seezunge,* Lemon, *Rotzunge*
Italian: Dover, *Sogliola,* Lemon, *Sogliola limanda* Spanish: Dover, *Lenguado,* Lemon,
Mendo limon

Rightly or wrongly I have put both dover and lemon sole together in this section. They are actually from different families – the Dover sole is from the family *Soleidae* whereas the Lemon sole is from the same family as plaice, halibut, dab and flounder (*pleuronectidae*). Each can, however, substitute for the other in most sole recipes, as can other flat fish such as witch or Torbay sole and megrim.

Lemon sole often suffers from the same problems of pricing as does the Dover and there are times of the year when demand for it from other countries is so great that the price disappears off the top of the scale! The flesh of the lemon is not as finely flavoured or as firm as that of the Dover but it is still a very fine fish to eat. The physical differences between the two are quite marked and it would be difficult to mistake one for the other. The lemon is a dull dark brown with varied and uneven markings in a range of colours from orange to green that seem to blend into the background colour of its smooth skin. In contrast, the Dover has a very rough skin, is much more elongated in shape and more charcoal in colour.

Dover sole is the one true sole *solea solea* but its habitat is not exclusively Dover as is suggested by its name. It is more likely to be called Dover because the port was the largest and closest supply of fresh sole to the London markets. It can be found from the Mediterranean to the north of Scotland and southern Norway.

It has long been considered by many as possibly the finest of all fish. *The Repertoire de la Cuisine* lists over 340 recipes for sole, and many of them are extremely elaborate. Its flesh is firm and white with a delicate flavour and simple dishes work best.

Many people consider sole best eaten two to three days after being landed as it needs time to mature and undergoes some sort of chemical change in its makeup. This is fine except that when it reaches the fishmonger it is probably already at least that old.

Poached Sole with Bacon and Chervil

Serves 4

Although the recipe was written for Dover sole you could substitute lemon sole in this light summery dish. If using lemon sole you need to be a little more careful as it is a softer fish than Dover sole and will be more difficult to handle.

4 x 280-350g/10-12oz of Dover sole

115g/4oz unsalted butter

salt and freshly ground white pepper

120ml/4fl oz dry white wine

350ml/12fl oz fish stock

8 thinly cut rashers of pancetta or dry cured streaky bacon

60ml/2fl oz whipping cream

15g/½oz fresh chervil leaves

METHOD Skin the soles and cut off the heads at an angle. Remove any roe and the blood clot from just behind the heads and rinse the fish well. Trim off the fins and the ends of the tails using a pair of kitchen scissors. Take a deep tray and using a little of the butter, butter the base. Lay the fish in and season. Pour in the white wine and the fish stock, cover with a buttered paper or foil and set the tray over a medium heat until the liquid starts to tremble. Transfer to an oven pre-heated to 190°C/375°F/Gas 5 for 5 minutes. The fish is cooked when the fillets just start to separate at the head end. While the fish is cooking grill the pancetta until crisp.

Once the fish are cooked remove them from the stock and drain, keeping them covered to prevent drying out. Transfer the stock to a saucepan and reduce over a high heat until almost gone. While the sauce is reducing remove the fillets from the fish using a palette knife, trim them of any bone and put them back together again to re-form the shape of the fish. Lay two rashers of pancetta on top and return to the oven for a minute to re-heat.

Once the stock has reduced add the cream, return to the boil then gradually add the rest of the butter away from the heat whisking continuously until it has melted. Place a fish in the centre of each plate and at the last minute add half of the chervil to the sauce and pour over and around the fish. Sprinkle the remaining chervil over the sauce.

Wine Note • Savigny Les Beaune, Simon Bize *(Burgundy)* • Such a stylish dish demands a special occasion and a stunning wine to accompany it. From a top producer, this sublime white Burgundy is really a 'spoil yourself' wine, with many levels of flavour and plenty of power to support this flavourful combination. They make a perfect pair.

Pressed Sole and Leek Terrine

Serves 18

9-12 fillets of sole with a total trimmed weight of about 900g/2lbs

1.3kg/3lb of leeks to give a trimmed weight of about 700g/1lb 9oz

45ml/1½fl oz olive oil

55g/2oz melted butter

salt and pepper

One of the easiest terrines you will ever make and once made it will keep for at least 4 days. Sole can mean witch sole, lemon sole or Dover sole; plaice could be used instead but will probably not set quite so well.

METHOD Trim the leeks of roots and outer leaves. Cut only the green centres of the leeks, not the outer silvery leaves, into rough 2.5cm/1in dice; wash and drain well. Heat 30ml/1fl oz of the oil in a saucepan, season the leeks and add them to the oil once hot; cover with a lid and cook the leeks very fast over a high heat stirring often to prevent colouring. When the leeks are just cooked tip them into a colander to drain and cool.

Make sure that the fillets of sole are fully trimmed of skin, skirt and bone. Grease a grilling tray with the remaining oil and lay the fillets on, brush them with the melted butter and season. Cook these under a very hot grill until only just done; this should take no more than about 3 minutes. Remove and allow to cool slightly.

Line a 28cm/11in terrine mould with cling film. Before the fish and the leeks are completely cold cover the bottom of the terrine with a layer of the fish (3-4 fillets); top this with about half of the leeks making sure they are of an even depth and lightly press down. Lay more fillets of fish in to form another layer and add the remaining leek, again making sure it is of an even depth and lightly press down. Top with the remaining fillets of sole. Fold the overlapping film over the top of the fish and place a heavy weight on top of the terrine until cold.

Wine Note • Sancerre, Beauregard, Dme Gitton *(Loire)* • No question here but to look to the Loire Valley for a squeaky clean Sauvignon that perfectly reflects the character of the terrine. The Gitton family is one of the top producers, still using traditional methods and lots of care and attention.

Fillets of Sole with Mousserons

Serves 4

I wish I could lay claim to this dish but unfortunately I must tell the truth. The first time I had it was in the restaurant of a hotel in Barbizon in France. I think it was in 1982, it was a beautiful spring day and we had lunch outside. That morning we had been to Rungis with the owner and chef and had bought the mousserons while we were there. This dish was just absolutely perfect, in fact quite stunning in its simplicity. The fact that it is a sauce made from mousserons may have something to do with why I liked the dish so much as they are without doubt my most favourite of all the wild mushrooms.

115g/4oz fresh mousserons

3 x 450g/1lb of Dover sole

55g/2oz cold unsalted butter

15g/½oz shallots, finely chopped

300ml/10fl oz fish stock (see page 23)

120ml/4fl oz dry sherry

225ml/8fl oz whipping cream

METHOD Pre-heat the oven to 190°C/375°F/Gas 5.

Remove and discard the stalks of the mousserons and wipe off any dirt and grass; do not wash unless really dirty.

Skin and fillet the Dover soles. Trim the edges and slightly flatten each fillet with the side of a heavy bladed knife or cutlet bat; this will help to prevent them from curling when they cook. Fold each fillet in half; if they prove to be a little long, then fold the tail over about 2.5cm/1in and fold in half. Lightly butter an ovenproof pan and scatter the chopped shallots over the bottom; lay the fillets on top, keeping them separate. Add the fish stock and the sherry, cover with a buttered paper and set the pan over a high heat until the liquid just starts to tremble. Transfer to the oven and cook for about 4-5 minutes.

When cooked, remove the fillets from the stock and keep them warm. Place the stock over a high heat and reduce by three quarters, then add the cream and reduce slightly until it starts to thicken.

When ready to serve return the fillets of sole to the oven for a minute to reheat. Add the mousserons to the sauce and return to the boil; remove the pan from the heat and gradually add the remaining butter to the sauce, shaking the pan continuously until it has all melted. Arrange the sole on plates and pour over the sauce.

Wine Note • L'Abeille de Fieuzal *(Bordeaux)* • Semillon, which dominates this blend, is a lovely smooth grape variety to drink with fish dishes that do not ask for too much acidity, i.e. in a rich, creamy combination such as this. The wine in question is the second wine of Château de Fieuzal, currently regarded as one of the top producers of white Bordeaux.

Turmeric Grilled Sole with Courgettes

Serves 4

METHOD Using a cannelle cutter cut grooves into the length of the courgettes then cut each courgette into eight thick slices at an angle. Blanch these in boiling salted water for 30 seconds and refresh in iced water then drain well. Oil a grilling tray, lay the courgette slices on this then brush with half of the melted butter and season.

Season the underside of each fillet of fish, sprinkle the turmeric onto a plate or tray, brush each fillet of sole with the melted butter then dip the fillets butter side down into the turmeric coating one side. Lay them onto an oiled grilling tray.

Combine the fish stock, the wine and the lemon juice together in a pan, bring to the boil and reduce by about two thirds. Meanwhile grill the courgettes under a pre-heated grill until they start to brown; remove and then grill the fillets of sole until these too are golden brown.

Once the stock has reduced add the cream and return to the boil. Gradually add the butter a little at a time whisking continuously until melted. Do not allow the sauce to boil once the butter has been added.

Place the courgettes, four slices to a portion, in the middle of the plates in a rough circle overlapping each other. Spoon the sauce around and arrange three fillets of the grilled sole on the courgettes.

2 large courgettes each weighing about 225-250g/8-9oz

30ml/1fl oz olive oil

55g/2oz melted butter

salt and freshly ground white pepper

12 trimmed fillets of sole each about 55g/2oz

20-25g/¾-1oz turmeric

300ml/10fl oz fish stock (see page 23)

125ml/4fl oz dry white wine

juice of ½ lemon

60ml/2fl oz whipping cream

25g/1oz unsalted butter

> **Wine Note** • Condor Peak, Old Vines Sangiovese *(Argentina)* • As the name suggests this wine is made from low-yielding, old vines and the result is suitably rich to accompany the Indian suggestion of the turmeric in this dish with a very supportive backbone of tannin.

Sole Veronique

Serves 4

48 white grapes (Muscat for preference)

4 x 350-400g/12-14oz of Dover or lemon soles

600ml/1pt fish stock (see page 23)

175ml/6fl oz dry white wine

salt and freshly ground white pepper

225g/8oz unsalted butter

Made correctly there can be no finer way of serving sole ever devised. If only I could call it my own! This is a real classic from way back and is a cornerstone of old-style classical French cookery, the food I learned to cook at college. This was in fact one of my exam dishes! Cooked correctly sole Veronique never has any cream in the dish, but most chefs add a little whipped cream at the end to help 'hold' the sauce and to assist in the glazing. If the fish stock is well made and reduced to the right level and the butter is added just right then the glaze will be glorious!

METHOD Preheat the oven to 190°C/375°F/Gas 5.

Peel the grapes and remove their pips – if the grapes do not peel easily then it may be necessary to blanch them in boiling water for a few seconds first. Allow them to cool and store in the refrigerator.

Skin and fillet the soles. With the side of a heavy knife or meat bat, slightly flatten each fillet and fold in half lengthways. Place the folded fillets into a lightly buttered ovenproof dish. Pour over half of the fish stock and all of the white wine, season, and cover with a buttered paper or foil and poach in the oven for 3-4 minutes. When the fish is cooked, remove the fillets, cover and keep warm.

Add the remaining fish stock to the cooking liquor, bring to the boil and reduce until it is syrupy. When the stock has reduced sufficiently, turn the heat down and gradually whisk in the butter until it has all melted.

Arrange the fillets on the plates, pour the sauce over and place under a very hot grill to glaze; this will only take a few seconds so keep a good eye on it. When browned arrange a pile of the chilled grapes on each plate.

Wine Note • Chablis 1er cru, Côtes de Lechet, Domaine Tremblay-Marchive *(Burgundy)* • A classic wine for a classic dish. It is worth going for the 1er cru version here, since it has a little more intensity coupled with the traditional minerally Chablis style. The added 'weight' will enhance perfectly the delicate, buttery sauce without overpowering it.

Trout, Sea Trout

French: *Truite, Truite Saumonee, Truite de Mer* • Italian: *Trota, Trota di mare*
German: *Forelle, Meerforelle* • Spanish: *Truta, Trucha Marina*

The sea trout (or salmon trout as it is also known) is actually more like a salmon than its actual blood relative the brown trout. It spends its adult life in the sea, only returning to the rivers to spawn, just as a salmon does, and this is when it is fished.

Many people will have difficulty telling salmon trout and salmon apart when whole, as they look so similar. The trout does have a tendency to look a little dumpier than a salmon and its tail is thicker and not as forked. Also, the spots on a trout are not, as in the salmon, confined to above the lateral line but are more widespread and there are also more of them. The flesh of the trout is much softer when cooked and the flakes are not as large as those of a salmon, nor is it as fatty. As with all species of trout, the sea trout has a longer line of pin bones than a salmon, extending further down the fillet. The sea trout can be found in a range of sizes from as a little as 900kg/2lb to as much as 6¾-9kg/15-20lbs, and can sometimes be up to 1m/3ft long, but the most common size is around 2-3kg/4-7lb.

The brown trout, which is very rarely seen for sale, cannot be mistaken for the sea trout. Whereas the sea trout is silver, the brown trout has a brown/bronze coloured back and a silvery-white belly. It, like the rainbow, is spotted with black and red, but the black spots of the brown trout do not extend to the belly as they do in the rainbow.

The farmed rainbow trout can be an excellent fish to eat, but this does depend upon its diet. In my opinion, a rainbow trout farmed purely for consumption has a very limited flavour, whereas a fish farmed for sport is free to swim and can live for a long time and so tends to be much tastier and better textured. Its back above the lateral line is a gold/bronze colour changing to silver underneath and is flecked all over with black marks and has a distinctive pinky/blue iridescent strip down its length.

The rainbow trout was imported here from America many years ago. The best size for eating is a fish weighing between 900g-1.8kg/2-4lb. Beyond that the flesh becomes very coarse and loses its distinctive delicate flavour.

Rillettes of Rainbow Trout with Chives

Serves 4

125ml/4fl oz olive oil

4 slices of French bread, cut at a slight angle and about 1cm/½in thick

450g/1lb trout fillets

salt and freshly ground white pepper

175g/6oz natural yoghurt

1-1½tbsp chopped chives

85g/3oz mashed potato

75ml/2½fl oz fish stock (see page 23)

½ clove garlic

55ml/2fl oz whipping cream

mixed salad leaves

This is a very simple recipe, especially for all those trout fishermen who are getting fed up with the same old ways of using their quarry. Try it by itself or with an assortment of other cold trout dishes.

METHOD Lightly oil an oven tray with a little of the olive oil. Place the French bread on this, drizzle each slice with 60ml/2fl oz of the olive oil and season them, then transfer to an oven pre-heated to 180°C/350°F/Gas 4 until golden brown. Remove and cool.

Fillet and skin the trout, removing the line of pin bones. Lightly oil a grilling tray using some of the olive oil and place the fillets of trout on it, lightly oil the trout and season, then grill under a very hot grill for about 2 minutes or until almost cooked. Remove and allow to cool. Before completely cold, flake the fish into a bowl. Once cold, fold in 115g/4oz of the yoghurt and the chopped chives.

To make the potato dressing: combine the potato, and the remaining yoghurt, stock and garlic in a food processor or liquidiser. Blend together and gradually add 100ml/3½fl oz of the oil then the cream; season to taste. If a little too thick then add more stock to achieve the required consistency. Break up and wash the salad leaves. Dress them with a little of the olive oil and season. Arrange a pile of leaves in the centre of each plate. Using two large spoons, form the rillettes into quenelles and place one onto each crostini. Sit the crostini on top of the salad and spoon the dressing around.

Wine Note • Cape Jaffa, Chardonnay • Wherever dairy products are present, Chardonnay is almost always the best bet and the yoghurt is definitely calling all the shots here.

Poached Fillet of Sea Trout with Tomato Fondue and Asparagus Tips

Serves 4

This is a very simple treatment of a superb fish; as with all recipes, if the basic ingredient is good, why do much more to it?

METHOD Scale and fillet the sea trout then remove the pin bones but do not remove the skin at this stage. Cut the fish into four equal portions. Peel and trim the asparagus tips to a length of about 8.5cm/3.5in long then blanch them in boiling salted water but keep them slightly under-cooked. Refresh in iced water and drain.

Season the portions of trout on the meat side then lay them in a tray just large enough to hold them, meat-side down. Heat the bouillon to boiling then pour on to the fish. Gently heat and poach for about 4 minutes then remove from the heat.

Bring the sauce to the boil and just before boiling gradually whisk in 55g/2oz of the butter, whisking continuously until it has melted. Keep the sauce hot but do not allow it to boil. Heat the remaining butter and toss the asparagus tips in this with a little seasoning until hot.

Spoon the sauce onto the plates. Carefully remove the sea trout from the stock and peel off the skin then remove the dark meat. Place the fish on the sauce skin-side uppermost; place four asparagus tips on each fillet.

1 x 1.3-1.8kg/3-4lb of sea trout

16 asparagus tips

salt and freshly ground white pepper

sufficient court bouillon to cover the fillets (see page 22)

12fl oz tomato sauce (see page 33)

70g/2½oz unsalted butter

Wine Note • Chinon, Dme de la Chapelle *(Loire)* • Like salmon, sea trout is a wonderful meaty fish that works well with red wine and if we stick to the Loire Valley and try a fresh, 'grassy' Cabernet Franc, the tomato and asparagus will also feel at home without becoming over-exaggerated.

Sea Trout in a Mushroom, Broad Bean and Courgette Bouillon

Serves 4

1 x 1.25-1.5kg/2½-3lb of
sea trout

6 tight button mushrooms

225g/8oz courgettes

115g/4oz broad beans

salt and freshly ground
white pepper

600-850ml/1-1½pts court
bouillon depending upon the
size of pan used
(see page 22)

75ml/2½fl oz whipping cream

175g/6oz unsalted butter

1tbsp finely chopped chives

Sea trout is such a delicate fish that it is easy to over-egg the pudding, as it were. Simple cooking and garnishes are what is called for here.

METHOD Scale the sea trout, fillet and remove the pin bones using a pair of pliers or tweezers. Cut each fillet into two equal portions. Score the skin in two or three places on each fillet.

Cut the mushrooms into a fine julienne. Top and tail the courgettes: cut two thin slices off each side of the courgette and then cut this into a fine julienne. Blanch the broad beans in boiling salted water for about 30 seconds, refresh in iced water then remove their husks.

Season the fillets of trout and lightly butter a deep pan; lay the fillets in this skin side uppermost. Bring the bouillon to the boil and pour onto the fish, then set over a medium heat and bring to the boil. Remove from the heat and allow to sit for a minute. Carefully remove the fish from the bouillon, cover and keep warm. Pour off 300ml/10fl oz of the bouillon into a saucepan and bring to the boil; reduce this by just over half. Once reduced add the cream, return to the boil and gradually add the butter (holding back 15g/½oz for cooking the garnish), whisking continuously until it has all melted. Keep the sauce warm but do not allow it to boil.

In a saucepan heat the remaining butter until it just starts to sizzle, add the mushroom and courgette julienne and a little seasoning. Gently sauté this without colouring for a few seconds then add the broad beans and the sauce.

Carefully remove the skin and the dark meat from each fillet of fish, pour the sauce and garnish onto the plates and place a fillet of trout skin-side up on the sauce. Scatter the sauce with the chopped chives.

Wine Note • St. Aubin, 1er cru, Blanc *(Burgundy)* • Like the ingredients of the dish, this wine is enticing and multi-layered. It is quite full-bodied, which will suit the sea trout well, and has a long nutty finish that will balance the vegetable julienne nicely.

Carpaccio of Trout

Serves 6

As a trout fisherman, I am constantly devising new ways to serve the catch of the day. This recipe came about when we had friends around for dinner one evening. I had absolutely no idea what I was going to serve them as a first course but as luck would have it I managed to catch a fair few of these little beauties the day before so this is what I made.

METHOD Fillet the trout and remove the pin bones.

Split the chillies lengthways and remove the seeds; cut the flesh very finely. Peel and then very finely shred the ginger. Combine these together with the lemon juice, water, mustard, oil and sugar and mix well.

Carve the trout fillets into very thin slices like smoked salmon and lay them out on the plates. Finely chop the spring onions and scatter these over the fish. Season the fish with sea salt and freshly ground black pepper. Give the dressing a good stir and spoon over the fish. Snip the cress from its punnet and scatter over the plates.

1 x 1kg/2lb 4oz of rainbow trout

3 small red chillies

10g/½oz fresh ginger

juice of 1 lemon

30ml/1fl oz water

1tsp whole grain mustard

75ml/2½fl oz olive oil

pinch of sugar

3 spring onions

sea salt and freshly ground black pepper

1 punnet mustard cress

Wine Note • Seppelt, Great Western Rosé *(Australia)* • Wow! 'If in doubt, drink fizzy pink', is not a bad motto to follow and the slightly Pacific feel of the marinade here would suggest that these two are perfect partners. The only real alternative would be a good quality Pouilly Fumé.

Roulade of Rainbow Trout with French Beans and Red Onion Vinaigrette

Serves 8

3 x 450g/1lb of rainbow trout

½tsp salt

1 egg white

30ml/1fl oz dry white wine

100ml/3½fl oz whipping cream

salt and freshly ground white pepper

175g/6oz French beans

1 red onion

60ml/2fl oz white wine vinegar

3fl oz olive oil

1tbsp sherry vinegar

1tbsp walnut oil

This may not be the easiest of starters in the world but it is very effective. Once made it will keep for a few days, but remove it from the fridge for an hour before serving as the cold stifles flavour.

METHOD Fillet and skin the trout. Using a small pair of pliers or tweezers remove the line of pin bones that runs down the middle of each fillet. Reserve four fillets and cut the remainder into small pieces. Process these along with the salt in a food processor until smooth. Add the egg white and process again until well mixed in then rub the mousse through a fine sieve into a bowl set on crushed ice. Stir in the wine and gradually add two-thirds of the cream mixing in well. Test the mousse and if a little too firm add more cream and re-test. Leave to rest in the refrigerator until needed.

Have ready a pan of boiling water, large enough to take the finished roll and deep enough to allow the roll to float.

To make the roulade flatten out the four fillets of trout with a cutlet bat or the side of a heavy knife until they are about 3mm/⅛in thick. Trim the edges to square up the fillets and lay them out, skin side up, side by side, on a sheet of cling film, filling any gaps with the trimmings. Lightly season the fillets and then carefully spread the mousse over them to form a layer the same thickness as the fish. Gently roll the fish over as if rolling a Swiss roll. Roll tightly in the cling film and tie off the ends as tightly as possible. Plunge the roll into the boiling water, reduce the heat so the water is barely simmering and cook for 10 minutes. Once cooked remove the roll from the pan and plunge into iced water till cold.

Top and tail the French beans and cook in boiling salted water until just cooked but still with a slight crunch. Refresh in iced water and drain.

Finely chop the red onion and place in a saucepan; cover with the white wine vinegar, season and bring to the boil. Boil for 30 seconds then allow to go cold. Add the olive oil and check the seasoning. Lightly season the French beans and toss these with the sherry vinegar and the walnut oil. Divide the beans out between the plates, forming a small pile in the centre of each. Slice the roulade into 24 slices about 5mm/¼in thick. Lay three slices over each bean salad and spoon the dressing around.

Wine Note • Julienas, Louis Latour *(Burgundy)* • Trout can be at the same time sweet and earthy so we are looking for a light fruity red or a full-bodied rosé here. Julienas is a perfect summer-drinking red with lashings of ripe cherried fruit and suitable for serving chilled, as this salad would suggest.

Mousse of Rainbow Trout

Serves 6-8

METHOD To make the mousse, place the trout in a food processor and blend until smooth. Add the egg whites and the salt and continue to process until the whites and the salt are well worked into the mixture. It will then become very firm.

Pass this mixture through a fine sieve to remove any sinew. Place in the refrigerator for about ½ hour to rest and chill well. Gradually add the cream to the mousse mixing it in well before adding more. After about half of the cream has been added, add the vermouth.

Once all the cream is incorporated then test a teaspoon of the mousse by plunging it into a pan of water that is barely simmering. Poach till cooked (two minutes); if the mousse is a little too firm then add more cream and test again until just right. Adjust seasoning if needed.

Blanch the spinach leaves in boiling salted water for only a couple of seconds then refresh in iced water. Drain these well and pat dry between two cloths. Lay the spinach out on a sheet of cling film to form an oblong about 25cm x 15cm/10in x 6in deep. Spoon the mousse along the near-side edge of the spinach. Gently roll the mousse in the film and tie off the ends.

Poach this roll for 12 minutes in water that is just under simmering; do not allow to boil as it will cause the mousse to become grainy. Transfer to iced water to chill well.

Once made, the mousse will keep well for three or four days if stored in water and still sealed in the cling film.

450g/1lb trout, skin and bone removed

2 egg whites

2tsp salt

600ml/1pt whipping cream

30ml/1fl oz vermouth

16-20 spinach leaves picked of their stalks

Tuna

French: *Thon* • German: *Thunfisch* • Italian: *Tonno* • Spanish: *Atun*

Tuna is a difficult fish to write about in general terms. The above translations are adequate but they go no where near describing all the different varieties we now have at our disposal.

The one regarded as 'the best' (if it is fair to say that as it does very much depend upon where in the world you are) is probably the bluefin, which is also known as *Thon Rouge* in French and *Roter Thun* in German. The bluefin, which can grow up to 4 metres/13ft in length and weigh up to a staggering 900kg/202lb, is a member of the tuna family and not only is it regarded as the best, but is inevitably the priciest too. The meat of the bluefin is a much darker red than other tuna as well as being fattier. It is only relatively recently that the bluefin has been so highly regarded – it was once considered unsuitable for sushi as it was so fatty.

We are much more familiar with yellowfin tuna in this country. An inhabitant of warmer waters than the bluefin, it weighs a lot less, usually between 20 and 25kg/45-56lb and is also usually cheaper. Skipjack, the tuna we are most familiar with in tins, is from more tropical waters and its flesh is much lighter in colour. Over the years it has been heavily fished, so much so that stocks are now diminishing.

Albacore or long-fin tuna (also known as *Thon Blanc* in French and *Weisser Thun* in German) grows to a maximum of just over 1m/3ft in length. The meat is lighter in colour than either the blue or yellowfin and is often used in the canning industry, along with the skipjack. But beware, as the meat turns a dull and unappetising brown once in contact with the air.

Until relatively recently fresh tuna was difficult to come by in Britain and the majority of people would only have eaten it from the tin. Nowadays it is more readily found in fishmongers and supermarkets. The flesh of the tuna is much closer to meat than fish, being very firm and compact with a dark red colouring. Tuna is best eaten underdone as it becomes dry very quickly, so seared in a very hot pan (leaving the centre rare) is the best method of cooking. It also needs to be fresh, as after even just a few days it begins to take on an almost acrid taste.

Herb Seared Tuna with a Tomato and Avocado Salsa

Serves 4

METHOD Follow the recipe for the herb seared carpaccio (see page 210) up to the point where the tuna has been seared, wrapped in the herbs and cling film and then refrigerated.

Blanch, skin and de-seed the tomatoes, and cut them into 1cm/½in dice; cut the red onion into similar-sized dice and mix with the tomatoes. Split the chillies in two and remove the seeds; chop them as finely as possible and mix into the tomato and onion along with the lemon juice. Peel the avocado and cut it into similar-sized dice as the tomato; mix into the salsa, season and add 60ml/2fl oz of the oil, then stir in the chopped chives.

Cut the tuna into 8 thick slices about 2cm/¾in thick, remove the cling film and season the fish on both sides. Heat 15ml/½fl oz of the oil in a frying pan until smoking, add the butter and very quickly sear the tuna in the frying pan over a very high heat for about 30-40 seconds per side. Remove from the pan and keep warm.

Dress the salad leaves with the remaining oil and season. Arrange these in the centre of each plate. Spoon the salsa around and place two tuna steaks on each salad.

60ml/2fl oz olive oil

550g/1lb 4oz fully trimmed piece of tuna preferably about 10cm/6in long by 7.5cm/3in square

salt and freshly ground white pepper

10g/¼oz unsalted butter

20g/¾oz finely chopped mixed herbs e.g. chervil, dill, tarragon, parsley, coriander, chives

Salsa:

2 plum tomatoes

½ medium red onion

2 small red chillies

juice of ½ lemon

½ avocado

salt and freshly ground white pepper

100ml/3½fl oz olive oil

2tsp chopped chives

15g/½oz unsalted butter

115g/4oz mixed salad leaves e.g. frizzy, lollo rosso, rocket, chicory and red oak leaf

---

Wine Note • Sauvignon Blanc, Hay Shed Hill *(W. Australia)* • As we all know, tuna is one of those versatile fish that work well with red as well as white wine. It is important to remember with such a meaty fish that if white, the wine needs to be pretty substantial. This stunning Sauvignon has so much character and freshness it will be perfect with the tuna and will really cut a dash with the salsa. A mouth-watering combination!

Seared Tuna Steak with Tomatoes and Sauce Gribiche

Serves 4

1 hard boiled egg

15g/½oz gherkins

25g/1oz shallot

20g/¾oz tiny capers

2tbsp chopped mixed herbs, e.g. chervil, dill, parsley, chives, tarragon

½tbsp whole grain mustard

130ml/4½fl oz olive oil

juice of ¼ lemon

salt and freshly ground white pepper

4 plum tomatoes

30ml/1fl oz olive oil for frying

15g/½oz unsalted butter

4 x 140g/5oz tuna steaks fully trimmed of skin

140g/5oz mixed salad leaves e.g. frizzy, lollo, red oak, endive

Classically sauce gribiche would be made from a mayonnaise base but this way is more modern as well as being lighter. Sauce vierge (see page 30) would also be a good accompaniment.

METHOD Cut the egg and the gherkins into small dice and finely chop the shallot. Combine these in a bowl with the capers, chopped herbs, mustard, 100ml/3½fl oz of the olive oil and the lemon juice; season with salt and pepper and mix well.

Slice the tomatoes very thinly and arrange in an overlapping circle on the plates allowing one tomato per plate.

Heat the oil for frying in a frying pan until just smoking, season the tuna steaks, and add the butter and then the fish. Sear these as quickly as possible on both sides. Allow one minute per side: tuna should still be pink when cooked or it will become too dry. Once cooked remove from the pan and keep warm.

Combine the salad leaves in a bowl, season and toss with the remaining olive oil. Carefully arrange the leaves in the centre of the tomato circles. Place a steak on the top of each salad and spoon the dressing around.

Wine Note • Spencer Hill Sauvignon Blanc • A typically Antipodean fresh, herbaceous flavourful Sauvignon will be very happy to engage with the zingy ingredients here.

Seared Tuna with Pak Choi

I am never sure how to spell pak choi – there seem to be so many ways, even the producers do not agree on its spelling, so there is no hope for me! Once only used by the Chinese in stir-fries and Chinese greens it has now become very fashionable although it can sometimes be hard to find. If you do have difficulty, try your nearest Chinese supermarket.

METHOD Trim the pak choi, removing any discoloured or wilted leaves and trim the root end so it is neat. Blanch these in boiling salted water for only about 30 seconds, until they just begin to go limp, then refresh in iced water. Drain well.

Peel the ginger and the garlic and cut them into a fine julienne.

In a saucepan bring the white wine, soy and 300ml/10fl oz of the fish stock to the boil; reduce until only about 100ml/3½fl oz remains. Add the ginger and the garlic along with the veal stock. Return to the boil and reduce slightly to thicken. In a frying pan heat the olive oil till just smoking; season the tuna steaks and add 25g/1oz of the butter and sear the tuna steaks in the hot fat very quickly, allowing only about 1-1½ minutes on each side. Once cooked remove from the pan and keep warm.

Place the pak choi in a saucepan along with the remaining butter and fish stock and season them lightly. Cover with a lid and gently reheat.

Drain the pak choi and place two or three in the centre of each plate. Place a tuna steak on top and spoon the sauce over and around.

8-12 baby pak choi depending upon size

25g/1oz fresh ginger

1 clove garlic

100ml/3½fl oz dry white wine

45ml/1½fl oz soy sauce

350ml/12fl oz fish stock (see page 23)

175ml/6fl oz veal stock (see page 33)

salt and freshly ground white pepper

30ml/1fl oz olive oil for frying

4 x 140g/5oz tuna steaks fully trimmed of skin and black meat

40g/1½oz unsalted butter

Wine Note • Carneros Creek, Pinot Noir 'Estate Grown' *(California)* • This deliciously soft, full-bodied Pinot is powerful enough to satisfy the meaty tuna yet fruity enough to cope with the spicy, oriental elements.

Herb Seared Tuna Carpaccio

Serves 6

150ml/5fl oz olive oil

400g/14oz fully trimmed piece of tuna preferably about 10cm/4in long by 6cm/2½in square

salt and freshly ground white pepper

10g/¼oz unsalted butter

15g/½oz finely chopped mixed herbs, e.g. chervil, dill, tarragon, parsley, coriander, chives

85g/3oz mashed potato

55ml/2fl oz plain yoghurt

75ml/2½fl oz fish stock (see page 23)

½ clove garlic

55ml/2fl oz whipping cream

175g/6oz picked and washed rocket leaves

55g/2oz shaved Parmesan

Served thinly sliced on a salad of rocket and shaved Parmesan with a top quality olive oil, it makes a wonderful first course or light lunch dish. Alternatively try it as in the recipe on page 207, with the same base but cooked on a little further and served with a tomato and avocado salsa.

METHOD Heat 15ml/½fl oz of the oil in a frying pan until very hot; season the tuna well on all sides. Add the butter to the oil then sear the tuna in the hot fat for about 30 seconds on each side in order to lightly brown it and cook only the very outside 5mm/¼in.

Spread a sheet of cling film out taut, sprinkle the herbs over an area as long as the tuna and about 23-25cm/9-10in wide. While the tuna is still warm sit it on the herbs at one end then roll it in the herbs while wrapping it tightly in the cling film. Tie the ends as tightly as possible. Leave to rest in the refrigerator for at least one hour.

Combine the potato, yoghurt, stock and garlic in a food processor. Blend together and gradually add 85ml/3fl oz of the oil then the cream and season to taste. If a little too thick then add more stock to achieve the required consistency.

When ready to serve toss the rocket leaves in the remaining olive oil and seasoning. Spread the leaves to cover the serving plates. Using a very thin, sharp knife slice the tuna into slices as thin as you can get them and lay them on the salad, allowing at least 5 slices per portion. Dribble the potato dressing over the tuna and rocket then scatter the Parmesan on top at the last second.

Wine Note • White Zinfandel, Robert Mondavi *(California)* • Almost impossible this one, so why not try something completely different? This 'white' wine is made from red grapes and is bright pink in colour – there is an explanation but probably the best idea is just to sample some and see how it works. This wine is fruity and spicy with definite hints of cinnamon that should work well in conjunction with the herbs while not being too timid for the tuna.

Tuna Steak on Cous Cous with Salsa Verde

Serves 4

½ **recipe for cous cous (see page 22)**

¼ **red pepper**

6 pitted black olives

1tbsp chopped chives

45ml/1½fl oz olive oil

4 x 140g/5oz tuna steaks fully trimmed of skin

salt and freshly ground white pepper

100g/3½oz unsalted butter

100ml sweet pepper fondue (see page 31)

225ml/8fl oz fish stock (see page 23)

55-85g/2-3oz frizzy

¼ **recipe for salsa verde (see page 29)**

METHOD Make the cous cous as in the recipe on page 22. Very finely dice the red pepper and chop the olives. Mix these with the chives into the cous cous.

Heat 15ml/½fl oz of the oil in a frying pan; season the tuna steaks; when the oil is hot add 15g/½oz of the butter and, over a very high heat, sear the tuna in the hot oil. Cook for about 1 minute on each side, remove and keep warm.

Place the sweet pepper fondue in a saucepan along with the fish stock and bring this to the boil. Lightly season the frizzy and toss with 15ml/½fl oz of the oil. Warm the remaining oil in a pan and add the cous cous, gently warming it through. Once the sauce comes to the boil remove it from the heat and gradually whisk in the remaining butter, whisking continuously until it has all melted.

Place a 10cm/4in cutter in the centre of each plate and fill with the cous cous, pressing it down well. Remove the cutter. Place a tuna steak on top of the cous cous, arrange a little of the frizzy on each piece of tuna and place a dessertspoon quenelle of the salsa verde on top of this. Spoon the sweet pepper fondue around the cous cous.

Wine Note • Gigondas, M. Chapoutier *(Rhône)* • As we have said before, rosé works well with cous cous, but this hearty dish needs something with a little more power to satisfy the tuna, salsa and black olives. These flavours conjure up a picture of a sunny terrace in the South of France so why not stay fairly close for the wine choice and sample this wonderfully powerful, slightly spicy and oaky fellow from one of the best producers of the Rhône Valley. You will not be disappointed.

Turbot

French: *Turbot* • Italian: *Rombo chiodato* • German: *Steinbutt*
Spanish: *Rodaballo*

Of all the flat fish turbot must be one of the easiest to identify. Firstly it has no scales and secondly it has 'stones' or what seem to be stones embedded across the dark brown skin on its back (which is probably why the Germans call this fish *Steinbutt!*). It is also rather round as its width is almost that of its length. In Scotland it is known as Bannock-fluke, because Bannock refers to a round oatcake.

This carnivorous fish is one of the finest of all the flat fish. Prized the world over for its firm and delicious flesh, it commands a very high price. Poached, grilled, roasted, pan-fried or steamed, served with delicate cream sauces or robust meat glazes, the turbot is fantastic. Do try to use only the larger fish though as small turbots (or chicken turbot as they are known) do not taste half as good as a fillet off a fish weighing approximately 3.6-5 kg/ 8-11 lb (or larger if available). Sadly, fish of this size are rarely found these days. Once they were commonplace, but thanks to the practice of fishing undersized fish, the stocks are greatly reduced and young fish are not getting the chance to grow and breed. There are other reasons than conservation (if more were needed) for using only large fish. The ratio of meat to bone on a turbot is poorly balanced in the favour of bone and on a smaller fish the ratio gets much worse. The bones of course need not be wasted as they make probably the best fish stock and are extremely gelatinous.

The farming of turbot has been quite successful over recent years and some very fine specimens can be turned out in a very short space of time. This will obviously help wild stocks as people choose to buy farmed fish instead of wild.

When buying whole turbot always turn the fish over and check the white underside for bruising. If the fish hasn't been bled properly then the flesh will be bruised which renders the meat unusable.

Turbot with Cumin Roasted Winter Vegetables

Serves 4

12 small button sprouts

115g/4oz carrot to give 12 pieces about 3.5cm/1½in in length

115g/4oz swede as above

140g/5oz parsnip as above but with the core removed

115g/4oz celeriac as above

115g/4oz turnip as above

140g/5oz small new potatoes as above

4 baby leeks

140g/5oz cauliflower

12 small peeled cloves garlic

12 small peeled shallots or button onions

30ml/1fl oz olive oil

4 x 175g/6oz fillets of turbot

25g/1oz melted butter

100ml/3½fl oz red wine

225ml/8fl oz fish stock (see page 23)

175ml/6fl oz veal stock (see page 33)

50g/1¾oz unsalted butter

salt and freshly ground white pepper

1tsp cumin seeds

½ recipe for mash (see page 25)

It's amazing how the addition of a little cumin seed can alter a whole dish. Cumin goes well with anything to do with winter and certainly works with the robust flavours you get from roasting vegetables like this.

METHOD Trim the sprouts, peel the carrot and cut into 12 pieces as described then turn each one into pointed barrel shapes. Repeat this process with the swede, parsnip, celeriac, turnip and potatoes but keep them all separate at this juncture. Trim the baby leeks and wash well; cut the cauliflower into 12 small florets. Peel the garlic and the shallots.

Blanch all of the vegetables individually in boiling salted water then refresh them in iced water. The carrot and swede should be cooked for no more than 2-2½ minutes, the rest for 1-1½ minutes with the exception of the shallots, which will take longer, and the potatoes, which should be fully cooked. It is import not to overcook any of the vegetables; they still need to be very crunchy at this stage as they are still to be roasted. Once refreshed, drain from the water and dry thoroughly.

Using half of the oil grease a grilling tray. Lay the fillets on the tray and season the fish; brush with the melted butter.

Bring to the boil the red wine and the fish stock; reduce until almost gone then add the veal stock, reduce this until it just starts to thicken, and keep warm.

Grill the fish under a pre-heated grill for about 3 minutes depending upon the thickness; once cooked, remove and keep warm.

Heat the remaining oil in a frying pan until smoking, add the butter and once sizzling add all the vegetables and season. Toss these over a very high heat until nicely browned, add the cumin seeds and toss through well.

Place a spoon of the finished mash in the centre of each plate; divide the vegetables out between the plates spooning them around the mash. Place a fillet of the turbot on the mash. Dribble the sauce around.

Wine Note • Quinta da Camarate *(Portugal)* • Portuguese wines are improving all the time and this is a very fine example, with plenty of fruit and a good strong backbone to accompany this real winter warmer.

Curried Turbot with Cabbage

Serves 4

It doesn't sound very inviting, does it? Don't let that put you off – it may sound simple, it is simple, but it also tastes ever so good! Pan-fried fish dusted with curry powder, and I mean only dusted, makes a great combination. As an alternative, you could try dusting the fish with the Thai spice mix on page 31.

METHOD Lightly season the fillets of turbot then sprinkle them with the curry powder, spreading it evenly over the fish.

Remove the central ribs of the cabbage leaves and break them up fairly small. Wash well and drain. Place the leaves in a saucepan along with 25g/1oz of the butter, season and cover.

In a saucepan combine the stock, white wine, and the lemon juice bring to the boil and reduce by three quarters. Meanwhile heat the oil in a frying pan, add 15g/½oz of the butter and as it starts to sizzle place in the fillets of fish curried-side down. Cook for about 2 minutes then turn and cook for a further minute; remove from the pan and keep warm. Set the cabbage over a fairly high heat and cook quite quickly.

Once the stock has reduced add the cream and return to the boil; just as it starts to thicken gradually add the remaining butter whisking continuously until all melted.

Place a pile of the cabbage in the centre of each plate and place a fillet of the fish on top. Pour the sauce around.

4 x 140-175g/5-6oz skinned fillets of turbot

salt and freshly ground white pepper

1tsp curry powder

450g/1lb cabbage

70g/2½oz unsalted butter

300ml/10fl oz fish stock (see page 23)

125ml/4fl oz white wine

juice of ½ lemon

15ml/½fl oz oil

225ml/8fl oz whipping cream

Wine Note • Highcliff Chardonnay *(S. Australia)* • A fairly straightforward dish that asks no more than a reasonable glass of Chardonnay preferably with some oak. Here we have a typical everyday Australian Chardonnay that is rich, full-bodied and oaky and fits the bill perfectly.

Fillet of Turbot with a Brioche and Black Olive Crust

85g/3oz brioche

15g/½oz chopped black olives

25g/1oz chopped mixed herbs e.g. parsley, tarragon, chervil, dill, chives

salt and freshly ground white pepper

25g/1oz melted butter

30ml/1fl oz olive oil

4 x 140g/5oz fillets of turbot fully trimmed

225ml/8fl oz fish stock (see page 23)

100ml/3½fl oz dry white wine

juice of ¼ lemon

125ml/4fl oz whipping cream

25g/1oz unsalted butter

This is a very simple-looking dish whose simplicity belies its richness. It is possible to use this crust on other fish but I would not suggest it for salmon. Salmon is very oil-rich and to top it with such a rich topping would be too much.

METHOD Roughly cut up the brioche and place in a food processor to turn it into crumbs. Add the olives and herbs and process until well mixed. Season with the salt and pepper and mix in the melted butter and half of the olive oil. Roll this paste out between two sheets of cling film into a rectangle about 30cm/12in x 10cm/4in; lay this on a tray and transfer to the refrigerator to set.

Once set, cut it into four pieces the same size as the pieces of turbot so that the crust fits the fish exactly, and peel off the cling film. Season each fillet of fish and place the crust on top. Using the remainder of the oil grease an oven tray then lay the fillets of fish on this. Place in an oven pre-heated to 220°C/425°F/Gas 7 for 8 minutes. Once cooked remove and keep warm.

While the fish is cooking combine the stock and the white wine in a saucepan and bring to the boil; reduce this until only a third remains. Add the lemon juice and the cream then return the sauce to the boil; reduce slightly then, off the heat, gradually add the cold butter whisking continuously until it has all melted. Pour the sauce onto the plates and place a portion of the fish on top.

Wine Note • Château Moulin Caresse, Vieilles Vignes, Bergerac • This dish sounds as though it should hail from Bergerac or Provence so it makes sense to match it with a powerful, rich wine from the same region.

Fillet of Turbot with a Thyme-infused Carrot and Pulse Broth

Serves 4

I absolutely adore the colours in this light yet rich dish; they are quite stunning. The lightness and slight sweetness of the stock coupled with the richness of the beans sets the turbot off well and makes this an ideal autumn dish. At first sight it may seem that this is a complicated dish to prepare but even the carrot essence is very simple.

METHOD Peel the baby carrots preserving their natural shape and leaving the tops on and cut to about 2.5cm/1in pieces. Plunge these into boiling salted water for about 1 minute until just cooked; refresh them in iced water and drain.

Lightly grease a grilling tray. Season the fillets of fish on the underside and lay on the tray. Brush with the melted butter. Place this under a very hot grill until just cooked – about 3 minutes depending upon the thickness of the fish. Remove and keep warm.

Rinse the pulses and put them in a pan with the carrot essence. Gently heat this till almost boiling. Add the spinach leaves and fold these through the stock until just wilted. Next add the thyme and the baby carrots then gradually add the butter, which should be cold, shaking the pan continuously until the butter has melted.

Spoon the beans into a pile in the middle of each plate and pour the stock around. Arrange the carrots around the beans and top the beans with a portion of turbot.

20 whole baby carrots

salt and freshly ground white pepper

15ml/½fl oz olive oil

4 x 140g/5oz of turbot

25g/1oz melted butter

400g/14oz cooked mixed pulses (chick peas, haricot blanc, borlotti beans, black eye beans, sweetcorn kernels)

350ml/12fl oz carrot essence (see page 21)

175g/6oz picked and washed spinach leaves

1tsp fresh thyme leaves

55g/2oz unsalted butter cut into dice

Wine Note • Brown Brothers King Valley Riesling *(Australia)* • The sweetness of the carrots, intensified by infusion, indicates a white wine with plenty of fragrance such as this pungent, fruity fellow. Always avoid any hint of tannin with sweeter types of food, as the opposite characteristics will clash terribly.

Whiting

French: *Merlan* • Italian: *Merlano* • German: *Wittling* • Spanish: *Merlan*

Often described as wholesome, the whiting's reputation has suffered somewhat in the past. Wholesome implies tasteless or bland and therefore only good for the sick or the elderly. Whiting is actually a much better fish than that. In years gone by it was often prepared with its tail poking out of its eyes and deep fried, then served with a tomato sauce known classically as *Merlan en colère*. It was one of the dishes you always cooked as part of the **City & Guilds Chefs'** course, which makes me shudder now.

Unlike the rest of the cod family to which it belongs, it is quite a small fish with an average size of about 900g/2lb. It has always been prolific and can be found from **Iceland** and **Norway** down to the **Mediterranean**, with over half the landings made from the **North Sea** and predominantly in **Scotland**.

As with any fish, go for the freshest you can find. Being a little delicate in flavour, the whiting will lose its taste very rapidly and so the fresher the fish the better. It is quite easy to check the freshness of whiting as its silvery to almost pearly white sides should look bright and positively gleaming. If it looks dull then don't buy it. There is no need to skin whiting as the skin is extremely thin with very fine scales.

Salad of Hot Smoked Whiting

Serves 4

This makes a very colourful and fresh-tasting salad suitable either as a starter or main course. You will need your own smoker for this recipe but if you do not have one then see page 159 for instructions on how to construct your own.

METHOD The day before, sprinkle the fish with the sea salt and season with the pepper and leave to stand for at least 12 hours.

Blanch, skin and de-seed the tomatoes. Cut into 1cm/½in dice. Trim the onions of any root and discoloured leaves then thinly slice them. Cut the cucumber into 1cm/½in dice discarding the core. Mix the tomatoes, onions, cucumber, capers, dill, lemon juice and olive oil together and season to taste.

Place 2-3 tablespoons of oak chips and a splash of water into the smoker. Put on the lid and set over a low heat to smoke. Once you have achieved a good head of smoke place the fish in and cook slowly for about 15 minutes.

Dress the salad leaves with a little of the dressing and divide between the plates. Flake the warm smoked whiting over the salad and spoon the remaining dressing on top.

Wine Note • Cloudy Bay, Sauvignon Blanc *(N.Z.)* • Not an 'off the shelf' wine but well worth waiting for as each new vintage comes out and is snapped up. Zingy, zesty and full of gooseberry fruit flavour. The salad is just as lively.

350g/12oz skinned and boned fresh whiting fillet

1tsp sea salt

freshly ground black pepper

2 plum tomatoes

3 spring onions

115g/4oz cucumber

55g/2oz tiny capers

1tbsp chopped dill

juice of ½ lemon

125ml/4fl oz olive oil

175g/6oz mixed leaves, e.g. frizzy, lollo, oak leaf, chicory, gem

Thin Tart of Flaked Whiting with Melted Brie

Serves 4

450g/1lb puff pastry (see page 27)

a little plain flour to dust the work surface

a little oil

350g/12oz whiting fillet

15g/½oz melted butter

salt and freshly ground white pepper

25g/1oz butter

225g/8oz spinach, picked, well washed and drained

4 plum tomatoes

115g/4oz ripe Brie

This dish makes a great lunchtime snack as well as a good starter. If using it as a starter then the ingredients would be enough for about 6; cut the bases a little smaller, e.g. 15cm/6in instead of 18cm/7in. It does not have to be made with whiting – any trimmings of a flaky type fish such as cod or haddock would do equally well.

METHOD Roll out the pastry to a thickness of 2mm/⅛in, cut four discs each 18cm/7in in diameter and prick these all over using a fork. Transfer to the refrigerator to rest for at least one hour.

Preheat the oven to 200°C/400°F/Gas 6. Cook the pastry discs in the oven for 15 minutes then transfer to a cooling rack till cold. Turn the heat in the oven up to 220°C/425°F/Gas 7.

Using the oil lightly grease a grilling tray, skin the whiting and remove any bones. Lay the fish on the grilling tray and brush with the melted butter. Season the fish and grill under a very hot grill for 2-3 minutes until barely cooked; remove and allow it to go cold.

Heat the butter in a saucepan and once sizzling add the spinach; season and cook over a very high heat for a few seconds until it goes limp. Squeeze out any excess moisture from the spinach and allow to go cold.

Thinly slice the tomatoes; lay these in a circle around the edge of each pastry disc allowing one tomato per tart. Divide the spinach into four and pile this in the centre of each disc. Divide the whiting into four and scatter this on the spinach. Remove the rind from the Brie and break the cheese over the fish and spinach. Season with salt and pepper.

Return the tarts to the oven for a further 10 minutes until the Brie has melted, the tomato has just started to cook and the tarts are piping hot. Serve immediately.

Wine Note • Condor Peak, Chardonnay/Chenin *(Argentina)* • It is tempting to go for a straight N.W. Chardonnay here to compliment the Brie but there are enough other elements that suggest something a touch lighter in style. This is exactly what the chenin does in the blend here, as well as adding a slightly floral, dry hint which will appeal to the delicate whiting.

Index